W9-ARW-107

My Times

A Memoir of Dissent

My Times

A Memoir of Dissent

JOHN L. HESS

SEVEN STORIES PRESS

New York | London | Toronto | Melbourne

Articles reprinted herein originally appeared in *Covert Action,*
Extra, Grand Street, The Masthead, MORE, The Nation, Newsday, the *New York*
Observer, The New York Times, and *Working Woman.*

Seven Stories Press
140 Watts Street
New York, NY 10013
www.sevenstories.com

In Canada: Hushion House, 36 Northline Road, Toronto,
Ontario M4B 3E2

In the U.K.: Turnaround Publisher Services Ltd., Unit 3, Olympia Trading Estate,
Coburg Road, Wood Green, London N22 6TZ

In Australia: Palgrave Macmillan, 627 Chapel Street, South Yarra VIC 3141

Library of Congress Cataloging-in-Publication Data
Hess, John L.
  My times : a memoir of dissent / John L. Hess.-- Seven Stories Press 1st ed.
    p. cm.
  Includes index.
  ISBN 1-58322-604-4 (alk. paper) -- ISBN 1-58322-622-2 (pbk. : alk. paper)
  1. Hess, John L. 2. Journalists--United States--Biography. I. Title.

PN4874.H475 A3 2003
070.92--dc22   2003015513

9 8 7 6 5 4 3 2 1

College professors may order examination copies of Seven Stories Press titles for a
free six-month trial period. To order, visit www.sevenstories.com/ textbook, or fax on
school letterhead to (212) 226-1411.

Book design by Cindy LaBreacht

Printed in the U.S.A.

Contents

Introduction

Hold the press. As these pages go to the printers, the world of journalism is transfixed by the drama at *The New York Times*. Its integrity has come under challenge, most severely within the paper itself, and its two chief editors have been obliged to resign. As an old *Times*man myself, I was saddened, and bemused. Clearly, Howell Raines and Gerald Boyd had committed a misjudgment in nurturing a pathological blowhard. But Jayson Blair's misdeeds, as recounted at staggering length, caused no real harm to anything but the credibility of the *Times*. Ironically, the sin that led the list of his trespasses was a fictitious description of the farm where Pfc. Jessica Lynch lived. So? But the Lynch saga did matter. It helped to glorify a preemptive war (which the *Times* supported), and it was a fiction from beginning to end. She was not caught in an ambush, not wounded in an exchange of fire, not abused by her captors, not rescued by gallant commandos; she had fallen from a truck and was cared for kindly by Iraqi doctors, who managed with difficulty to deliver her to nervous American troops. The *Times* did penance for its false sketch of the Lynch farm, but not for its role in relaying the Lynch saga. The BBC broadcast a day-by-day account of the preposterous fabulation, all citing unidentified sources in the Pentagon, but finally concluded that it was a put-up job. A *Times* article angrily accused the BBC of charging a conspiracy, and demanded that it produce documentary evidence. Just so, during this internal agony of soul-searching, the *Times* continued to feature the possible discoveries of suspected weapons of mass destruction by unidentified informants to anonymous sources who confided in Judith Miller.

Surely, Raines and Boyd meant well. Most *Times* people mean to do well, and sometimes they do well, but they still don't quite get it. That's what this book is about, so let me get on with it. As I was about to say—

For my sins, my first assignment at *The New York Times* was to edit Fin-Biz copy, which was so slugged after the hostile merger of two news desks, Financial and Business, whose jurisdictions were never clear; it had sometimes happened that both would report the same event on the same page. One day a sports editor and I spent a lunch break debating which of us had to cope with more appalling material. My colleague called it a scoreless tie, then conceded a point. He said he'd asked a friend who was a bank officer what he thought of the *Times*'s business coverage. The banker replied that it was excellent, authoritative—"except in banking, where they don't know their ass from first base."

That is the conventional view in a capsule: The *Times* is great, except on anything one happens to know something about. It dominates even those who should know better, like the authors of the unintentionally devastating biography of the *Times* Family, discussed in Chapter Four. As I note therein, the *Times* was never "the greatest newspaper in the world," nor even very good except, like the vicar's egg, in spots. What it was and continues to be is the most influential newspaper in the world, the most relied upon source of information in the most powerful nation in the world.

A bedrock axiom of market analysis holds that the public is always wrong. This is not cynical, at least not very, but rather a statement of the obvious: the public is the last to learn of any significant development, and by then it's too late. It follows that the press, on which the public relies, is always wrong. Not necessarily on details like yesterday's closing prices, though even these may be rigged or misleading, but on the cutting edge of history, which a line that Gibbon pinched from Voltaire calls the tale of man's crimes, follies, and misfortunes.

These days the news is depressing enough. To take my observation literally, that our guiding light is always wrong, would be to abandon hope. A more optimistic outlook sees the media as a battlefield, though hardly a level one. For fifty-seven years in journalism, I have sought to even the balance, by my lights. This book is a further effort. It is not primarily about me, but about what I witnessed, particularly in my twenty-four years at the *Times* as an editor, rewrite man, foreign correspondent, investigative reporter, and food critic. To indicate my bias, let me precede my memoir of dissent with a sermon I preached to the National Conference of Editorial Writers in its organ, *The Masthead,* in the spring of 1982.

ARE WE THE TOWER OF PISA?

For an outsider, it was hard to tell the candidates apart. It was hard for the voters, too. They split so closely that nobody can be sure who won. But the publishers had no problem; every daily in New Jersey backed the Republican for governor.

So in a manner of speaking, one might say that half the electorate voted against the press.

The situation was much the same around the country. It was not particularly new; way back in New Deal days, the overwhelming majority of newspapers upheld the traditional values (now known as supply-side economics) against the overwhelming majority of their readers. Nor is it surprising, for publishers reflect the sincerely held views of the business community. But it is disturbing today, perhaps frightening, because in the typical market there is only one daily left.

There are television and radio, to be sure, but they cannot replace the press as media for thoughtful information and analysis. In any case, their owners vote the same way as the publishers, when they are not the same people. Such a one-sided outlook in a near-monopoly situation can only promote mistrust and moves toward judicial and legislative curbs.

Somebody has likened the American media to the Tower of Pisa, narrow and tilting. For us who dwell in it, it may seem that it is the world around us that is aslant. (We could not, for example, understand why a passing remark by President Reagan about nuclear strategy, which was ignored by the U.S. editors who heard him, was front-page news in Europe.)

Why can't everybody see that we are standing straight and tall? If anything, we lean over backward to be fair. Don't we publish letters, op-ed pieces, and columns by a wide range of pundits?

Well, how wide?

"In the field of opinion writing, conservative syndicated columnists now dominate the field," bragged Hugh C. Newton, lobbyist-publicist for the Heritage Foundation. There followed a list of a score of (to me) dreary Right-thinkers, a couple of ex-centrists now sliding to the right, and a ragtag remnant of "hard-line" liberals.

I am forced to agree. Beginning perhaps with Spiro Agnew's attack on the nattering nabobs of negativism, editors made a more or less conscious effort to cultivate right-wing columnists, for balance. With the Reagan victory of 1980 and the so-called conservative tide, many editors predicted there would be a pickup for liberal columnists. The contrary occurred. My own column, which might be described as hard-line dissent, has gradually added subscribers, but the hawks and supply-siders have picked up more. [United Features did not renew my contract; it invited my surviving subscribers to substitute the "liberal" Morton Kondracke, a Reaganite bore.]

One might say that liberalism is old hat. In fact, that is precisely what one says: "Only the conservatives have new ideas." Well, I admit to a bias, but I cannot see what is new about proposals to cut taxes, repeal a century of social legislation, and go nose-to-nose with the Russkies.

New ideas are surely needed. But like generals, journalists are often fighting the last war. What is Ronald Reagan's "window of vulnerability" but a remake of John F. Kennedy's "missile gap"? Yet many have accepted the former as they did the latter.

Look up your own files of a generation ago on nuclear energy, on tobacco, and on DDT. Read the learned arguments of the establishment, and compare them with those used today on similar issues. We are often wrong.

News is, after all, what the public does not know. The press should always be pushing against the wind, rebutting the established truth—if not in our editorials, then in our news columns, and if not there, then in our op-ed pages. If we must be a leaning tower, then that's the way we should lean.

CHAPTER ONE

Learning a Trade

When there was an accident at the Copper Queen mine, the ambulance wasn't allowed to use its siren, and the *Bisbee Daily Review* wasn't allowed to report it. The mine, the ambulance, and the paper all belonged to Phelps Dodge, and so did I when I took up the trade of journalism there in 1944.

That was something of an accident, too. On my seventh wartime voyage in the merchant marine an old spinal injury laid me low, and a bone doctor told me to do no more heavy lifting. He said a dry climate might help, so I hobbled to Arizona. Spotting a fellow arthritic in a diner, I asked if the Arizona air had done him any good. He said, "I don't rightly know. I was born and raised here." However, there I was, and there was a job opening in Bisbee. I'd never been a reporter before, but I'd never been a seaman before I boarded my first ship. Actually, it requires more craftsmanship to qualify as an able-bodied seaman than as a journeyman reporter. In both cases I learned the trade the old-fashioned way, by doing it.

It was not a demanding job. The paper was made up by a deskman with a "pony wire" from the United Press—a saddlebag of teletype copy that rode in on the daily bus from Tucson, backed up by bulletins received on a Morse key amplified by a tin of Prince Edward tobacco—plus pages of syndicated boilerplate, eked out with local news gathered by me and the city editor, a man who was fond of shooting pool. To a serene character, it should have been a pleasant stint. Bisbee was a picturesque town—or rather, two towns, one Anglo, one Mexican—in Cochise County, near Tombstone. In addition to Rotary luncheons and savings-bond drives, I was free to write about locals' hobbies, about my war at sea, about hunting coyotes with hounds, and about the death of a legendary woman who ran a miners' boarding house (a story that was picked up by the UP wire). I was not free to write about the town budget; the clerk told me it had not yet come back from Phelps Dodge. I was not free to write about the sulfurous plume from the smelter at Douglas, which had to pay for damage to crops but not to lungs. I was not free to write that the election for sheriff was to determine who would collect the payoff from the casinos; as in many mining towns in the West, gambling was wide open on the main street but strictly forbidden in private homes. I was not free to report a sequel to a historic event, the Bisbee Deportation. Just after World War I, vigilantes loaded hundreds of striking miners and their families on cattle cars and stranded them in the desert in New Mexico. Now, after all those years, the miners won bargaining rights, defeating a company union in an NLRB vote. I persuaded the city editor that we had to report the event. He did, in a short under the headline, "Miners Union Loses Out in Local Election."

A poet or a folklorist might have settled down in Bisbee, but it was no place for a man who wanted to play John Reed. Having learned in a few weeks all that the *Daily Review* had to teach about the craft, I accepted an offer by a traveling agent of the United Press and flew to Los Angeles. When I presented my air ticket for repayment, the bureau chief said sorry, I was not on the payroll until I got there. It was my introduction to the celebrated parsimony of UP, whose alumni call themselves the Downhold Club, after the cablese injunction to DOWNHOLD EXPENSES. Los Angeles was briefly stimulating, exposing me to a whiff of Hollywood and a minor earthquake, but I was soon sent off to Salt Lake City, which after a time I quit to join the Associated Press in San Francisco and then New York.

Reflecting now on what the wire services had tried to teach me, I suppose the main things were speed and cynicism. We were always on deadline, and always in competition. What counted was not being right but being first—in fact, being right could be costly. The wire services kept score on their play in major newspapers, and the quicker and noisier lead invariably won. When we at the UP in Salt Lake counted fewer victims in a train wreck than the AP did, our home office told us grimly that we'd been skunked; it did not congratulate us for having got the count right.

We were conditioned from the start to fudge. The first word of any story was likely to be a lie: the dateline. It says the piece was written there, and chances are it was not. The event may have happened there, or near there, or some of it may have happened there, and the place has a nice offbeat sound. At many publications, like New York's *Daily News* when I was there, a phone call to the scene was held to warrant a dateline.* The wire services recognized no limit. At the AP bureau in San Francisco, a bank of talented rewrite men (yes, the bureau was all male, and all white) would take a spare five-line communiqué from the Pacific command in Hawaii and translate it into two columns of thunderous combat. Pictures and captions were also subject to creative treatment. A photographer from the bureau took what is often called the greatest picture of the war; the few editors who set aside the flag-raising on Iwo Jima as too obviously posed and kitschy lived to regret it. (In a sense, the picture may downplay the courage of the photographer and the Marines who posed for him by making it seem too easy and triumphal; they had surely been through hell getting there, and would go through more.)

As they say in show business, sincerity is everything; if you can fake it, you've got it made. Ronald Reagan, who began as a radio

---

*The *Times* used to be fussier, but that scruple seemed to collapse with the World Trade Center. For example on December 18, 2001, the lead story bore the splendid dateline of Tora Bora, but one of the two reporters who signed it was in Washington, and nearly all the information in it came from the Pentagon spokesman, Admiral John Stufflebeam. The *Times*'s military expert filed from Tora Bora, but *his* main source was Defense Secretary Donald Rumsfeld, who was in Belgium. Actually, none of the reporters who got to Tora Bora was permitted to witness any combat, but the prose was often intense.

sportscaster, once demonstrated his skill to an audience of U.S. information agents. Pretending to read from a ticker tape, he turned a few
symbols into a breathtaking putout at second base. He said it might
not have happened quite that way, but it came out right in the end,
and that's how he wanted our truth to be put forward to the world.

Technological progress keeps putting a crimp into this sort of cre-
ativity. An old British correspondent in North Africa told me that the
romance went out of the business when the first underwater cable
was laid, and an old French sportswriter following the Tour de France
grumbled, "Before the telly, we could write up a storm." They did
keep trying, though. When TV first appeared in American saloons
after the war, it was great fun to watch a prizefight on the screen while
listening to the version on the radio. I marvel at the skills that TV has
developed since then, and empathize with referees, now exposed in
turn to the evil eye. But TV introduced its own methodology of hype:
the close-up that makes a small group look like a throng, the voice-
over that contradicts the picture, the picture that does not really
belong to the story, the countervailing source that is ignored.

Routine TV and AP hype hexed a bizarre story that I covered for
the *Times*. It was a page out of the Arabian Nights: King Hassan of
Morocco, his viziers, and the diplomatic corps had been taken
hostage at his birthday party. That is all we heard on the radio in
Paris; communications had been cut. Hours later Hassan's voice
appeared briefly, announcing that Allah had prevailed. An ABC team
and I caught the first flight to Rabat. As I ran toward customs, the
TV correspondent lingered to do a standup he'd scribbled on the
plane, reporting all quiet in Rabat and under control. He explained
to me that he had to hand that film to the pilot for the return flight
to make the evening news back home. I found a cab. On the highway files of armored vehicles appeared, and then came the rattle of
small-arms fire around the military headquarters. Confused cadets
were being rounded up, and some of them lined against a wall and

shot. The Belgian ambassador was dead. On the evening news back home, presumably, all was quiet and under control.

At a news conference the next day the King, a sleek Don in Italian threads, glowed like a cat over a fresh kill. Regarding foreigners' objection to summary executions, he said, "*Je m'en fous royalement*" ("I don't give a royal fuck"). Asked whether we might have access to the rebel officers, he replied, "I regret, gentlemen, that this time tomorrow night, after giving the required information, they will be dead." The AP took him at his word. The following night I was awakened by a message from New York, saying that AP was reporting that the officers had been shot. Could I confirm? Not at this hour, I replied, and said New York must decide whether to run AP.

The executions actually occurred the following morning and were broadcast by radio. It was unforgettable: shouted orders, the tramp of boots, the cries of "God bless the King!" from the condemned men, the orders to fire, the volleys, each of which set off a chorus of barking from all the dogs roundabout, and finally the order to the troops to march past and spit on the traitors. It was unforgettable, but it was old news. We'd been scooped by AP.

The Associated Press, a news cartel founded in an era when publishers displayed strong and conflicting political passions, is credited with fashioning the cloak of objectivity—the straitjacket, if you will—worn by our press. It was designed to avoid offending individual members, but it came to be presented as a virtue: no opinions, just the news, extruded in strings like sausage that could be cut to fit. Early on, *The New York Times*, under Adolph Ochs, became the model for this apparently bloodless journalism. Every day the wire services would advise all users how the *Times* was playing the news on Page One. Especially on those big, complex issues that seem boring to boring minds, the *Times* became a handy desk reference. And so it remains.

Journalists and the public need to know it better.

Jobs of Summer Are Rare Rest of the Year

Headline in the World's Greatest Newspaper, July 18, 1989

CHAPTER TWO

Tyranny of the Clerks

A first immersion into the city room of *The New York Times* had to come as a shock to anybody who had worked in a normal news shop. Russell Baker, who could be philosophical about it because he was only visiting, was bemused by the swarm of idle reporters. Homer Bigart was driven to despair by the swarm of busy editors. At a desk adjoining mine, he grumbled one night, "I never knew newspapering could be dull till I came to *The New York Times.*" He surely did not mean that our trade had turned dull but that *Times* editors, whom he called clerks, could take the life out of it. When he came to the *Times* in the late 1950s, Bigart was widely regarded as the finest reporter in the land; when he died, a passage from one of his dispatches was set in type as poetry. But he said he could not bear to look at his copy after the *Times*'s "clerks" had been at it.

The *Times* was doubtless the most edited newspaper in the land, and one of the least efficient. Reporters were required to type on "books," with carbons that yielded ten copies, for distribution to that many licensed second-guessers. One night, after a day that should have been exhilarating, when I was pursuing fast-breaking developments in a major scandal that I had precipitated with earlier reporting, I complained in a memo that I had had to deal with eight editors, separately; I suggested that they meet, agree on goals, and designate a hitter. Bigart found it hard to deal with them. Summoned to confer with A. M. Rosenthal, he growled, "What do those assholes want now?" To comfort us, that other legendary reporter, Meyer Berger, displayed a paperweight with the legend

ILLEGITIMI NON CARBORUNDUM EST, for "Don't let the
bastards wear you down."

   Times management preferred to produce its staff from scratch, hiring Ivy League graduates as copy boys, culling them, and in due time
promoting survivors to desk jobs or news beats. I thought it foolish
and callous. The routine certainly was not calculated to produce good
copy boys. At the deadline for front-page copy one night, I was moving a bulletin in short takes, calling "Copy!" each time. On the second
take, I looked up and there the boy stood, studying the first take I had
handed him. On deadline. Only at the *Times*... This was not a great
way to detect potential talent, either. Anthony Lewis, for one, found
promotion too slow, quit, and went to the *Washington Star*, where he
won a Pulitzer Prize and then was rediscovered by the *Times*. The system did come up with some very good people, and many drones, all
of them subject to the illusion that the *Times*'s way was normal. To a
degree the *Times*'s huge staff could make up in quantity of coverage
what it lacked in quality, but I presume that members of the owning
family in their social rounds were continually being advised that the
Herald Tribune was better-written, that lots of other papers were more
fun to read, that the *Wall Street Journal* was more useful. So from time
to time they hired writers who had established their talent elsewhere—
and then added new layers of editorial desks, like the stomachs of a
cow, to process their prose into *Times* cud.

   This clutter of clerks was a caricature of a professional shop. At
the *New York Daily News* (where I had worked earlier), when the bells
on the Teletype signaled a flash, the room fell quiet, the aisles cleared,
copy moved without haste from hand to hand, and the flash was on
the street in no time. Meanwhile at the *Times,* chaos would have broken out. Upon the flash, editors would emerge from nowhere, hud-
dle in clusters and then scatter, shout for clips, summon reporters
to write sidebars, call all bureaus for reactions,★ and hover over the

---

★Awakened by such a request signed Gerstenzang (Nat Gerstenzang, night foreign
editor), Arnaldo Cortesi is said to have replied: "Man on street in Rome is in bed. And
by the way, what is a Gerstenzang?"

poor devil who had been chosen to write the lead, exhorting him to get everything up high. And the *Times* would be the last paper in town to appear with the story.

The flash did not have to be a surprise. During my spell on the foreign desk a pope took a week to die. Every afternoon I pulled four sets of page proofs of his obituary for perusal by our canons and saw to the changes they proposed. Finally his eminence drew his last breath, and zounds! Out of nowhere they swarmed, the big canons, too. The pages were torn apart and remade. The presses rolled an hour late... I understand that much the same happened upon the expiry of Richard Nixon, and it still goes on.

This I heard with my own ears: In the men's room, side by side facing the wall were a low-level editor I'll call Kugelhopf and a terminally unhappy beat reporter. Pause. "Kugelhopf, I hear you had a baby. Congratulations." Kugelhopf (unaccustomed to civility from reporters): "Why, thanks!" "What did you name her?" "Rachel." "No, I mean, what did you name her the first time? You know you change everything."

I envied the wit. For my part I am not proud to have cried across the city room one day, "Kugelhopf, my name was on that story. You made me look as stupid as you are!" I forget the specific provocation. There were so many. One that had entertained the newsroom was a dispatch from Paris, under my name, in which "Boul' Mich'" was helpfully spelled out Boulevard Michigan.* The clerks endowed me with a tin ear: a man in Amsterdam spoke English not with a BBC but a British Broadcasting Corporation accent. "At a time when *according to officials* the stock market was going down...."; the words in italics (mine) were one clerk's demented effort to denote my objectivity. (Such fudging on the part of editors is not really all that different from the multiplicity of informed sources that reporters routinely pretend to have canvassed.)

---

*The house newsletter *Winners & Sinners* cracked: "Boulevard Michigan in Paris? It develops that the reporter wrote 'Boul' Mich',' the familiar (but obviously not to everybody) term for Boulevard Saint-Michel."

Ted Bernstein, the news editor, campaigned valiantly to elevate our style but was often defeated by confusion among his troops. When he exhorted them to preserve the difference between "that" and "which," every "that" was liable to be changed to "which," and every "which" to "that." He fought the subversion of the adverb "hopefully"; as a result, when I wrote during the demolition of Les Halles in Paris that the famous bistros were staying on hopefully and the little bars hopelessly, "hopefully" was changed to "it is hoped." Ted did not like to see a corporation identified as a firm, so a law firm I mentioned became a law business. This syndrome was so common that Betsy Wade, a pioneer woman copy editor and a superior one, sent me a teasing cable saluting me for my correct use of the word "transpire"—adding that it had, of course, been caught in time and changed.

When the *Times* published a selection of my features, *Vanishing France,* the book's editor, Roger Jellinek, was baffled by differences between the pieces as written and as they appeared in print; he went with the originals. And gratifyingly, of the fifty pieces he chose, about ten had not been used at all. My little waifs. It was not that the editors did not like them; on the contrary, they assured me that they loved them, and told me my batting average was very high. But it was not so high on offbeat pieces. On a visit to Paris, Clifton Daniel, then managing editor, offered a tip that he said used to work for him: if they ignored a piece, he'd wait six months and file it again. I dug into my folder of unused pieces, found one that was two years old, and filed it again. This time it was used; it also reappeared in my book.

The most common and, I fear, sincere excuse that *Times* editors give for excluding worthy material is one that lay readers and journalists on other publications may find incredible: a lack of space. Quite evidently they have more space than they can manage well. The space in question is charmingly known in the trade as the news hole, which is determined by the amount of advertising that is sold.

Every morning, the advertising department gives the managing editor a dummy for that day, and he apportions the blanks among the various desks. Although the hole is evidently enormous, the desks are all overwhelmed by the flood of copy pouring in from wire services and the huge *Times* staff. As in any bureaucracy, the editors' first concern is to avoid criticism from above; hence they seek to match every story, however dull or trivial, that might appear in another publication and to regard with trepidation anything offbeat. The brass can't complain about a piece they're not aware of, so the offbeat feature may safely be put aside, and is often then forgotten.

On night rewrite, Tom Buckley once said, "We had a nice human-interest story going there, but the desk caught it just in time." Our rewrite bank that year had a more chronic frustration. Every night at 9 PM, Bernstein and his aides, known collectively as the bullpen, would adjourn to the composing room to put the paper to bed. Minutes later, the bulldog editions of the *Herald Tribune* and the *Daily News* would arrive. A desk subaltern we called the Colonel, who was trying out as night city news editor, would clip out every local news item that the *Times* did not have and deal them out to us with orders to match them. At 10 PM the bullpen would come back down and pick up the *Trib* and the *News*. After a while the Colonel's phone would ring. He would reply, "Yes, we have it." Then he would pick one item from his new pile, send it on its way for the next edition, sweep the rest of our work into the wastebasket, pick up his homburg and his walking stick, and go home.

Advertising grew steadily, so the news hole grew, but a sort of Parkinson's law ensured that space would always be tight. In his staff bulletin Bernstein argued reasonably that four hundred words should be quite enough for the average article. Nobody paid attention, not even his own bullpen. One afternoon I picked up a modest human-interest story and filed three hundred words. The desk called with glad tidings, "That's going on Page One. Give us more." I said fine, but that was all it needed. No, no, they insisted, if it's on Page One, it has to jump (be continued) inside. (That is an unacknowledged and of course idiotic rule—one of many whose only explanation is that it has always been done that way.)

Forty years after Bernstein's appeal, a *Times* staff bulletin again called on writers to keep it short—this time to eight hundred words, implying an inflation of 100 percent. Readers will recognize that nobody's paying attention to that appeal, either. *Times* people still evidently expect the goods to be judged by yardage—which is surely one reason their stories often take so long to get to the point.

The same reproach may be addressed to me, since after two chapters I have not yet reported my arrival at the *Times* nor admitted that I signed on as a copyreader—i.e., a clerk. An explanation, if not a wholly satisfying one, is that my wife and I had come to New York with lofty dreams, no money, and in short order three small hostages to fortune. Desk work was easier to find than reporting and paid a bit more; my headlines won cash prizes at the *Daily News* and kudos but no more money at the *Post*. Finally, Richard Burrett, the *Times*'s newsroom personnel chief, called with a modest offer I was glad to accept. Apologetically he asked me to sit in for just three months on the Fin-Biz desk. Unfortunately my headlines there drew kudos, too. But one day, an old colleague on the foreign desk told me, "Hess, you do readers a disservice. You get them to read stories that are a waste of their time."

And he was right.

"The *Times* is not a crusading newspaper."

City editor Frank Adams

CHAPTER THREE

Fin-Biz

The business pages of *The New York Times,* when I landed there in 1954, were a veritable magic pitcher for press agents. Hordes of them made a living from it, and in return they fed, wined, and entertained its reporters. At Christmastime the loot arrived literally in handcarts. Free booze may have been the undoing of Jack Forrest, the financial editor, an amiable alcoholic who was often away vacationing with boozy tycoons and seldom ended a day upright at his desk. The department was managed by his assistant, Tom Mullaney, a teetotaler who needed no liquor to lubricate his regard for business. When I pointed out to him one day that company reports of earnings for nine months, which we printed as received, obscured late developments, he replied that they must have a good reason to do it their way.

The *Wall Street Journal* would subtract the six-month figures from the nine and report "imputed third-quarter earnings." Its news editors took no nonsense from company flacks. They evidently figured that their readership did not mind the propaganda on the editorial page but wanted useful information up front. They took delight in foiling Detroit's annual effort to keep design changes secret while clearing out stocks of the expiring year's models. When General Motors pulled its ads to punish such a scoop, the *WSJ* hooted happily, until GM backed down. But for Fin-Biz, the industry had its reasons, and it was not for the *Times* to contest them.

The contrast goes far to explain a phenomenon I have never seen discussed. The *Times* emerged from World War II as the nation's premier source of business news, with a circulation ten times that of the *Wall Street Journal*. Looking toward nationwide distribution, the *Times* was then experimenting at great expense with transmission by facsimile. A decade later the *Wall Street Journal* was passing the *Times* in circulation without compromising its tombstone makeup, without photographs—only the news. And it began printing at remote sites by teletyping code to linotype machines. The *Times* sought to follow suit with editions in Los Angeles and in Paris. Both failed. (I believe it tells worlds about *Times* management that Tom Mullaney was assigned to edit the west coast misadventure, then returned to Fin-Biz when it folded.) Which also helps explain why the popular barometer of the stock market today is the Dow Jones and not the *Times* average. The *WSJ* periodically replaced stocks and adjusted weightings in its Dow Jones averages. The *Times* indexes, fossilized, had become a joke in the trade. Burton Crane, our stock market reporter, worked for months with some clerks on their own time to bring the indexes up to date, but in the end these efforts were turned down, Crane told me, because the editors did not want to admit publicly that they'd been in error. (Later they just quietly abandoned the *Times* indexes. Nobody mourned.)

Readers today may find it difficult to imagine how bad Fin-Biz was. In the decades since then the writing has much improved—how could it not?—but has remained as faithful as ever to the establishment, and often as naive. In those earlier years there were perhaps fewer illusions about our mission. Fin-Biz reporters made no waves. From time to time one of the brighter ones would cross over to where the money was; several became rich, and at least two became filthy rich. But most of the troops stayed on, either because the living was easy or because they had never really learned a trade. They lived off press handouts and didn't always bother to change the words. One night I had to ask a fellow what a line in his story meant. He expressed pleasure that I'd asked. "You know," he said, "I was wondering that myself."

One columnist built a long relationship with an outfit called, if memory serves, the Foreign Bondholders Protective Council. It consisted of speculators who bought defaulted securities at pennies on the dollar and then nagged Washington to hassle the issuers for a settlement. My colleague had stocked up on Czarist bonds; his column would periodically berate the Eisenhower administration for groveling to Moscow while ignoring the American widows and orphans who had built the Russian railroads. I don't think his gamble paid off. He was not a lucky type.

Another colleague played a key role in a scam that has taken New Yorkers for many millions of dollars, though I doubt he got any more out of it than an occasional lunch and an occasional article bearing his byline. The articles would warn that the city was on the verge of a conflagration because of the condition of residential wiring. Under the cover of this sustained fire scare, lobbyists for the electrical trade eventually put through a law that would grant any landlord who replaced his wiring a rent increase sufficient to recover the cost in a year and a half—with the increase continuing thereafter in perpetuity.

An orgy ensued. The electrical trade was overwhelmed. Hustlers advertised in the *Times*, offering to do the job and handle the paperwork for landlords, no cash down, pay them later out of rent increases. Gangs of huskies with crowbars stormed through apartment houses, reducing plaster to rubble. Many had evidently never handled a soldering iron before; in my dust-coated apartment they installed the fuse box upside down. The work obviously could not pass inspection. But it did.

By then I had escaped copyreading and was on night rewrite. In a memo I sketched the situation and suggested an investigation. The city editor, Frank Adams, a stout, ruddy gentleman with a laugh like a sonic boom, called me over and said kindly, "John, the *Times* is not a crusading newspaper."

The scandal did make the front page a few months later, in the proper way, via a handout. The state attorney general accused a dozen city inspectors of taking bribes to approve wiring. The story then died. A couple of bribe-takers were lightly punished; those who paid the bribes took their profits, and to this day tenants are paying those rent increases, compounded, for rewiring that was often unnecessary and often unsafe. Until now nobody has blamed the *Times*.

LIGHTS THAT SHINE LESS BRIGHTLY

P oor Adams never realized it, but the *Times* was and is indeed a crusading newspaper. It's just that others write the marching music, and the *Times* plays it. In Adams' own bailiwick the paper kept blowing the horn for Robert Moses' crusade against the urban understructure while ignoring or denying abuses by Moses that were then being exposed by the *Post* and the *World-Telegram*. On every front of the Cold War—the nuclear arms race, Berlin, Cuba, Vietnam—the *Times* could, to paraphrase Adlai Stevenson, be considered the quasi-official organ of our crusades. For a quarter of a century now it has echoed the refrain of the crusade against Social Security. So the rewiring scam was routine, petty stuff.

I need now to confront my own complicity. I edited copy and wrote headlines for the rewiring caper and many other misdemeanors. That was what I had been hired to do, and I was quickly advised that objections were not welcome. On my very first day comparative figures in a brief item looked odd. As occasionally happened, a reporter copying from a handout had got one number wrong. I showed the anomaly to the chief of the Fin-Biz copy desk, whom I'll call Sarge because he began his career as a military clerk. He snapped, "Looks all right to me." When galley proofs arrived, I hesitated, then restated my misgiving and drew the same response. On my arrival next day, Sarge tossed me a tear sheet with a red line around the error and said, "You shouldn't have let that get by."

My immediate thought was that I had made a poor career move. Perhaps I should have quit on the spot. I'll get to why I did not in a moment, but at this distance in time, the incident just seems funny.

Sarge didn't have a clue. He had been hired as a stenographer and risen in the ranks by following routine without question. He was bewildered by the reaction to a routine type of headline he'd used a hundred times:

Tampax, Inc., Fills Executive Vacancy

That one occurred during a period when we were not on speaking terms; I noticed it in proof, and I am ashamed to say that I held my tongue. And, I had not quit. I have mentioned my family obligations. Also, I began freelancing in off hours: short, humorous comments for the then-liberal *New Republic*, longer pieces for the *Atlantic*, the *Saturday Review*, and the *Reporter* weekly (all three of which, I now believe, had ties with the CIA—as did the *Times*). The economic jungle dimly visible from the Fin-Biz desk fascinated me; I made my way to Wall Street, rewrote a respectable handbook on market analysis for one firm, wrote a radio news report for another, and absorbed the pungent realism of the Street ("The public is always wrong"; "There ain't no free lunch"; "It's no use being right when the market is wrong"). I tilted my freelance against puffery that was passing through the Fin-Biz desk. One of my magazine articles spotted "a cloud over Detroit no larger than a Volkswagen"—a line that John Keats borrowed the following year in his best-selling *The Insolent Chariots*. A piece of mine on federal tax policy was the subject of a CBS commentary by Eric Sevareid and was entered into the *Congressional Record* (not widely enough read, or people would not persist in considering President Kennedy to have been a genuine liberal). Another article described the war of the railroads against passenger travel. Tycoons were sabotaging service, bleeding the roads by neglecting maintenance and selling off assets (like Penn Station). Meanwhile they were devouring one another and heading for bankruptcy and a vast government bailout—all being reported in the *Times* as if their press agents were covering the story.

A relief from the frustration of the Fin-Biz desk was the presence on the rim of Mel Barnet, a Harvard graduate who spent his idle moments translating Greek classics and studying great chess games and who tried to stretch my mind with philosophy. He mentioned casually that he had been a Communist in the 1930s at the *Brooklyn Daily Eagle*, during one of the battles that founded the Newspaper Guild, but after going off to war, he had quietly concluded that Marxian dogma was not for him. He saw the follies of Fin-Biz much as I did but with serene humor—until his subpoena arrived. Senator James Eastland of Mississippi had mounted an effort in late 1955 to put a red taint on the *Times*'s exemplary reporting on the struggles over segregation and voting rights in the South. Eight or ten staff people were summoned and ordered to name names of former comrades. Most did. They remained on the payroll, although their careers were permanently blighted. Barnet and a copyreader on the foreign desk refused to testify, citing the Fifth Amendment, and were fired on the spot.

Our union contract barred dismissal except for due cause. But the Guild had, like many other unions, purged Left influences, and its leadership was in fact involved in the CIA's covert wars, as is now widely confirmed. Its Washington office sponsored a program of outreach to foreign journalists that was secretly subsidized and staffed by the Agency. The New York Guild officials held that taking the Fifth was indeed due cause for dismissal and declined to contest the firings. I posted a petition on the Guild bulletin board calling for arbitration. A referendum was held. The motion failed by a margin of about 3 to 2. I believe it carried the newsroom but was beaten in the commercial departments—an irony, because it was the Left that had persuaded the Guild in its formative years to include nonjournalists.

Barnet's departure left a wide gap on the Fin-Biz desk. Sarge had become accustomed to shoving most of the copy over to us in a pile, leaving the rest to himself and two invalids (one an alcoholic and the other in what we took also to be an alcoholic haze until he collapsed and was diagnosed as an advanced diabetic). Three applicants were called in for a week's trial. My opinion was not asked, but I had to observe their performance, since I took over the slot when Sarge left each night. In jousting with unions, publishers pretend that it takes three months or six months or whatever to judge a craftsman. Nonsense. I would have hired A on the spot, B was no prize, and C was impossible—who let him in? At the end of the trial week, Sarge told A and C that they weren't what we were looking for and approved B.

It is I suppose characteristic of all organizations that people in authority prefer to be flanked by lights that shine less brightly. This phenomenon was visible at all levels of the *Times*. What was surprising was that Sarge was allowed to select his helpers. How they turned out I cannot say, for my unjust incarceration in Fin-Biz finally came to an end when some friendly influence obtained my promotion to the foreign copydesk. Sarge did not linger; he requested his own release to the rim of the city copydesk, and then early retirement.

Before I move on to abuse other troops, I think I should pin responsibility for the *Times* where it belongs, on Adolph Ochs and the men who succeeded him as publisher. For a brief study, in the following chapter I submit my review of *The Trust: The Private and Powerful Family Behind The New York Times*, by Susan E. Tifft and Alex Jones. The book is like some other biographies I have had occasion to review in that I thought revelations leaped from the page yet were ignored by most critics. I think the critics' impassivity illustrates my observation that journalists see what they are looking for. I recall Dwight Macdonald, who demolished the critical establishment with his review of James Gould Cozzen's *By Love Possessed*—or should have demolished it, anyway. Or check out Mark Twain on James Fenimore Cooper. But I digress. Meet the Family.

The Family
Key Members of the Ochs-Sulzberger Publishing Dynasty

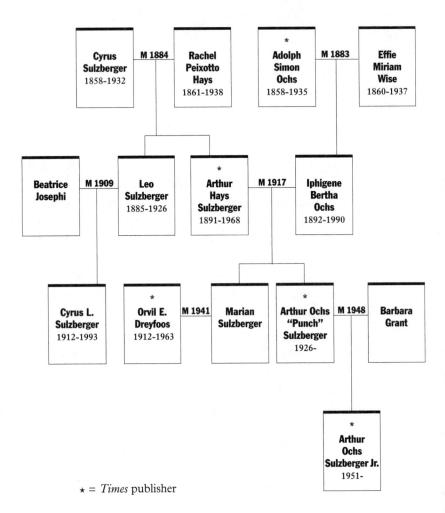

| Cyrus Sulzberger 1858-1932 | M 1884 | Rachel Peixotto Hays 1861-1938 | | * Adolph Simon Ochs 1858-1935 | M 1883 | Effie Miriam Wise 1860-1937 |

| Beatrice Josephi | M 1909 | Leo Sulzberger 1885-1926 | | * Arthur Hays Sulzberger 1891-1968 | M 1917 | Iphigene Bertha Ochs 1892-1990 |

| Cyrus L. Sulzberger 1912-1993 | | * Orvil E. Dreyfoos 1912-1963 | M 1941 | Marian Sulzberger | | * Arthur Ochs "Punch" Sulzberger 1926- | M 1948 | Barbara Grant |

* Arthur Ochs Sulzberger Jr. 1951-

★ = *Times* publisher

CHAPTER FOUR

Meet the Family

On one memorable evening in mid-century, a Hungarian charmer cried across the *Times* city room, "Darling, zay are changing my story!" When the echo reached the publisher of the *Trib*, he garumphed, "Drink is the curse of the *Herald Tribune*, and sex is the curse of *The New York Times*." We who toiled for the Good Gray Lady cherished that tale, implying that she was not as prissy as she looked.*

Little did we know. There was gossip downstairs about our publisher, Arthur Hays Sulzberger, escorting actresses and prostitutes up the back elevator, but nobody told us that he also required his wife, the sainted Iphigene, to tolerate them as houseguests. I never heard that Adolph Ochs, the patriarch, would squeeze women visitors against the wall at the *Times*, or that he once chased a nephew's bride around his apartment in her nightie.

It was hardly news that Adolph would consider fit to print, yet these and many other unflattering disclosures pepper *The Trust: The Private and Powerful Family Behind The New York Times*, by Susan E. Tifft and Alex Jones, an authorized and reverent history of the clan that appeared in 1999. Actually Punch Sulzberger, the Dan Quayle of the clan, who flabbergasted us all by inheriting the throne in 1963, had sensibly rejected the project, but the authors say they persuaded him to relent by assuring him that they would not be salacious. Nor were they. Alex Jones, who won a Pulitzer covering the media for the *Times*, is very much a *Times* man. What might emerge as a *Peyton Place* in

---

*The following material originally appeared in similar form in *Extra!*, January/February 2000.

other hands is treated here with detachment, chiefly for its bearing on the succession.

For example, we are told laconically that Punch's first marriage came apart when he returned early one day to his Paris apartment and found his wife with Don Cook of the *Herald Tribune*. Punch was then serving an apprenticeship as a reporter, a hitch famous in our lore for his neglecting to call in after seeing a racing car mow down eighty-three spectators. His divorce and remarriage coincided with an unrelated paternity suit, which the Family settled. We are filled in on multiple couplings, liaisons, and breakups among his sisters and cousins, chiefly as they bore on whose Ochs was being gored in the internecine strivings that make up much of *The Trust*, ending with the strident objections of Punch's second wife to the ascent of her stepson, Arthur Junior.

We are also advised of problems in the clan with alcohol and drugs and manic depression, which last ailment laid Adolph low for extended periods. The authors tell us that the Family was seriously afflicted with dyslexia, thus accounting for a remarkable rate of failure in private schools and mediocre grades through college; they suggest that Punch had trouble reading long articles in the *Times*. Indeed, the only member of the extended Family to show unquestionable talent was John B. Oakes, a cousin whom Punch fired as editor of the editorial page because of his liberalism. The record may, however, reflect unfairly on the women, who never had a chance. At least until the present fourth generation, their menfolk were, to put it bluntly, chauvinist pigs.

When Jeanette Rankin, the first woman to be elected to Congress, voted against going to war in 1917, a *Times* editorial called it "final proof of feminine incapacity for straight thinking." When the troops came home from the first world war and race violence broke out, the *Times* mourned for the prewar days when most blacks "admitted the superiority of the white race and troubles between the two races were unheard of." Fond as Adolph was of his only child, Iphigene, he was furious when she tried behind his back to wangle a job at the paper. Hers is a moving story, which evokes that of Eleanor Roosevelt. She had returned from college a liberal and a feminist; late in life, she said she'd always been a bit of a socialist. But there was no question of her pursuing a career other than producing a male heir. Her first three tries were girls, and the fourth, Punch, turned out to be conspicuously unsuitable, so rivalry for the succession seethed among many cousins and their wives. Adolph left voting control of the Trust to Iphigene, but she obediently left management to her husband, Arthur Hays Sulzberger, who shortly before his death in 1961 passed it to a dim son-in-law, Orvil Dryfoos. Finally, when Orvil died suddenly in 1963, Iphigene overrode general opposition and enthroned Punch. He does not emerge here as excessively grateful. On the day of Iphigene's funeral and cremation, an Ash Wednesday, Punch noticed a smudge on the forehead of a *Times* staffer and jested, "Oh, dear! I hope that isn't Mother!"

Iphigene's loyalty to the Family, her kindness to its many crippled birds, and her discretion were legendary. So it is a revelation to learn in *The Trust* about a taped message that she caused to be played at a stag dinner celebrating her husband's 20th anniversary as publisher. "Dear Arthur," she said, "Once more, you must admit, I am right. If this were not a man's world, as I've always insisted it is, I would not be left out in the cold tonight. If I'd been the boss's son instead of his daughter, this party might have been for me instead of you." Then, disappointingly—and, I think, erroneously—she added that she would have been a disastrously inferior publisher. "All I want is to be your wife, even when I'm left at home."

There is in fact scant evidence of superior management by the male side. On the contrary, the menfolk failed against the odds in their home town, Chattanooga, and in efforts to publish editions of the *Times* in Paris (twice) and Los Angeles. They blew countless millions on badly planned printing plants and on a facsimile system of transmission, long before the *Wall Street Journal* and *USA Today* showed them how to print at long distance. They provoked long and costly strikes, which in the end were settled on terms they should have negotiated at the start. They so botched a venture into book publishing as to lose control of the Times Books rubric.

It may properly be argued that they must have done some things right, but even these tend to lose luster on examination. For example, Adolph's "stroke of genius" in cutting the newsstand price to a penny, said to have saved the paper at the start, turns out to have been a desperate move to finesse exposure of his padding of circulation figures. And while those strikes waged by Orvil Dryfoos and Punch temporarily cut into the *Times*'s profits, they also sped the demise of the other three broadsheet dailies in New York, leaving the *Times* in an impregnable position—which renders absurd an often repeated myth that Editor A. M. Rosenthal then saved the *Times* by introducing those special sections. In fact, the paper was never in danger, and the sections were imposed on a reluctant Rosenthal by Punch, who presumably got the idea from similar formats in the *Washington Post* and the *Miami Herald*. All of which raises the question: How did such a family build the most influential newspaper in the world?

The answer, I firmly believe, lies in the oath published by Adolph Ochs in 1896 in his first issue of the *Times*, "to give the news impartially, without fear or favor, regardless of party, sect or interests involved."

Not that he meant a word of it—as Tifft and Jones show when they tackle another mystery: how did Adolph Ochs, a virtual bankrupt from Chattanooga, persuade Wall Street to set him up with the moribund *New York Times*? Answer: The financiers were anxious to keep the paper alive as a Democratic voice against the Populist Democratic candidate for President, William Jennings Bryan, who was stirring the masses with that speech about the Cross of Gold. Ochs bought a fine new suit, set up a fake bank account as reference, and persuaded J. P. Morgan and others to bankroll the purchase. His "impartial" paper pilloried Bryan, and Ochs marched with his staff in a businessmen's parade against him. In 1905, he let a financier who had been exposed by the *World* as a crook write a *Times* editorial in rebuttal; at the time, the financier held a controlling bloc of *Times* stock in escrow. (Ochs appears to have paid his way out of hock in 1916, though details remain cloudy because he had records destroyed, apparently in fear of a tax audit.)

And yet. Ochs's noble vow defined the image of the *Times* forever after, even for those who honored it in the breach. Which made for extraordinary paradoxes. We are told that Scotty Reston crowed for years, as well he might, about how young Punch rebuffed President Kennedy's request in 1963 that he pull David Halberstam out of Vietnam. Yet Reston himself had at Kennedy's request toned down *Times* coverage of the Bay of Pigs and of the Cuba missile crisis... Punch's grandfather, Adolph Ochs, wasn't surprised by the Teapot Dome oil scandal of the early 1920's; he had sat on the story to avoid embarrassing the Harding administration. Punch's father, Arthur Hays Sulzberger, let the CIA park agents in an undetermined number of *Times* bureaus and at the Agency's bidding pulled a *Times* reporter out of Guatemala on the eve of a coup that in the end cost countless lives. (Punch's cousin Cyrus Sulzberger was a willing asset of the CIA, code name Fidelis.) Punch himself on one notable occasion challenged cousin John Oakes to say whether he'd take an editorial stand that would damage the *Times*'s interest simply because it was in the public interest—and blew his stack when Oakes said yes, he would. "Without fear or favor, regardless of interests involved," indeed.

And yet, Punch and his news staff rose splendidly to the challenge of the Pentagon Papers, the secret history of the Vietnam War. It was an exploit that honored all of journalism, but it needs to be put in perspective. It had little effect on the course of the war except that it led Nixon to Watergate—and the *Times* blew that story. Tifft and Jones overlook one reason for its playdown of the burglary: bureau chief Max Frankel had been assured by his friend Henry Kissinger that the White House was not involved.

The *Times*'s coverage of the Indochina war, as indeed all its news coverage, may be viewed as a battleground. On the one hand (to employ a favorite *Times* usage), a handful of reporters did noble work; on the other hand, editors reined them in, toned down reporting on the peace movement, passed up chances to break the news of the My-lai massacre, and followed the basic administration line on peace terms to the bitter end. I reserve my modest witness to these events for later on but note here that, far from challenging the fictitious Gulf of Tonkin incident that led to our virtual declaration of war in 1964, Reston was then advising Lyndon Johnson on how it would play. The *Times* eventually reported the truth, tragic years later. This was typical. Every day the paper carries distressing reports about the results of policies it supported or ignored when they were going down.*

"KEEP YOUR HAND ON THE TILLER . . ."

The *Times* succeeded because advertisers valued its readership and because readers respected its explicit commitment to integrity and its implicit role as the voice of the establishment. Especially in times of crisis, they were reassured by its heft and its sobriety... "All the News That's Fit to Print"... "the newspaper of record"... the long gray columns, unrelieved by comics or even, while Ochs lived, by crossword puzzles. In turn other media came to accept the *Times* as the voice of authority. Newspaper editors all over the country took daily guidance from an AP advisory on how

---

*A random example: The *Times* savaged New York's Mayor David Dinkins for granting a cost-of-living catch-up to teachers, and lauded his successor, Rudolph Giuliani, for freezing their pay. Then in November, 1999, a front-page story described as a crisis the exodus of qualified teachers from the mean city to the better-paying suburbs. The story spoke of an urgent need for increases on the order of 20 or 30 percent. But when the Giuliani contract expired in 2001, the *Times* returned to its customary parsimony, calling for longer hours in exchange for a 3 percent raise.

the *Times* was playing the news on Page One. Broadcast news desks relied on it as a desk handbook on complex issues of policy. When Kennedy was reminded that the buildup for the Bay of Pigs invasion had previously been reported by *The Nation*, he retorted, "But it was not news until it appeared in the *Times*."

So it became the most powerful newspaper in the world. But despite the persistent conceit shared by Tifft and Jones, it never was "the greatest newspaper in the world," or even a great newspaper. Leaving aside the foreign press, the *Trib* and others were far better written, the *World-Telegram* and the New York *Post* covered the city more thoroughly and with less fear or favor, the *Wall Street Journal* was light-years better and bolder on business news, the *Washington Post* covered the capital better, and individual reporters on various publications would frequently beat our socks off. The *Times*'s journalism is forever making up in quantity what it lacks in quality.

Quality is there, to be sure, and it is visible every morning, like raisins in oatmeal, though one should examine each one before swallowing. Some of the Pulitzer awards were deserved, some were appalling. Talent is constantly attracted by the *Times*'s aura, its clout, and its money, but for a recruit to sustain individuality and idealism in that mill of mediocrity is exhausting. Some of the best escaped to other battlefields, some were forced out, some adapted. A Darwinian selection favors the survival of people who see the world as the Family does.

Jones, for example. Asked on a book show which of the Family they most admired, he and Tifft promptly named Ochs and Punch. Only after prodding did Tifft think to mention that Iphigene, who had held the Family together, was nice, too. If there is a villain in *The Trust*, it is Bert Powers of the printers union. Jones and Tifft wholly agree with management that the *Times* had to become a media conglomerate to obtain the resources to smash the unions. In the end Powers saved his members' jobs for life; Jones and Tifft are shocked that some now draw money from the *Times* without producing anything. It never occurred to them that that could be said of most of the Family.

Having previously recorded the breakup of the Bingham dynasty, which ruled the *Louisville Courier*, the authors are convinced that family control is a sine qua non of journalistic virtue, and they end with the triumphant assurance that it will survive for another generation or two. Ironically, the publication of their book coincided with the ouster by the *Times* of the family that long ran the *Boston Globe*. Anyhow, their thesis is questionable in the abstract and in the particular. Consider the standards of Hearst, McCormack, Chandler, Newhouse, Annenberg, Pulliam, and a host of other dynasts. Consider also the history of the *Times* under the Family. The Newspaper of Record recorded a century of the crimes, follies, and misfortunes of mankind, generally as a faithful voice of the Eastern establishment. It supported all its wars, hot and cold. It supported witch hunts during and after World War I and temporized with the one after World War II; it fudged the menace of Hitlerism and played down the Holocaust. (Jones and Tifft are interesting on the uneasy relationship of this very American family with its Jewishness.) At the cutting edge of major events, it could be found against women's suffrage, against unionism (always), against minimum wages and national health insurance. In its New York base it backed Robert Moses and his bulldozers against the countercrusaders Jane Jacobs and Lewis Mumford. Like the rest of the business establishment, it preferred corrupt politicians to liberal reformers; in the 1997 mayoral election it conceded that the Republican Giuliani was "ethically challenged" and racially "insensitive"—as it endorsed him against a woman Democrat whom it regarded as ethically unchallenged and racially sensitive.

It should be noted that the new generation, represented by Arthur Junior, has been exemplary on women and homosexuality (though one might find troubling his agreement with his wife that she should end her independent career in journalism). He also moved the editorial page from center-right to center. But the right retains strong positions on the paper, established during the reign of Rosenthal as executive editor. Rosenthal's first successor, Joe Lelyveld (who was replaced by Howell Raines only to replace him in turn when Raines stepped down in June 2003), is quoted here: "Abe would always say, with some justice, that you have to keep your hand on the tiller and steer to the right or it'll drift off to the left."

So that was about where the *Times* stood at the arrival of the new millennium. Like all the media, it is in a period of extraordinary turbulence, and great changes no doubt lie ahead. Whether the Family actually will prove able to keep control remains to be seen. Does it matter? Stay tuned.

"Most of us at the UN, and I think this is true of foreign delegates as well as ours, have come to rely on the *Times* coverage of the UN as almost quasi-official."

Ambassador Adlai Stevenson, in an October 27, 1964 letter to Arthur Ochs Sulzberger

CHAPTER FIVE

Clerks to the World

When Adlai Stevenson died, the only book at his bedside, and indeed the only book he was known to have consulted in years, was the *Social Register*. The foreign desk kept one handy, too, but referred perhaps more often to Debrett's *Peerage* and the *Almanach de Gotha*. No other American publication can have been as punctilious about titles. Our managing editor, Clifton Daniel, was quick to spot any gaffe regarding the British gentry; he was sensitive also to such distinctions across the Channel, as among Freiherren, barons and baronets, counts, dukes, and princes—and their ladies. Cables would arrive regarding momentous events; our first task was to fill in the appropriate Misters, Herren, Monsieurs, Señores, and Signori, according to protocols lost in history. I think a Rumanian had to be Monsieur, though I can't remember why. But it was more important to get the title right than to get the story right.

Tales were legendary of correspondents in the field being hassled about the spelling of names and places whose transcription into English is at best arbitrary. The desk found it difficult to accept that some cultures don't use first names and that the U of U Nu, the UN secretary general, was an honorific, implying Mr. Nu. Much time, energy, and passion went into getting such details right. At the same time monstrous falsehoods were passing into print, unchallenged.

I refer especially to our coverage of the coups, conspiracies, betrayals, assassinations, and black propaganda that festered during the Cold War—covert action, which Henry Kissinger said should not be confused with missionary work, and which Scotty Reston tolerantly called dirty tricks. Instructive in this regard is the sad tale of Kennett Love. He was our correspondent in Tehran during the overthrow of Mohammad Mossadegh on August 19, 1953, a momentous turning point in world history. We got Mossadegh's name right (by our rules), but little else of importance.

To this day, American textbooks tell it as it was conveyed by Love and other American reporters: how Mossadegh, a sniveling clown in pajamas, was threatening to turn Iran over to the Soviets when a patriotic populace overthrew him and restored its beloved Shah. Actually, as Iranians have known all along, Mossadegh was a conservative nationalist who had outlawed the Communists and who opposed foreign domination. What doomed him was his nationalizing the oil fields. The West embargoed Iranian oil; when that trick did not suffice, the CIA organized a coup in detail, down to hiring hoodlums, drafting proclamations, and directing the street fighting.

In the *Times*, Love gave us an eyewitness account of a homegrown revolt. But six years later he wrote a different account in a term paper for a professor at Princeton. It told how he and an AP man were taken to an American residence in Tehran to meet the coup's native military chieftain, watched the photocopying of a decree by the Shah dismissing Mossadegh, and took copies to distribute to other journalists.

He noticed that American diplomats never seemed surprised at the news he brought them from the streets. He also remarked that the black-market rate for the dollar was going down instead of rising, as one might expect during an upheaval; it was not until long afterward that he deduced that this was because the CIA was pouring dollars into the slums to pay for gang violence. In his thesis Love wrote:

> I myself was responsible, in an impromptu sort of way, for speeding the final victory of the royalists.... A half-dozen tanks swarming with cheering soldiers were parked in front of the

radio station. I told the tank commanders that a lot of people were getting killed trying to storm Dr. Mossadegh's house and that they, the tank commanders, ought to go down there where they would be of some use.

They did go, and they were of use. Mossadegh's guard was routed; he was captured and died in prison. The Shah was brought back and imposed a police state enforced by the CIA-trained Savak, whose name became a byword for terror. It crushed moderate and left opposition, leaving the way open to the fanatic mullahs who seized power in 1979.

In 1980, while Americans were transfixed by the plight of the embassy hostages, somebody found a copy of Love's term paper in the sealed archives of Allen Dulles, the former CIA chief, and leaked it to *CounterSpy*, a journal that specialized in exposing covert action. *CounterSpy* accused Love of having been a CIA agent. He denied it. He was quoted as saying that he'd acted out of "misguided patriotism." He later denied that, too, but it would seem to be his best defense, and is almost certainly true.

Persuasive evidence came in a suit he brought against Jonathan Kwitny for calling him a disgrace to journalism and for quoting too much of Love's term paper in Kwitny's book on U.S. foreign policy, *Endless Enemies* (Congdon & Weed, 1984). The libel complaint was dismissed, but the copyright infringement count went to trial. (It was eventually upheld.) Inevitably, Love's truthfulness came under scrutiny.

It was only five months after the coup, Love testified, that a senior *Times* colleague, Robert Doty, told him who was running that show, adding, "but you cannot file it."

Considering what Love had witnessed, he certainly seems to have been naive. Under cross-examination he explained his failure to report those activities in his dispatches as reflecting "our policy."

Q. You mean the U.S.'s policy, isn't that correct?

A. The U.S. and *The New York Times* were dead against Mossadegh.... *The New York Times* editorial board would write these editorials about this, portraying Mossadegh as an insane old clown that spent all of his time in bed weeping... they seemed never to have read my copy.

Love said he became so troubled about his copy that he wrote three letters to the foreign editor, Emanuel Freedman, confessing that he had avoided mentioning the role of American agents in the coup because it was "too good grist for the Russian propaganda mill," but now felt the story should be told.

"Why do you think I did it three times?" he said. "I was trying to get Freedman so angry that he would go for the story."

Needless to say, Freedman never did go for the story. In fact, while Love was pleading in 1954 for permission to report it, the *Times* was covering up another coup. Elated by its triumph in Iran, the CIA set out to repeat it in Guatemala, which had moved to redistribute some idle land held by United Fruit. With light feints by land and air from Nicaragua, subversion of the Guatemalan army, and a heavy propaganda offensive, the Agency overthrew a democracy and brought on decades of terror. Years later we learned that our publisher, Arthur Hays Sulzberger, had acceded to a request by Allen Dulles to keep the correspondent Sydney Gruson away until the deed was done.*

The extent of Sulzberger's services to the CIA has never been fully disclosed. George H. W. Bush, who headed the CIA from 1976 to 1977, has said it did not then employ *Times* correspondents as agents, but Tifft and Jones say he was referring only to fulltime staffers. Carl Bernstein reported that during the 1950s about ten CIA agents were employed as clerks or part-timers in *Times* bureaus overseas. Gossip

---

**The Trust, p. 313.

mentioned two or three full-timers as well. The subject is intriguing, but whether journalists were actually paid by the CIA is surely less significant than what they reported, or did not report.

The easy Guatemala caper no doubt encouraged the arrogance with which our covert warriors took over from the defeated French in Indochina the same year, and began a war of lies, some of which are repeated in the *Times* to this day. Then came another crisis in the Middle East, in 1956. In response to a rebuff by Secretary of State John Foster Dulles, the Egyptian strongman Gamal Abdel Nasser nationalized the Suez Canal. In a synchronized assault, Israel crossed the Sinai Peninsula and France and Britain moved in, ostensibly to block Israel and protect the "lifeline of the British Empire." The empire was gone but the *Times* still worried about its lifeline. In the event, the rescue effort cut the lifeline. However, Eisenhower forced the allies to withdraw, and the canal was cleared of sunken ships and reopened. I recall showing Freedman a clipping quoting shippers as saying that the canal was operating more efficiently than it had been under the Suez company. Since that contradicted what we had predicted, I suggested we look into it. He did not reply.

ALWAYS ASKING QUESTIONS

On the home front, *Times* reporters were covering the segregation battles with courage and distinction; abroad, most of them fit Stevenson's perception of them as quasi-officials. One shining exception was Herbert Matthews. During the Spanish Civil War, which the *Times*, like the State Department, treated with studied neutrality, Matthews had covered the republican side sympathetically, while a colleague carried the flag for the fascist side. Now a resistance was flickering in Cuba, and Matthews's sympathies were again engaged.

So, I must say, were mine. Cuba has seemed special to me since I first stepped ashore there as a seaman in 1942. It was an enchanting respite from the worst of the war at sea. But long afterward, when the picture of Elian Gonzales came to dominate our TV screens, I was struck by how he resembled the small boys who greeted us at the foot of the gangplank—offering to lead us to their sisters. The island was rich and beautiful, most of its people poor and hungry. I remember telling myself that this country needed a revolution. Ironically, Fulgencio Batista told me the same thing when I interviewed him on behalf of the Associated Press, in a luxury suite at the Waldorf-Astoria soon after the war. Having as a sergeant led a revolt against dictatorship in the early 1930s, he had eventually handed power over to duly elected civilians, who thereupon engaged in looting the country. Bored in exile, Batista said he was planning to return and get into politics. He did. Still popular, he seized full power in 1952 and set up a growingly cruel tyranny, with the collusion of the Mafia, American business interests, and the U.S. government.

Then came Fidel Castro and his quixotic adventure. His little band disappeared into the Sierra Maestra and were long unheard from. The regime said it was over and Castro was dead, which seemed plausible, given the relation of forces. But Matthews made his way into the Sierra and found the rebels alive, spunky and determined. His exploit was a shining page in a dark chapter of the history of the *Times*. No doubt it encouraged the resistance in Cuba and its sympathizers abroad, whence the famous poster of the Bearded One with the legend "I got my job through *The New York Times*." In truth, Castro was not a Communist in the Sierra but rather a radical nationalist. He mistrusted and despised the Communists, and vice versa; only during his triumphant march on Havana did they join his parade. When he closed the gambling casinos and moved to nationalize large foreign holdings, the Eisenhower administration decided he had to go. It began by cutting Cuba's sugar quota and taking a few covert counterrevolutionary jabs. Castro then turned to Moscow for help, took over the Cuban Communist Party, purged its leadership, and made the party his own, thus turning the myth into reality.

In 1960 Miami was abuzz with war preparations. *The Nation* and a few other publications reported that exiles were training in Guatemala. Paul Kennedy of the *Times* went there and found no evidence of it. In the presidential campaign John F. Kennedy, who presumably had some idea of what was going on, accused the administration of tolerating a Communist menace ninety miles from our shore; his opponent, Vice President Nixon, felt obliged to call him reckless. (Kennedy also brandished the missile gap. There was a huge one—in our favor.) Anyway, JFK won the election, and approved plans for the Bay of Pigs. Now Tad Szulc gave the *Times* another chance to shine; from Miami he reported the buildup and said the invasion was imminent. It is notorious that, at Kennedy's request, Scotty Reston had the story played down and struck the word "imminent."

On 43d Street, we followed the debacle by shortwave radio. The newsroom was gripped by a deepening sense of humiliation—not because our government had committed a cowardly aggression, but because it had been defeated by a tiny foe and exposed to all the world as a liar. Planes from Florida disguised as Cuban had bombed Cuban airfields before the invasion; at the UN, Adlai Stevenson waved fraudulent photographs and lashed the Cuban delegation with contempt. He claimed later to have been deceived by Kennedy, but he did not resign; nor did he lose the affection of the *Times*. Matthews, however, became an embarrassment. He was moved upstairs to the anonymity of the editorial board, and his career effectively ended.

In all these events the foreign editor remained silent. Freedman was, in fact, painfully shy. A quintessential clerk, he tried with expensive tailoring to dress up to his eminence, but he shunned eye contact. A short man (like me), he chose a shorter clerk, Nat Gerstenzang, to be night foreign editor. Nat in turn passed over the obvious choice to succeed him as head of the copy desk, a bright fellow who occasionally questioned his judgment, and named instead a man who was subject to hot flashes and occasionally took leave for psychotherapy. Call him Sigmund. One evening he passed to me for editing a dispatch from a desert region in the Mideast. Agreeably surprised at its quality, I just checked off the punctuation, wrote a headline, and slid it back. A few minutes later I heard a squeak. Then, "Did you pass this?" "Yes, what's wrong with it?" Redfaced, Sigmund pointed to a mention of camel dung being dried in the sun for fuel. "Do you realize," he said, "that people will read this at the breakfast table?" For once I found an appropriate retort. "Do you realize what our readers do before they get to the breakfast table?" Sigmund slashed his pencil across the offending passage.

The nit-picking reached my breaking point during an immensely colorful visit to the United States by Nikita Khrushchev—the one in which he tossed corncobs at reporters in Iowa and wagged his bottom at movie moguls in Hollywood. Harrison Salisbury wrote the leads, splendidly, and for a change a story deserved all the space we could give it. One night I was ordered to cut eight hundred words from Salisbury, to make room for some of the sidebars that the editors thought every big story required: a profile, a history of the site, whatever. Under protest, I complied. Next day, a furious Nat Gerstenzang confronted me. I had unknowingly deleted the name of a security official who happened to be the subject of that day's "Man in the News."

Last straw. I went to Freedman and told him I would no longer work on a desk where copy came out worse than it went in. I thought he'd likely reply that he accepted my resignation. Instead, he looked down at the crease in his trousers and the polish of his shoes, murmured that he didn't think the copy came out worse, and asked what I wanted to do. I said I aimed to go back to reporting. Still looking down, the foreign editor of *The New York Times* said, "I don't know why everybody wants to be a reporter—always asking questions."

The upshot was that I chose a job not many people wanted, night rewrite. It fit in with my freelancing and would minimize the controversy I thought I'd run into on news beats that had been suggested to me. I did not altogether escape foreign news, however. Gerstenzang occasionally would ask me to rewrite dispatches from David Halberstam in Saigon. I recall asking him, "What's wrong with it?" He said I'd see. I ran the cables through my typewriter, making no substantive changes. Halberstam's work deserved the Pulitzer Prize it would receive, but it made the foreign desk nervous. On the front page one day a powerful eyewitness report by Halberstam was twinned under a joint headline with a dispatch from Washington that in effect called him a liar.* On the other hand, the *Times* rebuffed President Kennedy's suggestion that it bring Halberstam home.

I'll discuss our Vietnam coverage in another chapter, but I am struck again by the contrast between what we knew about the Kennedy administration and what we reported. Secret wars, coups, assassinations, sabotage, black propaganda, cultural corruption, regressive fiscal policy—the basic outlines were quite visible, but we covered them as Kennett Love did the coup in Iran.

In my seat on the rewrite bank I was a fascinated but helpless onlooker. I wrote an occasional freelance piece, signed an occasional petition, swore an occasional oath. Then, at home one night, I got a call from the bullpen. The *Times* had begun printing in Europe an early edition edited in New York but it was not working out well. A few men were being picked to put it together in Paris. Would I care to go? Paris. Would I!

The New York Times, August 23, 1963. The Saigon regime had begun violent raids on Buddhist temples two days earlier. The U.S. government scrambled to deflect blame for the raids from President Ngo Dinh Diem, implicating army commanders in the plot. Halberstam's lead cited "highly reliable sources" that "the decision to attack Buddhist pagodas and declare martial law in South Vietnam was planned and executed by Ngo Dinh Nhu, the President's brother, without the knowledge of the army." Alongside this report the *Times* ran its dispatch from Washington, which led off, "The United States Government believes that a group of Vietnamese commanders convinced President Ngo Dinh Diem that he should order a crackdown on the Buddhists and proclaim martial law."

Pepe le Pew,
le skunk.

Photofest

From "Week in Review,"
The New York Times,
November 29, 1998.

CHAPTER SIX

Paris Edition

It should have been a cinch. Our only competition was the Paris *Herald Tribune*—a livelier paper, to be sure, with better sports writing and columnists from home and a breezy string of expatriate talent, including Art Buchwald. Plus comics. But Europe offered a wide-open market to the quasi-official organ of the Western superpower. And we had one major advantage: the closing stock tables from New York, transmitted in an electronic burst and fed into our linotype machines in Paris.

My first chore was to organize, edit, and write half a page of financial news from the wire services and to write an occasional feature. B. J. Cutler, the *Trib*'s editor, said ours was the only section he could never match. But I kept hearing complaints about missing stocks, which I relayed to the editors to no avail. I found out why one night when I was putting my page to bed and saw a printer reach into the page and toss lines of lead at random into the hellbox. I emerged crying to Tom Daffron, the editor, "Tom, they're throwing out stocks!" His deputy growled, "How else you gonna justify the page?" The problem was that while the space allotted to the stock tables was rigid, the number of stocks traded would vary from day to day. It dawned on me that our editors had told the printers to solve the problem that way. I pointed out that the makeup editor could simply take out a few alphabetical headings and footnotes as needed. Instead, Tom asked me to stay out of the composing room.

My first chore was, in any case, done. I turned the page over to one of the bright expatriates who lined the copy desk and set out to compete with the *Trib* on another front, as a one-man bureau serving the several American communities in Paris. That year many people were alarmed by the provocative language of the Republican candidate for president, Senator Barry Goldwater, who was widely perceived as threatening war in Southeast Asia. I followed their campaign for Lyndon Johnson with sympathy, though I gently warned some of them that he was no dove. I did other community news, interviews, features, and with my wife's guidance, a weekly restaurant review that would lead us to pleasant adventures.

One day the *Trib* carried on its front page an AP report of a strike of schoolteachers at an American air base near Madrid. I said it was too bad we had missed it. "We didn't miss it," the deputy editor grunted. "It made the overset." Meaning that the AP story had been set in type as a short but had been squeezed out for lack of space. I grabbed a phone and worked the bases. The teachers' walkout had spread around Europe. I stayed ahead of the story until the strike was settled a week later. Then a teacher phoned to ask that I fax clippings of our coverage. Why don't you buy a paper? said I. We can't, he replied, the *Trib* had vending machines in the PX's, but not the *Times*. I charged up to circulation, where three supervisors were sitting waiting for the hour of the aperitif, when they would adjourn to their informal club across Rue Lafayette. Their chief put my news to a colleague, who said yes, we also had permission to install vending machines, but hadn't got around to it yet. It became clear why newsdealers around Europe were often running out of the *Times* and said they got no response to inquiries. In season, our circulation department worked the Côte d'Azur, but service was no better there. Referring to these and other anomalies, a woman bookkeeper told me, "*Le New York Times est pourri*"—rotten, corrupt, incurable.

It was a slow death. I witnessed it from another vantage point, since Daffron decided that his editorial budget had no room for a reporter, and I moved to the Paris bureau of *The New York Times* as a temporary fill-in. The publisher sank millions into a new printing plant in Paris but kept the old management. Finally Sydney Gruson was brought in as editor, and the quality of the paper visibly improved—but it turned out that he had been named skipper only to scuttle his ship. He negotiated a deal under which the *Times* and the *Washington Post* became joint owners of the *International Herald Tribune*. Punch Sulzberger had promised Gruson the editorship, but his new partners balked at replacing the captain of the winning team. (It would not be until January 2003 that the *Times* would buy out its final partner and place the editorial content under direct control of the New York paper, thus ending an interesting hybrid and beginning an international edition for the third time.) Gruson quit in anger, but eventually returned as Punch's amiable and shrewd adviser. This is, of course, far ahead of my story, but Gruson figures in several memorable chapters of it.

The first came soon after I arrived at the Paris bureau. A dinner companion related that Morgan & Cie., the investment banking subsidiary of Morgan Guaranty, had sailed into stormy weather. It was in trouble with the European cartel led by Deutsche Bank, with the Swiss and Danish authorities, and with the Feds in Washington, who were concerned about the conflict between Morgan Guaranty's role as a commercial bank and trust company and its subsidiary's floating of new securities for related companies. To resolve the legal issue, the bank had arranged to hand 80 percent of the subsidiary over to Morgan Stanley of London (no kin, formally). These were several stories that had the banking world abuzz. I spent a day checking them out, filed my scoop, and went to bed.

In New York the story was routed to Tom Mullaney, who was back in Fin-Biz after the debacle in Los Angeles. He turned it over to his banking reporter, H. Erich Heinemann—who had just been hired away from Morgan Guaranty. Heinemann replaced my dispatch with a piece purporting to rebut a disobliging rumor that had never been published, a no-no under *Times* policy. It quoted the bank as saying its Paris venture was thriving—so well, in fact, that it would be taking in Morgan Stanley as an 80 percent partner. Embarrassingly, however, a carbon copy of my cable had gone to the Times News Service. It received good play in the *Times* of London and elsewhere, including our Paris edition. I've been told that the chairman of Morgan Guaranty complained to the publisher. The news service then carried a message declaring that questions had been raised about the accuracy of my cable and inviting subscribers to print a corrective dispatch from New York, which followed. As far as I know, none did. There were no inaccuracies to rebut. Bankers I talked to, including a couple at Morgan, had been pleasantly surprised to see my candid account of its tiff with the European cartel. I was of course outraged. I drafted a protest cable. David Halberstam, who was temporarily in charge of the Paris bureau, spiked it and sent one of his own. No response. I phoned Gruson, who was then serving as foreign editor, and blew my stack. He pleaded ignorance about finance and said, "John, it's just another story." Then he added that he had been planning to call me anyhow, to invite me to stay on as a staff correspondent in Paris. It was a curious sensation: bad news and good news in tandem. It was a sensation I would experience again and again.

GOTT IN FRANKREICH

On good days I now had the best job in the world. The only foreign correspondents I'd have changed places with were the free souls who were paid by the *Baltimore Sun* or the *Los Angeles Times* or, like Hemingway, the *Toronto Star*. They didn't have the clout of *The New York Times*, but they didn't have its editors, either. Nonetheless, I was living high in France and should have been, as the German saying goes, happy as *Gott in Frankreich*. And I suppose I was, except when I wasn't.

The bureau chief handled the top diplomatic and political stories and entertained important visitors. My job was occasionally to substitute for him or back him up with sidebars and field the flow of requests from New York. In my spare time I followed my own star. It moved in an eccentric orbit, even when I covered such apparent frivolity as the Bachelors' Fair.

A retired banker seeking to revive a dying hamlet in the Pyrénées sponsored a carnival to attract wives for its unmarried men. It was picked up as a fun story by the world media, with one exception. "The sightseers came by the thousands," my lead said. "Cupid never had a chance." Journalists and other gawpers frolicked in the square, where a few small, dark villagers in floppy berets sat apart, glumly. I left to seek out their womenfolk, whose daughters and landless sons had fled to the lowlands. A white-haired mother of seven, with an eighth on the way, told me she did not know why the fair was being held. "My faith," she said, "life must be better elsewhere."

And of course it was. But the revolution that was wiping out small farming (in the United States as well) was also destroying the cunning husbandry that preserved the fertility of the land and the rich variety of its produce. I tried to record its passing and interpret it without undue sentimentality, and to examine alternatives (a topic I'll return to at the end of Chapter Thirteen). On one assignment I detoured to a small collective farm in the Savoie, whose organizer, a worker priest, told me that the right size was eight to twelve families; fewer than that would be insufficient to get the benefit of the division of labor (a civilized work week, vacations), more than twelve would nurture friction, factions, jealousy, and shirking.

I never found time to get that bit of wisdom into the *Times*, but paging through *Vanishing France*, a selection of pieces I wrote for the paper, I am impressed by how much dissent did get past the desk. The first article in the book mourned the demolition of Les Halles, the great central market of Paris, and reported that Paris was eating less well, and paying more, as a result. I pursued that issue later in New York and encouraged the founding of Greenmarkets. In the same didactic spirit I sought to record the picturesque and the sad, the good and bad that were being destroyed in the name of progress,

and to salute those arrangements that made life better for most people in West Europe than in our country.

I once divided the number of trees and acres of park in Paris and
New York, respectively, by the number of tree surgeons and gardeners they employed and concluded that Paris loved trees one hundred times more than we did and flowers ten times more (see
Appendix item one, "A Blooming Wonderful City"). Parisian park
workers I talked to worried that if my column got back to France, it
might encourage Mayor Jacques Chirac to cut staff. Foreigners often
seem to emulate our faults more than our virtues. That was a point
I tried to make in Paris, in panel discussions and in occasional guest
columns in *Le Monde*. In passing I put in my two centimes to help
save the Rond-Point of the Champs-Élysées. The great aircraft
designer Marcel Dassault told me in an interview that in view of the
objections he would reconsider his plan to deface the site with two
office buildings. And, as all can see today, he did drop it. The plan
surely clashed with the spirit of the man who said his secret of design
was that if it was beautiful, it would fly. His son, announcing a new
venture, was asked what had been done in the way of market
research; I was delighted to hear him reply, "We asked Papa, and he
said, 'Go ahead.'" Just then the notion that management science was
the secret of U.S. power was being heavily propagated by Jean-
Jacques Servan-Schreiber's slapjack best-seller, *Le Défi Américain*. To
several audiences in Paris I argued that America was not rich because
it had MBAs but rather had MBAs because it was rich.

I doubt I changed many minds. Of course I was there to report
and not to preach, but my outlook had to shape what I observed. No
two reporters perceive the same event; we generally find what we are
looking for. I reckon that is evident in every article in *Vanishing
France*—for example, the one about the murder of a nurse by two
convicts in the prison at Clairvaux. I went there a week after the
French press corps had left, having whipped up a hysteria that would
send the perpetrators to the guillotine. I found an unreported scan-

dal: harsh conditions, a work slowdown by guards, the assembly of prisoners to witness the bonebreaking clubbing of would-be escapees. At another prison rebelling inmates chalked grievances on roof tiles, which they threw into the street. One that grabbed my attention said that in the local palace of justice, where two judges alternated, sentences handed down on Mondays, Wednesdays, and Fridays were far harsher than those on Tuesdays, Thursdays and Saturdays. Blind justice, indeed.

As noted, features about common folk were liable to be mislaid in New York. But our editors shared the appetite of the masses for news about aristos—and still do, as witness recent frenzies involving Lady Diana, William Kennedy Smith, John F. Kennedy Jr. et al. Charlotte Curtis, whom we then still called our women's editor, took umbrage at a trendy reference to jet setters as Eurotrash. For my part I found it hard not to smile at a procession of frumpy Hapsburgs and Hohenzollerns attending a funeral in Liechtenstein; it was instantly clear why movie directors choose actors from the working class to play royals. Two reigning monarchs whom I interviewed while they were killing their subjects struck me as gangsters, though I could hardly so describe them in dispatches; the *Times* valued Hassan of Morocco and adored Hussein of Jordan. On the other hand, I was charmed to meet the liberal dowager queens of the Belgians and of the *Times*. The former volunteered that the fascist-leaning King Baudouin I was an imbecile; the latter, Iphigene Sulzberger, would never speak ill of her son but probably harbored no great illusions.

THE NEW ROME

My *Times* credentials were a magic key. I walked the streets of Paris with William Saroyan. I visited dirt-floor huts of peasants, caves of winegrowers, kitchens of great cooks, the last horsedrawn barge in France. The fabulist author of *Papillon*, in his hospital bed dying of cancer, spun me a yarn about death row. The brilliant chemist and compulsive swindler Philippe Ariès chatted with me

about the arts of outwitting corporations, doping horses, and coun-
terfeiting paintings. I hitched a ride through the Alps with the Tour
de France, where Tom Simpson, a Yorkshire miner's son and world
champion, told me why bike racers used stimulants ("Kiddies moost
eat, moostn't they?"); a year later he fell from the saddle during a
steep climb and died. Claude Lévi-Strauss, the anthropologist,
explained structuralism to me in terms he thought I might grasp.
(He forgave an error about him inserted by a copy editor and wrote
me a flattering note about *Vanishing France*.) I enjoyed comparing
his insight about the way primitive legends vary according to
whether food is baked or boiled, with the insight of Père Troisgros,
the primitive patriarch of the greatest restaurant in France, about
the difference between raw and cooked salt.

I asked the renowned biologist Jean Rostand, a Résistance hero
and peace advocate, whether "survival of the fittest" had not promoted the vicious aggressivity that ravaged our century. "*Ah non,
monsieur!*" he exclaimed. "Man is a loving animal!" He viewed the
instinct to defend the family as a self-sacrificing impulse essential to
its survival, although social forces had so misdirected it as now to
threaten the survival of life on earth. It was a bit of a coup to get this
sort of message into the *Times*, which then as now reflected the
Establishment's outlook on the great events of the day. I could
scarcely tackle them head-on in dispatches, so when James Finken-
staedt, a partner in William Morrow & Co., invited me in 1967 to
write a book about France, I jumped at the chance, after warning
him that what I had in mind was not folkways but something more
urgent.

Back home people were reported to be pouring French wine into
gutters, burning French lingerie, canceling travel to France. The
phobia was whipped up by a media whose mindset may be judged
from a question posed by Don Cook of the *Herald Tribune*, then dean
of the American press corps in Paris, at a background briefing by
the American ambassador, Charles E. Bohlen: "Mr. Ambassador,

don't you think Charlie's foreign policy boils down to this: He gets up in the morning and says to himself, 'What can I do that would hurt the United States?' then goes ahead and does it?" Bohlen replied patiently that he didn't think Charles de Gaulle was anti-American at all but simply did not believe that a small or medium-size country should get drawn into the orbit of a great power. (I checked my notes later with Bohlen.) This diplomat, dedicated cold warrior that he was, had a better handle on reality than did many of my colleagues.

In my spare hours I pounded out a 150-page pamphlet, which I called *The Case for de Gaulle*, though actually it set out a case against U.S. foreign and economic policies as presented by our media. It received pro and con reviews in the *Times*, and permitted me to broadcast my dissent during a cross-country book tour (though there were seldom copies in the bookstores).* Rereading it today, after more than three decades, I find it painfully current. My thesis was that on each of the big issues on which de Gaulle was bugging us, he had a moral right to his position; in some cases his position was possibly even in the interest of the United States. On Indochina and on Israel, which I shall treat in separate chapters, I said he was prophetic. When he sent our troops away, I asked, was he not doing us a favor? Was it not aberrant that our armies were still there, twenty years after VE-Day? Our answer at that time was as obvious as the Berlin Wall, but the Wall fell long ago, and our troops remain in Europe. NATO no longer has a plausible mission, yet nobody today seriously questions the need to expand it. In the year 2000, presidential candidates debated whether our military budgets had been increased sufficiently.

---

*A French translation was kindly reviewed. I presume it helped account for my being awarded the *Ordre du mérit*. Publications like *Le Monde*, by no means favorable to de Gaulle, found it newsworthy that an American should defend France at that juncture. My defense was qualified and limited; I indicated, for example, that I did not agree with de Gaulle that France needed an atomic *force de frappe*, but added that we Americans were hardly the ones to lecture anybody about the bomb. Readers interested in my view of de Gaulle as a leader may consult the two final articles in *Vanishing France*.

If our policies remain the same in the absence of the Soviet menace, what then was our driving motive? I propose the reply of an American official, dining near the Quai d'Orsay, to my troubled observation that we were behaving like a new Rome: "I *like* being the new Rome!" The same hubris marks nearly all commentary on foreign affairs in the *Times* today, if not with the evident delight of, say, Thomas Friedman, then with the gloomy acceptance by all hands of the white man's burden. Manifest Destiny and the American Century were born long before the Bolshevik Revolution and have survived its demise, I fear stronger than ever. Even the resentment of France has persisted.

De Gaulle rejected the role of satellite not only for France but also for Eastern Europe. He defended national sovereignty, economic as well as military, against what we now call globalization. He described the European Common Market, then being organized with encouragement of the U.S., as a *machin*, or gimmick, and he delayed the admission of Britain, which was reluctant but also offended. Today, Euroskeptics and critics of GATT, NAFTA, the IMF, and the World Bank may find de Gaulle's view as I presented it very much to the point. His call for a return to the gold standard may now seem quaint. It did then, too, at least to American financial reporters. And yet it had an intellectual clarity worthy of attention, while our reporting thereon was a lesson in bad journalism.

"I do not think Nasser wanted war. The two divisions he sent into the Sinai on May 14 would not have been enough to launch an offensive against Israel. He knew it, and we knew it… fundamentally, the war was provoked by an ensemble of factors…. The Arabs must understand that one does not provoke wars with impunity. This one, like the previous ones, will have to cost them something."

Gen. Yitzhak Rabin, Israeli commander-in-chief, in an interview with Le Monde, *February 29, 1968.*

CHAPTER SEVEN

Tragic Victory

In Paris, the Six-Day War played out against a setting of unreality. On the sunny morning of June 5, 1967, when I strolled through Parc Monceau on my way to the office, the city was at its loveliest. But clusters of pedestrians gathered around the news kiosks at the Gare St. Lazare, staring at an extra of *France-Soir* headlined *"L'Egypte Attaque Israel."* Appalled, I made my way to Rue Caumartin. Our bureau chief, Henry Tanner, said worriedly that he hoped it would become clear beyond doubt that the Arabs had struck first. In a few hours that pretense had been abandoned. Israel's Mirages had destroyed Egypt's MiGs on the ground in a preemptive strike, and its armor was racing to the Suez, just as in 1956. In the following days Syria and Jordan entered the fray in accordance with their treaty with Egypt and were swiftly crushed. In Paris processions wound through the streets chanting *"Israel vaincra!"* ("Israel shall conquer!"), and automobile horns responded with the three-two beat that a few years before had signified *"Algerie Francaise!"* In the street below our window a marcher threw a rolled-up ball of paper at a North African workman. By the sixth night Israel occupied all of Jerusalem and the West Bank, the Golan Heights, Gaza, and the Sinai. It was a famous victory.

Sydney Gruson had managed to get there by chartering a plane in Zurich. Returning by way of Paris, he exclaimed, "What a lovely war!" "Sydney," I said, "Six hundred *Jewish* boys died in that war." (It was as clear then as it would be today, alas, that ten thousand Arab lives would not weigh in the balance.) I didn't understand, he replied. Had I read the threats in the Arab press? Had I seen how close Arab guns were to Tel Aviv? Had I seen the Golan Heights, menacing the kibbutzniks tilling the shore of Galilee below? It is no doubt vain to debate who began this showdown. There had been a bloody clash in that disputed area in April. Moscow charged that Israel was mobilizing to attack Syria. With typical bluster, Nasser declared the Strait of Tiran closed to Israeli shipping, sent UN peace observers away, made a defense pact with Syria and Jordan, and declared he was ready if Israel wanted to fight ("Israel Encircled," said a headline in *Le Monde*). As Rabin later told *Le Monde*, Israel's leaders did not think they were in peril of attack.

Nor did de Gaulle. Abba Eban, the dovish Israeli foreign minister, found him agitated by the threat of a world war. "I had much more reason than him to be nervous," Eban said, "but I was not." On May 24 de Gaulle called upon Washington, Moscow, and London to join him in an effort to avoid war. Washington agreed, Moscow declined. The *Times* commented, with gloomy satisfaction, "Even President de Gaulle, who is apparently willing to throw Israel to the sharks... has been rebuffed in his effort to achieve a four-power conference." That day de Gaulle received Eban in a meeting that he would recount in a famous November, 1968 news conference at the Élysées:

> If Israel is attacked, I told him then in substance, we will not let you be destroyed, but if you attack, we will condemn your undertaking. Certainly, despite the numerical inferiority of your population, considering that you are much better orga-nized, much more unified, much better armed than the Arabs, I do not doubt that if it comes to that you would obtain mili-tary success. But then you would find yourselves engaged in growing difficulties, on the ground and from the international point of view... so that they will little by little put the blame on you, as conquerors.

War was not yet inevitable. Diplomats were busy in many capitals. President Johnson, preoccupied with Vietnam, called for restraint. The Egyptian vice president was on his way to Washington, apparently to seek a face-saving deal. The Israeli cabinet was split on whether to attack, until June 1, when Moshe Dayan came in as defense minister and broke the tie.

One of the myths that have blighted peace hopes since then was born that week. As recently as March 25, 2002, Bill Safire could express outrage at suggestions that the Jews "occupy Judea and Samaria... the land on the west bank of the Jordan [that] was used by Arab armies in 1967 as a base to surprise and destroy Israel." And on May 10, 2002, the myth echoed in a dispatch by Steven Erlanger on the suicide bombings and reprisals: "Thirty-five years ago, during the six-day war, Israel's soldiers bravely defended their doughty little country from a combined attack of Arab nations."

The actual war and its aftermath went as de Gaulle had predicted. He carried out his promise to condemn the attack and announced an embargo on arms sales to Israel. The United Nations nearly unanimously called upon Israel to evacuate the occupied territories, but it was de Gaulle who served as lightning rod for the anger of Israel's sympathizers. My book, *The Case for de Gaulle*, proposed the heresy that there were no winners, only losers in that war and held that de Gaulle's conduct had been exemplary except for one lapse of judgment. In that November news conference he prefaced his scolding of Israel with what he surely intended as a compliment: a reference to the Jews as "an elite people, sure of itself and *dominateur.*" The translation caused some tension between the Paris bureau and New York. We preferred the first meaning given in our dictionary, "dominating," as in overcoming travails, whereas others took it as "domineering." I held that in either case it was uncalled for. David Ben-Gurion defended de Gaulle's intentions, but his was a minority view. Even in France, de Gaulle's stance had few defenders. *Le Monde* was particularly harsh, but a few months later it summed up the situation in the Holy Land as follows: "Terrorism, border incidents, repeated warnings, reprisal raids, cease-fires painfully negotiated while awaiting new battles: One might think oneself carried back a year.... It suffices to say that, *as was easy to foresee*, the victory of last June has resolved nothing" (emphasis added).

AN UNWITTING LIABILITY

That will do as a description of the next two years. The Paris bureau had other business to attend to: the Vietnam peace talks, the youth uprising of May 1968, de Gaulle's recovery and eventual self-defeat. Meanwhile bureau members were frequently pressed into duty to help report other fires: Prague, Biafra. I visited gunmen in Ireland and churchmen in Western Europe, got an early glimpse of Libya under Qaddafi, did my book tour in the States, and continued when I could to report about vanishing France. Then, in June 1970, I was sent to relieve our Cairo correspondent for a spot of home leave. I think my experience there tells something about the history of U.S. involvement in the Middle East. It also tells something about journalism and the CIA. Long afterward I recalled that time in an article headed "The Company I Didn't Keep" for the journal *Covert Action*:

> Daniel Schorr put us all on the spot years ago when he acknowledged that as a correspondent for CBS he routinely swapped intelligence with the CIA (*The New York Times*, January 5, 1978). It then behooved every journalist to come in out of the cold, I thought....
>
> The Company, as we often refer to it with casual familiarity, apparently categorizes journalists as witting contacts, unwitting contacts, witting assets and unwitting assets. I suspect that the agency, if in fact it did use me once or twice, put me down as an unwitting liability.

In the eight years I wrote for the *Times* overseas, I never met anybody I knew to be working for the CIA. I knew journalists who had been approached, and I met many who would, like Schorr, occasionally call on a station chief for a briefing. Not I.

I had never cultivated or used such contacts. I was struck by this once, at a Franco-American conference of journalists, when a compatriot complained that the Quai D'Orsay kept only two officials available to serve the entire English-speaking press corps. I wondered why, with fifty million French citizens to talk to, he needed more diplomats—but after all, he was a diplomatic correspondent. I have known reporters abroad who would not file a story before checking it out at the embassy. They give it away in their dispatches: "according to Western diplomatic sources . . ." They could cover the scene just as well from the State Department, which gets the same reports.

Schorr himself, in recounting how he exchanged information with the CIA, seemed insensitive to the possibility that it loaded his reportage. His agency informants may indeed have been "generally more knowledgeable and objective than their diplomat counterparts," but as he noted, they only told him what they wanted known. In light of what we now know about the CIA, it takes an act of faith to believe that they never slipped him any disinformation. "As long as my sole purpose was getting a story and my employers were aware of what I was doing," Schorr wrote, "I felt ethically secure."

The CIA never made an overt approach to me, nor I to it. Publicly, and in writing, I disagreed with nearly all aspects of U.S. foreign policy in those years (1964–72). However, there was one move by Washington that I did approve of—the now almost forgotten Rogers Plan, which may have been the most benign effort of the Nixon administration.

In early 1970, Nixon and his National Security Adviser, Henry Kissinger, were handling all the "major" foreign policy matters involving Indochina, Chile, and Europe. They let the nominal Secretary of State, William P. Rogers, take responsibility for the Middle East, where the situation appeared hopeless. A war of attrition between Israel and its neighbors was taking lives daily along the Jordan river and the Suez canal. The Israelis refused to negotiate until the Arabs came to them without conditions. The Arab states refused to negotiate unless the Israelis agreed to withdraw from the territories seized in 1967.

Rogers proposed a cease-fire, accompanied by an agreement to negotiate a peace based on U.N. Security Council Resolution 242. This document called on Israel to withdraw from occupied territories and for the Arab states to recognize Israel's right to exist. Both sides greeted the Rogers plan with growls.

It was in this context that the CIA may have used me to convey a message or two.

An acquaintance in Cairo claimed to be the correspondent for a small European radio station. At a social occasion he took me aside and showed me the text of a U.S. aide memoire (confidential diplomatic communication) to Foreign Minister Mahmoud Riad, assuring him that the U.S. understood Egypt's insistence on the return of the occupied territories, and would press Israel to agree in principle, as a basis for a cease-fire. The correspondent asked that I not reveal my source, because an Egyptian official would be gravely compromised if the leak could be traced to him.

I trusted my informant not at all, so I did what reporters often do in such circumstances. I went to a U.S. diplomat who had often declined comment but was not known to have lied to us, and asked him something like this: "If I were to file a report along these lines, would I fall on my face?" He said no.

To protect my source, I flew to Beirut and filed from there, asking New York not to use my byline or a Mideast dateline. The desk went me one better and folded the story into a dispatch from Washington.

Months later, a colleague with good CIA relations told me what followed. The Egyptian Foreign Ministry complained to the State Department that while Cairo had been compelled to keep quiet, Washington had leaked news of its proposal. This was an obvious assumption, because of the Washington dateline. Secretary Rogers replied that the *Times* had obtained the story through a correspondent in Cairo, who had filed it from Beirut. My *Times* colleague and his sources thought this diplomatic embarrassment an excellent joke on the CIA.

A more portentous story was to follow. One weekend in mid-July, my young informant advised me that Nasser had been persuaded by Moscow and Washington to accept the Rogers Plan, and would announce a cease-fire in a few days. I checked this one not only with the U.S. Embassy but also with a well-informed Egyptian, and filed the story on July 18, 1970, datelined Cairo.

On that day, Israeli fighter-bombers were raiding Egyptian anti-aircraft positions. In Washington, Kissinger had just held a backgrounder in which he spoke of expelling the Russians from Egypt. In a television interview, Nixon asserted that the Arabs "want to drive Israel into the sea" and that a shift in the balance of power against Israel would mean war. Assistant Secretary of State Joseph Sisco was talking tough as well, and it looked as if Secretary Rogers, the dove, was being pushed aside.

It is unclear why the CIA (assuming it was the CIA) was willing to scoop Nasser on his announcement of a cease-fire. Washington may have feared that Nasser would change his mind and decide to hang tough. The leak, then, might have been a nudge. It may also have been designed to restrain Israeli aggressiveness on the Suez front, which was clearly a danger to Arab acceptance of the peace plan.

Like most such exclusives, this story reflected little real credit on the reporter. Unfortunately, some of my competitors took it as a reflection on them. Replying to "rockets" from their home offices, they cabled that the *Times* story was a hype. They filed dispatches to that effect, and they repeated it loudly in the Nile Hilton restaurants.

Continuing attacks on Washington and Tel Aviv in the Cairo press seemed to support their view. My own dispatches in succeeding days fleshed out details of the coming agreement, and my editors, bless them, ran my copy. But as the week advanced, I began to get uneasy.

On Thursday, July 23, Nasser addressed a party assembly, and berated Israel, the U.S. and the Rogers Plan for forty minutes. In the press box, reporters were punching out bulletins about Nasser's rejection of the plan, and occasionally glancing at me with smirks. Then in a glaring non sequitur, Nasser concluded by saying that, silly and hopeless as it was, he would give the Rogers Plan a whirl.

The wire service bulletins' new leads all said Nasser had accepted the plan "conditionally," and my own desk, which had backed me bravely until then, now cautiously inserted that qualification into my own dispatch. In fact, despite the bluster, Nasser had put up no reservations, and his letter of acceptance to Rogers actually used the adjective "unconditional." I am persuaded that the grudging treatment by the U.S. press of Nasser's bold gesture contributed, in a small way, to the plan's eventual failure.

Although none of the coverage I saw made a point of it, it was the Israelis who balked at peace. In the Knesset on June 29,

Golda Meir criticized the plan, holding that a three-month cease-fire was not enough, that the Egyptians should come to the Israelis directly and that it should be made clear that not all the occupied territories could be returned. In the end, the Suez cease-fire was the only positive achievement of the Rogers Plan. Negotiations for a peace agreement were never begun. Instead, cease-fire followed temporary cease-fire. The Palestinians, for whom no explicit provisions were made, rejected the plan from the beginning. While shooting stopped on the Suez front, commando raids continued across the Jordanian and Lebanese frontiers. Against Arafat's opposition, PLO hardliners extended the warfare to travelers, culminating in the synchronized hijacking of four airliners. In Jordan, King Hussein responded with his tanks and crushed the PLO there. Nasser, exhausted by his effort to halt the strife, died on September 26.

A joke in Cairo the next year went: "Name a suave, handsome man whose hobby is extending cease-fires." Anwar el-Sadat did more: he expelled the Soviet military missions and resumed relations with the U.S. But he failed to get any movement toward a settlement. On the contrary, with an election approaching, Nixon undercut any hopes for peace by waffling on his earlier commitment to U.N. Resolution 242's call for pre-1967 borders.

In a talk I had with Assistant Secretary Sisco in Washington in late 1971, he said the Rogers Plan could not be called a failure, because nobody had been shot along the Suez since mid-1970. The shooting resumed on Yom Kippur, in October 1973. It cost more than 10,000 lives to restore the cease-fire and move the front a few miles across the canal. Then came the civil war in Lebanon, clearly a byproduct of the impasse, followed by Sadat's daring deal for the Sinai, his assassination, the Israeli invasion of Lebanon, and still no peace.

Looking back I'm struck by the transitory nature of the scoops that, if my colleague is right, the CIA fed me. The really big stories, of course, are the ones the Company would protect with its life: its intelligence failures, its role in the civil wars, the politics behind the turn away from Rogers and the victory of the hawks (*CovertAction*, Summer 1991).

The question may reasonably be asked: How qualified was I to cover the Middle East? The answer is, not very, but neither was the Anglo-American press corps as a whole. I never met a member who spoke Arabic. That meant we could converse only with the few "natives" who knew English or French, or we relied on translators—often our drivers. I believe that the situation persists to this day; the fact that editors tolerate it speaks worlds about the imperial mentality. I kept trying to convey my handicap to readers (which is why I mentioned the BBC accent of that Dutchman in Amsterdam); I remember a British correspondent, looking over my shoulder as I wrote, marveling at my scruple in that regard. In my Mideast missions I found the French best qualified by and large. The British had a few fine reporters as well as some of the most unscrupulous ones I ever met. Two of them tried to slip me phony scoops on Russian subs in the Dardanelles and in the Suez Canal, respectively, figuring that if *The New York Times* reported it, they could get away with it too. It was that sort of experience that caused me to predict, when Rupert Murdoch bought the *New York Post* in 1976, that we Americans would now learn how low journalism can get. (He had his revenge; he bought the TV station on which I said that, and I was fired forthwith.)

WAR WITHOUT END

Qualified or not, I was sent back to help cover the hijacking of the four airliners by the leftist Popular Front for the Liberation of Palestine. One was flown to Cairo, evacuated, and blown up, apparently to rebuke Nasser for his cease-fire. The other three were parked on a sweltering desert airstrip in Jordan. Hostages were released in installments as mediators toiled in vain. Amman was in a state of anarchy. Rival factions of Palestinians guarded roadblocks. Boys pointed AK-47s in our faces and examined our press cards, then waited for a chieftain who could read them and let us pass. Bursts were often fired into the air, for no apparent reason; there never seemed to be a shortage of ammunition. The last lot of hostages was taken to a secret location and the planes destroyed. A Palestinian uprising against Hussein seemed imminent, but Arafat, who disapproved of the hijackings and expelled the PFLP from the Palestine Liberation Organization, would have none of it. A dispatch of mine identifying him as a moderate in that scene shocked some readers in New York—as no doubt it would in the year 2003.

Eric Pace of the *Times* and I alternated in flying our copy from Amman to Beirut each evening, to avoid Jordanian censorship, and returning next morning. I drew the long straw—what turned out to be the last flight before Hussein closed the airport, cut communications and sent his armor against the Palestinians. Eric and several dozen other journalists were confined to the Intercontinental Hotel in Amman under spartan conditions, unable to report the fighting, while I tried with John Lee, a *Times* financial reporter, to cover it from one of the world's great hotels, the St. Georges, in Beirut. We had to work with scraps, mainly from Arab media (translated), rumors, and a couple of nervous sorties to the Syrian and Israeli borders. Lee found the U.S. Embassy singularly unhelpful; indeed, the military attaché could not identify pictures of military tanks on the move that a reckless freelancer photographed for us in Syria. Day after day Hussein's armor would shell the Palestinians, meet some resistance, and pull back. The Iraqis threatened to intervene—against whom was not clear. The Syrians sent a column across the border to relieve the Palestinians. We gathered that Israel and the U.S. persuaded them to pull back. Nasser, gravely ill, struggled to bring about a cease-fire. When it came, it required the Palestinian militias to

depart from Jordan to Lebanon. Exhausted, Nasser died, setting off
a paroxysm of grief in the Muslim world. That was Black September.
In Beirut I renewed contact with the PFLP spokesman, Ghassem
Kanefani, a young poet, novelist, and artist famous in the Arab
world. At a news conference in Amman during the hijacking crisis,
I had asked him (in my un*Times*ian manner), was it not morally
indefensible to risk the lives of innocents, and would it not be self-
defeating if any were hurt, no matter how just their cause? He
replied, I thought evasively, that before the hijackings the world had
ignored the Palestinians; now it was paying attention. I could not
deny that; until then the very word Palestinian was suspect in New
York, implying as it did the existence of a people other than Jews
with a claim to the Holy Land. Now the word occasionally got by.
In Beirut, Kanefani returned to my question: he pointed out that
every one of the hostages had survived, and he said PFLP members
had died under orders to protect them during Hussein's attacks. I
later visited the house in the combat zone of Amman where they had
been held and saw fresh graves in the garden.

I also saw Arafat again, in a refugee camp at Beirut that would
one day be the site of a massacre by Maronite Christians under the
protection of Ariel Sharon's troops. In Jordan, Arafat had impressed
war correspondents as indecisive and disorganized, but Kanefani
acknowledged that when the Jordanian armor struck, Arafat shoul-
dered a bazooka, improvised a barricade, and fought back. In Beirut,
Arafat gave me pieces of mortar shell with Hebrew markings, which
he said had been fired by Hussein's army into the refugee camps in
Jordan. I had only his word for that, which would be worthless in
New York, but the claim was plausible. On a tip in Amman that
Americans were flying materiel, including some from Israel, to Hussein, a CBS TV crew and I had driven back to the desert airstrip and
watched a U.S. cargo plane unloading under the guard of a few Jordanian tanks. An officer politely gave us coffee heated on the engine

of his tank while, out of our sight, one of our drivers was beaten for having brought us there.

Not much of the real history of that small war was visible to us, and rather less ever reached our readers. Groping in the dark, we had to compete with more strategically situated colleagues. A. M. Rosenthal, the managing editor, arrived in Beirut on a quick tour to inspect his troops. His foreign editor, Jimmy Greenfield, was a casualty; he fainted literally in our arms from what a French doctor diagnosed at a glance, and an American doctor confirmed after elaborate tests, as abuse of his liver.

While he was mending, we took Rosenthal for a peek at the region south of Tyre and Sidon that threatened to become a war zone. En route, he asked a question that he had apparently just faced in Cairo: did we think the *Times*'s coverage was biased? We were not then aware that Rosenthal would one day emerge as a superhawk on Israel,★ but I wondered: doesn't the man read his own paper? After an uncomfortable pause I mumbled that dispatches from Washington and Tel Aviv tended to get preference in play over any from an Arab capital regarding the same events. I fear I did not express a more important point—that although we contemptuously rejected Arab leaders' complaints, we accepted as truthful their hollow threats

---

★The Rev. Billy Graham apparently understood Rosenthal better. Not long afterward, when Graham and Nixon ranted about the "Satanic Jews" and the necessity of breaking their "stranglehold" on the media, Graham added: "But I have to lean a little bit, you know. I go and keep friends with Mr. Rosenthal at *The New York Times*, and people of that sort. And all—not all the Jews, but a lot of the Jews—are great friends of mine. They swarm around me and are friendly to me. Because they know I am friendly to Israel and so forth. They don't know how I really feel about what they are doing to this country." Even when they did know, they forgave. When the foregoing tape was made public in 2002, the Anti-Defamation League came to the defense of Graham and Nixon, on the ground that they had rescued Israel. William Safire, who had long claimed the late president as a friend and shared his wisdom with readers, withheld comment on the revelations of his anti-Semitism. But in another context, Ed Koch explained to an interviewer why he raged at the Rev. Jesse Jackson but remained friendly with Senator Jesse Helms: "You don't understand. Jesse Helms may hate the Jews, but he loves Israel."

against Israel. The different weight given to news about casualties among Israelis and Palestinians has not changed over the years. As I write, a report by American pathologists accusing Israeli troops of using excessive force in the current intifada is played down inside under the headline "Doctors Back Many Palestinian Accusations, but Not All" (*The New York Times*, November 4, 2000, p.8A).

The threat of violence was palpable in Lebanon. Arafat reportedly never slept in the same place two nights running; one met him only by appointment, after a circuitous, blindfolded tour. Leaders of rival factions were even harder to reach. By contrast, the PFLP press office in Beirut faced the broad Corniche, within walking distance of the luxury hotels where Western journalists mingled with visiting oilmen, bankers, diplomats, agents, and Gulf sheiks. When I called there, I found Kanefani, a slender, tense figure rather resembling Omar Sharif, standing at an easel, drawing a horse with carbon and crayons—one of his avocations. He sipped mineral water and took a pill for his ulcers, then tucked an automatic into his belt and headed for home. At the curb, as he opened his car door, I remarked that there were hundreds of windows facing us that could conceal a weapon. He replied with a smile that a fusillade aimed at him just then would also hit a middle-aged American journalist. Seriously, he said he did not care for his role as a spokesman but could not perform it in hiding. That was the last I saw of him.

At a luncheonette in Tel Aviv a bit later I had an off-the-record chat with a former Israeli Labor minister who was reputed to be a dove. I asked what he might envision in the way of peace terms. He told me he thought a majority of Israelis might be willing to give up 85 percent of the occupied territories. I was startled. After a moment's thought I said, "You mean, you'd give back the Sinai?" He said yes. And nothing else?—not Gaza or the Golan Heights or the West Bank or old Jerusalem? He said no, not them. When I got back to Paris, I told my wife I never wanted to return to the Middle East because the people we met there were doomed to war without end.

A few weeks later Kanefani and his niece were killed by a bomb in his car. His assistant opened a letter that exploded, leaving him half blind and deeply scarred. An Israeli missile hit the apartment of our Beirut office manager, killing his wife and daughters, who had entertained us and given my wife a lesson in Palestinian cuisine. No, I never wanted to return. Besides, I had another war on my conscience.

"I need to feel that somebody is reading what I write and cares about it. I'll tell you a story that illustrates what I'm talking about. I was in Paris with a delightful, interesting man who works for the *Times,* John Hess. John was in the Paris bureau, and he was one of the people who sort of straightened me out about Vietnam. He bugged me about it and told me I had to learn more—and I did. One day John said to me, 'That was a good column you did today.' And I said, 'Do you really think so?' and he said, 'Do you see that? Writers always want to be told twice.' And he's right."

Anthony Lewis, interview in Harvard Magazine, *November, 1976.*

CHAPTER 8

How We Blew My-lai

It gave me a lift to learn that Tony Lewis thought I helped straighten him out on Vietnam, but I fear he flattered us both. I never did quite straighten him out, or persuade him to share my sense of guilt for our sins, such as our failure to report the massacre at My-lai. Conceivably we could have affected the course of the war.

That was in 1968. We were in Paris, and yes, you could say it was the best of times and the worst of times, the year of the flower children and the year when the blossoms were crushed in Paris and Prague, in Memphis and Los Angeles and Chicago. It was a year of hollow talk about making peace, accompanied by the heaviest bombing in history. To cover the peace talks in Paris, the *Times* sent two of its best and brightest, Hedrick Smith from Washington to do the blow-by-blow and Lewis from London for the deep analysis. For us in the Paris bureau this turned out to be a break; we had more than enough real news to cover, including the student upheaval of May 1968. The error of the *Times*, and of Smith and Lewis, was to think that the peace talks were any more than a charade.

They should have known better. The pattern had long been set: every hint of a move toward peace would be followed by an escalation. When Hanoi, on the first day of 1968, offered to negotiate if the bombing stopped, President Johnson replied that he would stop bombing in the North if Hanoi would stop its aggression in the South; meanwhile he stepped up his secret wars in Laos and Cambodia and sent the Americal Division on a sweep of Quang-nai Province. At the end of January the Tet offensive proved to the world that this was a colonial war, against people who were not about to surrender. Johnson responded by sending over another division.

At My-lai on March 16 our troops systematically slaughtered hundreds of defenseless women, children, and old men. Americans were not told about that operation but were told of a massacre by the Vietcong at Hue. Then LBJ, following the strong showing of Eugene McCarthy in New Hampshire, withdrew his candidacy for reelection, announced a halt in bombing of that part of North Vietnam above the 20th parallel, and offered to talk with Hanoi (see map page 100). After some fencing the two sides agreed to meet in Paris on May 10. In flew Smith and Lewis.

Four days earlier, however, a secret order to American field commanders directed them to mount an "all-out drive." In Paris, Hanoi's delegate denounced the escalation and demanded a total halt to the bombing of the North as a condition for negotiation. LBJ's "peace ambassador," Averell Harriman, insisted that Hanoi first agree to withdraw from South Vietnam. He told reporters, "One day they will get tired and get down to constructive discussion."

Plainly, that meant the U.S. would punish the Vietnamese until they quit fighting for the independence promised by the Geneva agreement of 1954. So the two delegations would not even begin to talk peace terms until LBJ did stop bombing North Vietnam—which he did on November 1, too late to save Hubert Humphrey, too late to stop Richard Nixon. The American public had been bamboozled.

In those critical months in 1968, the *Times*men in Paris could have played a significant role in exposing the charade; instead, they took part in it. Unwittingly, to be sure. These were, as I said, two of our best and brightest: intelligent, liberal, and conscientious. Tony Lewis had earned fame for his reporting on human rights and Rick Smith would become famous for his reporting on the Soviet Union.

Smith was fabulously organized; in a large ledger he kept track of every phrase in the negotiating record, every shift in tense or syntax. Conscientious. One evening, as we headed out to dine, he surprised me by asking what I thought of the dispatch he'd just filed. I said perhaps the reference in his lead to the strident voices of the Vietnamese should have been balanced by mention of the nasal twang of the Americans. Rick stood there, expressionless, as the old wrought-iron elevator arrived, then told us he'd join us later. He turned back to file a new lead.

Conscientious. The problem was that these men identified with *our* side. At the briefings that followed each session of the talks, reporters for the major American media occupied the front right-hand pew and addressed the U.S. spokesman (himself a former *Times*man) by his first name. When, nearly a decade later, I caught Rick on a panel broadcast from Washington ("Were we notified that Sadat was going to do that, Rick?" "No, we weren't." "Well, what position will we take if... ?" "Well, our position is . . ."), I was reminded of those news conferences in Paris. Among the neutrals, where I would sit on my rare visits, a French reporter punned that when my compatriots up front said "we" (pronounced of course "*oui*") they meant *non*.

H. L. Mencken once wrote about reporters in Washington: "A few months of associating with the gaudy magnificoes of the town, and they pick up its meretricious values, and are unable to distinguish men of sense and dignity from mountebanks. A few clumsy overtures from the White House, and they are done." I believe Tony Lewis once played touch football with the Kennedys, and he was undone; I could never dent his infatuation. The aura of power is especially inebriating in the foreign sector.

There was a savoring of that seduction in the Harvard interview in which Tony flattered me. In 1969 he was promoted from London bureau chief to op-ed columnist. "I got Reston's call—this is an elit- ist item—at the Royal Opera House, Covent Garden. We were at the ballet, sitting in the director's box. This is a very grand thing. You wear evening clothes; you dine between the acts in a sort of ante- room. And it's very funny, very nice."

He went on: "The first few [columns] I did were rather tentative and took a sort of Harriman line: we must have an agreed solution. A year later I was committed to a Vietnam position in total opposition to American policy." That would be about the time of Nixon's thrust into Cambodia and the killing of protesters at Kent State and Jackson, Mississippi, in April 1970.

Now scroll back to June 1968. Martin Luther King has been assassinated in Memphis and Robert Kennedy in Los Angeles. American campuses are in revolt, peace advocates are girding for the Democratic convention in Chicago. At the *Times* offices on Rue Caumartin, Cyrus Sulzberger writes in his diary on June 16, "Lunched with Harriman.... Averell says there is not a chance of Hanoi's making any concessions at this time in exchange for us halting the bombing. We must be patient and tough" (*An Age of Mediocrity*, p.439). Rick Smith has borrowed the desk next to mine to share my splendid view of the jeweled dome of the old Opéra. Rick asks Tony, who is standing, whether they ought to cover a hearing of the war crimes tribunal founded by Bertrand Russell and headed by Jean-Paul Sartre. Tony replies with the hauteur of a London clubman (think of William Buckley) that he made it a rule to pay no mind to anything "Bertie" ever did. I remember the scene vividly because I chose not to butt in, and that came back to haunt me.

A year and a half later, I was alone in temporary charge of the bureau when the tribunal met again. The second page of its news release was a shocker. It recalled that its 1968 session had described the Son My (or My-lai) massacre—which had only then, in late 1969, penetrated our media and shaken the American conscience. I sent for the published proceedings. Sure enough, there it was in unmistakable detail, the systematic extermination of a village, whose name now entered history alongside those of Lidice and Oradour.

What if the *Times* had exposed My-lai during that summer of rage in 1968?

One can of course imagine many other what-ifs (e.g., what if Dr. King had survived, or Bobby Kennedy?), but my concern here is with our work in Paris. Timely news about My-lai would surely have set off a shock wave, as the revelation did when it came a year and a half later. It might well have caused LBJ and Humphrey to reconsider their positions, and a shift of 260,000 votes (less than half of one percent) could have reversed the outcome of the 1968 election.

An objection presents itself: readers today may find it hard to believe that a single war crime could have made that difference. A generation of forgetfulness and falsification has done its work. In the mid-1990s, the *Times*—the newspaper that had published the Pentagon Papers—could report a consensus that "we have done all we can" for Vietnam, which lingers in poverty because Hanoi, in 1954, "decided that the conquest of South Vietnam, not national development, was the top priority"; a book reviewer could wax indignant at the suggestion that our planes deliberately bombed hospitals; Malcolm W. Browne, revisiting Vietnam, could detect "a predatory undertone... beneath the outwardly friendly curiosity toward Americans," and a survey of American opinion could be headlined: "Forget Vietnam? No. Forgive? Perhaps" (see *The New York Times*: June 22, 1997; May 18, 1994; and February 2, 1994, respectively). In the year 2000 the *Times* could endorse for the Republican presidential nomination John McCain, an unrepentant bomber of people he persisted in calling gooks.

The following year the *Times* distinguished itself by disclosing a crime committed by another presidential candidate, Bob Kerrey. One night in 1969, he led a Navy SEAL team that butchered an old man and as many as twenty women and children in the village of Thanh Phong. The story had been impeccably reported by Gregory Vistica for *Newsweek* in 1998, but his editors spiked it as of no interest, because Kerrey pulled out of the race a few days after Vistica confronted him. To their honor, the *Times* and *60 Minutes* found the story of interest in 2001. Horrifying in detail, fascinating in human terms, it cried out for hearings and further journalistic exploration. Instead it met a storm of abuse. The media pack (with a few honorable exceptions) joined Kerrey in first denying he did it, then minimizing it and concluding that for American servicemen to kill helpless civilians was not a war crime.

A cautious suggestion by the *Times* that the matter deserved a public inquiry was described by Mark Shields on PBS as "an act of moral arrogance rarely seen." That was fairly typical. In the columns of the *Times*, Clyde Haberman saw Kerrey and other Vietnam veterans as brave targets of unfair criticism, like the New York policemen who shot Amadou Diallo by mistake (as all will recall, forty-one times). William Safire denounced the Kerrey story as "another manifestation of the self-flagellation that led to the Vietnam Syndrome— that revulsion at the use of military power that afflicted our national psyche for decades after our defeat." He worried too much. In the event, the story vanished from the *Times* in ten days. And then, after September 11, 2001, the mainstream media could soberly discuss the desirability of murder, arbitrary detention, and torture in the war against terror.

But it was different in 1968. Many of us then were haunted by the images of a little girl burning with napalm, of a Saigon general killing a prisoner, of an American officer destroying a town to save it, of monks in flames, of tiger cages. Belief in our righteousness had been damaged by revelations about the CIA's campaign of disinformation. I referred above to the storm of outrage that hit the streets when the story of My-lai broke in November, 1969. (Cy Sulzberger told his diary that the protests frightened his dinner guest, the Duke of Windsor.) So it does not seem out of the question that exposure of that massacre in America's most influential newspaper in 1968 could have tipped the electoral balance.

Another story that we missed surely would have. On the campaign trail Nixon was proclaiming that he would end the war even as he was lobbying the Saigon regime to stall the peace talks, to avoid an "October surprise." Henry Kissinger was in Paris that summer, counseling Harriman and secretly coaching Nixon. Lyndon Johnson learned about Nixon's treason from the FBI but chose not to let on. So a malignant conspiracy was being acted out in Washington, Saigon, New York, and Paris—and the *Times* blew that story, too.

Now, to have missed it need not embarrass a common journalist who is outside the loop, but the *Times* has always prided itself on its intimacy with the movers and shakers. In his autobiography Max Frankel gloried in the access; he bragged, for example, that Kennedy's secretary of state, Dean Rusk, confided to him that "Laos is not worth the life of a single Kansas farmboy." Later Rusk and Frankel would come to hold publicly that Indochina was worth many Kansas farmboys, but Max could not share Rusk's earlier vision with readers because it was off the record. "We respected confidence," he explained, "not just as a matter of ethics, but as a transaction of commerce."

The balance of that trade has always been overwhelmingly one-sided. Reporters deliver sympathetic coverage; they are commonly paid back with tips on news that would become public in any event. In his memoir Turner Catledge of the *Times* nostalgically recalls helping one of his Senate drinking buddies to bury a peccadillo; the one scoop he mentions getting in return was beating FDR to the announcement of a trade meeting with either Belgium or Holland, Catledge could not remember which.

Such commerce remained a staple of the Washington bureau. Scotty Reston practiced it with succeeding administrations, enjoyed splendid access, and got lots of exclusives, but their value was questionable. The assassination of Kennedy struck him as ironic because "his short administration was devoted almost entirely to various attempts to curb this very streak of violence in the American character"—this about an administration that began with the Bay of Pigs, gave birth to the Green Berets, seethed with assassination plots, risked a nuclear war, and ended with the execution of Ngo Dinh Diem.

LBJ occasionally consulted Reston on how his Vietnam policy would play and found him "quietly approving"(see Robert Dallek's *Flawed Giant*). It appears that the president never shared with Reston his doubt whether Hanoi had actually made unprovoked attacks on two U.S. destroyers in the Gulf of Tonkin, reports of which led to a virtual declaration of war; Reston and his colleagues never doubted the story. A *Times* staff bulletin gave kudos to all hands for their coverage of a battle that never happened.*

THE NATIONAL INTEREST

After a savage power struggle with A. M. Rosenthal in New York, Reston handed the Washington bureau over to his able disciple, Frankel. During a visit in late 1968 I watched Max preparing to beat President-elect Nixon, by a matter of hours, to the announcement of his Cabinet. As Max assigned his troops to tap their long-cultivated sources in each department, the eminent reporter Tom Wicker murmured to me, "So much talent, for so little."

The greatest failure of Frankel's career resulted from abject trust: it was widely believed in the trade that he blew the Watergate scandal in part because his friend Kissinger touted him off. And the greatest victory on his watch, the publication of the Pentagon Papers, was the fruit not of commerce with officialdom, but of combat against it.

Like most American reporters in Vietnam, Neil Sheehan was gung-ho when he arrived in 1962. It was a lovely war: days in the field manhunting with American "advisers," nights in Saigon with beautiful native women. The reporters all had weapons, and some used them; Malcolm Browne pinned the severed hand of a Viet-

---

Winners & Sinners, August 13, 1964: "Editors' exploit. When North Vietnam PT boats made their second attack (Aug. 5), copy poured in from all over, much of it from Tom Wicker, Jack Raymond and Arnold Lubasch in Washington. It entailed a massive post-midnight task of organization, and processing. [Twelve editors and helpers listed.] . . . A fine piece of teamwork, and the product reflected it."

namese on the wall over his typewriter.* Their adventure is well told in *Once Upon a Distant War* by William Prochnau (Times Books: 1995). Only Homer Bigart, the best of them, grasped the horror, the folly, and the mendacity of it, but he soon left. The younger men— Sheehan of UPI, Browne of AP, David Halberstam of the *Times* and Charles Mohr of *Time*—all believed it was a noble cause.

Their epic began when they learned that we were losing the war. Guided by field officers like John Paul Vann (who would turn out to be the murderous psychopath of Sheehan's *A Bright Shining Lie*), they found that our proclaimed victories were actually defeats, that Diem's mercenaries wouldn't fight, and that the countryside belonged to the guerrillas, who were arming themselves with American weapons seized or purchased from the mercenaries. The reporters' photographs of Buddhist monks immolating themselves and their witness to a savage assault on their pagoda doubtless sealed Kennedy's decision to eliminate Diem. But they kept giving the lie to the victory claims of the American brass. Admiral Harry Felt, the Pacific commander, snapped at Browne, "Why don't you get on the team?" Kennedy had told the publishers association, "Every newspaper now asks itself, with respect to every story, 'Is it news?' All I ask is that you add this question: 'Is it in the national interest?'"

When *Time* magazine spiked Charles Mohr's copy and published a general attack on the reporting from Saigon as false and biased, he resigned. But he never had any doubt about the morality of the war. Nor, it seems, did Halberstam. Speaking in defense of Bob Kerrey in 2001, he emphasized that the incident in the Delta had occurred at night, in "the purest bandit country—by 1969, everyone who lived there would have been third generation Vietcong." Further evidence

---

*R. W. (Johnny) Apple, who was A. M. Rosenthal's favorite protégé, bragged of having killed several Vietcong, potting them from a helicopter. A *Times* colleague muttered, "Women and children, I presume." (See Timothy Crouse's unsparing portrait in *The Boys on the Bus*.) Apple relates that he gave Lieut. Commander John McCain a lift in his copter, beginning a friendship that has marked Apple's coverage ever since.

that this was an American war is the fact that no Vietnamese accompanied Kerrey's death squad and others like it at the time. Halberstam and his comrades had observed similar conduct in 1962, and none ever questioned its morality—except Sheehan. After serving another tour in Saigon for the *Times*, and after years of agonizing, he came to suspect that the war might be, as William Shawcross put it, not a mistake but a crime. John Leonard gave Sheehan an entire issue of the *Times Book Review* to express his misgivings; Leonard believes he was on the verge of being fired for approving it when praise poured in from around the country.

That exploit doubtless led Daniel Ellsberg to turn the Pentagon Papers over to Sheehan in 1971. In his memoir Frankel misses the irony that the aide named by Robert McNamara to edit that secret history of the war was Leslie Gelb, the quintessential *Times*man in the revolving door, who went in and out of the government but never shared with readers his knowledge that it lied. Frankel gives himself two chapters on his role in the publication of the papers and gives Sheehan a gratuitous slap for "excruciating slowness."

Neil flew to Paris in September, 1968, to apply to the North Vietnamese for a visa, and asked me to go along. We took an official of their mission to lunch at the nearby Closerie des Lilas, Hemingway's old hangout. It was strange: Neil, still conflicted about the war, and I, who had a son in naval air and had lost a nephew in that service, entertaining an enemy colonel over white linen on a sunny terrace, with the great fountain playing opposite the Observatoire. He was a brown, wiry man, who looked like what he was, a veteran of more than two decades of war. Our business was quickly done; he promised to forward Neil's application to Hanoi (which never responded, alas). The balance of our conversation produced two memorable moments. When the colonel pressed us to explain U.S. policy, one of us mentioned warily that many Americans thought of Hanoi as a client of the Soviet Union and China. He retorted angrily: *"We owe them nothing! It is we, and we alone, who have been fighting!"* And with regard to the paralyzed peace talks, he demanded, *"Would you negotiate with a country that was bombing you?"*

I abandoned *Times*ian detachment. "Sure I would," I said. "Soviet tanks are in Prague—hasn't Dubcek gone to Moscow?" The colonel froze. After a long pause, he said: *"You know my government does not agree with your government about what is happening in Prague...But suppose, just for the sake of argument, we did agree with you*... (pause)... *WE... WOULD... NOT... GO TO MOSCOW!"*

I remember thinking, Boy, did we pick the wrong enemy!

Back home, the country was shaken by the police riot at the Democratic convention in Chicago. Editor Rosenthal changed what Tony Lukas witnessed from "brutality" to "overreaction." When Harrison Salisbury complained on behalf of his staff at the convention that Abe was "taking the guts out of the story," Rosenthal retorted that he was taking out "the goddam editorializing" (*The Trust*, p.444). Hubert Humphrey turned a blind eye to the outrages around him and a deaf ear to Mayor Daley's anti-Semitic rant, accepted the nomination (and the *Times*'s support), and threw away the election by sticking to the Harriman line.

Too late, LBJ halted the bombing in the north on November 1, opening the way to peace talks at last. An absurd scuffle then began over "the shape of the table," involving the recognition of the Saigon regime and the National Liberation Front in the South as independent parties. (The *Times* would edit my copy to identify the front as "the so-called provisional government of South Vietnam"; it never said "the so-called Saigon government"—which would far better reflect the truth as our leaders knew it.)* Sulzberger told his diary

---

*Off the record, U.S. policymakers talking to Sulzberger spoke with awe about the vitality of the National Liberation Front combatants (as distinct from the North Vietnamese regulars) and with despair and contempt about the so-called Saigon regime. Frederick Nolting, a former ambassador to Saigon, told Cy (in paraphrase), "Our only chance was ended when we decided to dump Diem, and there has never been a government since." On July 22, 1964, Cy told his diary, "I asked [Defense Secretary] McNamara if he wasn't alarmed by the recent statement of General Nguyen Cao Ky demanding a direct attack on North Vietnam. McNamara said he didn't know why Ky had made such aggressive statements. General Ky had better shut up or they will find themselves with a new air force commander." Two weeks later, the Navy claimed that two of its destroyers had been attacked in the Gulf of Tonkin, and LBJ rushed a prepared resolution through Congress and bombed the North. The *Times* applauded. Ky kept his job, and Cy kept his mouth shut.

on December 19, 1968, that Harriman was "absolutely furious" with what he called double-crosses by Saigon and "almost has more sympathy for Hanoi than for Saigon at this stage," but what Sulzberger deplored as Harriman's shift to an "extremely dovish position" occurred on the ambassador's way out.

EXTREME CAUTION

With the shape of the table settled, the four entities began a dreary speechifying that would continue for years, while the war ground on. Tony and Rick left it to the resident drudges; analysis and summary thereafter came out of the Washington bureau, which got its news straight from the highest sources. In Paris I seldom drew the Vietnam detail, but as noted, in December of 1969, I found myself temporarily alone in the bureau, and it was not about to snub another war crimes hearing on my watch.

Again, Sartre presided. There was a GI deserter, whose testimony I played down as hearsay (and besides, deserters made our editors nervous). There were two American and two Canadian doctors whose accounts of treating victims of napalm and toxic gases and of the terror called Operation Phoenix were entirely believable, but they had given their report earlier in Toronto, and I thought, overoptimistically, that the *Times* might have picked it up there. And there was a young woman who broke down as she described the death of her village eleven months earlier. At my side, a cub reporter for AP wept. If he filed anything, it made no stir. The significance of the story was that it refuted the notion, still current today, that My-lai had been an aberration, which the Army deplored. Here was a massacre in the same area ten months after My-lai; we now know also that Kerrey and his Navy SEALS were about to strike far to the south, and a Marine-CIA death squad was on a similar mission up north. I cabled a summary of what I had to New York, with a request that our Washington and Saigon bureaus check out whether the Army unit implicated was indeed at that place at that time and would confirm or deny the account. Then I filed my dispatch and went home. A few hours later, this short appeared on the *Times* newswire:

© 1969 New York Times News Service

PARIS, Dec. 19—A sobbing Vietnamese girl asserted at a news conference here today that American troops had slaughtered 300 men, women and children in her village, Binhchau, in the commune of Balangan, in Quang-nai Province.

This, she said, was on Jan. 13 of this year—nearly 10 months after the alleged [sic] massacre at Songmy, which is also in Quang-nai.

The girl [sic], 21-year-old Pham Thi Ling, was one of a series of witnesses introduced by the International Center of Information for the Denunciation of War Crimes. They were presented by Jean-Paul Sartre, the chairman, in an effort to prove that Songmy "was not an isolated incident." Sartre was a member of the so-called [sic] Bertrand Russell War Crimes Tribunal, which met last in Denmark, in 1967.

Two American and two Canadian physicians who had studied or worked in South Vietnam discussed the ravages of chemical warfare, and an American deserter now living in Canada told of alleged atrocities he had heard about or seen.

Next morning, I learned that some of the foregoing had been tacked as a shirttail to another article inside the paper. In my view that was worse than not to have printed it at all, since it signified that the *Times* considered the report neither credible nor important. A cable from the foreign desk confirmed it.

your question on massacre seems fair enough. our feeling was that the nature of the sponsoring organization, the absence of substantiation and the recent spate of similar allegations from many sources all pointed to extreme caution in handling a story with the emotional impact of this one. we have attempted in the last few weeks to check out many allegations, through the washington and saigon bureaus as well as correspondents at military bases in the u.s., and we have been unsuccessful so far. we continue to be interested in checking them out, and are in fact running a short tonight saying that u.s. command in saigon is going to investigate the girl's accusation. regards.

Obviously, the spate of allegations and the flurry of inquiries would never surmount the extreme caution of the editors—especially considering the sources. Therein they exposed a crippling malady of the *Times*: its allergy toward sources that challenge the establishment's truths. While divided about Vietnam, it took offense at the presumption of foreign critics like de Gaulle and Nehru and Sukarno and "Bertie" Russell and Sartre, and of Americans like Dr. Benjamin Spock and Noam Chomsky and Linus Pauling—yes, and Dr. Martin Luther King, Jr.

King's role calls here for what may appear to be a digression but is far from it. Waging his Rainbow Campaign against poverty, he argued that the Vietnam war was devouring the needed resources. "Somehow this madness must cease," he declared in a statement that alarmed the establishment and the *Times*. Earl Caldwell, a black reporter for the *Times*, was assigned to follow King, and he witnessed King's assassination in Memphis. Caldwell has testified in court that the national editor, Claude Sitton, had exhorted him to "nail Dr. King," saying he "had to be stopped or there's going to be a bloodbath." Sitton was a hero of ours; a white Georgian, he had covered the civil rights struggle in the South with courage and distinction. I would have found Caldwell's account hard to believe but for an encounter of my own.

The intellectual world was then being shaken by revelations about the CIA's foreign and domestic program of subversion and disinformation. As Frances Stonor Saunders related in *The Cultural Cold*

War, a task force report to President Eisenhower in 1954 called for "an aggressive covert psychological, political and paramilitary organization more effective, more unique, and if necessary, more ruthless than that employed by the enemy." In face of the Communist threat, the report declared: "Hitherto acceptable norms of human conduct do not apply. If the U.S. is to survive, longstanding American concepts of 'fair play' must be reconsidered... It may become necessary that the American people be made acquainted with, understand and support this fundamentally repugnant philosophy" (p.234).

American historical "norms of human conduct" toward peoples of color may not be so high-flown as those implied. In any case, the program grew so enormous that it eventually blew its cover. In 1964, *The Nation* reported that the CIA was subsidizing magazines in London and New York; in 1966, the *Times* carried allegations that the CIA was funding the Congress for Cultural Freedom, based in Paris; in April, 1967, *Ramparts* magazine published a broader exposé, which embarrassed leading intellectuals and journalists around the world. The *Times*'s editors asked all bureaus to gather data on the agency's covert activities, for a roundup under the supervision of Sitton's national desk. It also asked staffers to report privately any ties they may have had with the agency. The *Times* has never made public the results of either effort.

Assigned to look into CIA doings in France, I filed preliminary memos on its past use of the underworld in Marseilles for strike-breaking and its ongoing subsidy of Force Ouvrière, a schismatic labor federation, and I began inquiring about rumored cash payoffs to politicians. There was much work to be done but no response to a request for guidance from New York. On a home visit, I asked Sitton whether the paper really wanted this stuff. He looked aside, toward 43d Street, then murmured that in matters like this he put the national interest first—precisely what John F. Kennedy had urged with regard to reporting on Vietnam.

So nothing came of my dispatch on the Balangan massacre. I would have been wise, no doubt, to take the advice of colleagues, bite my tongue, and move on. Instead, I unloaded years of guilt and frustration. In a letter, I reminded Rosenthal that he had written a book about people in Brooklyn who did not heed the cries of a woman who was being assaulted, telling him, "I have a shattering feeling that you and I are doing the same thing." With all the hand-wringing going on just then about My-lai, I asked, "Why was it necessary for a kid at Claremont College to break the story? Why did twenty newspapers (was one of them ours?) ignore his letters?" I recalled that I had told the foreign desk long ago that there was a Pulitzer Prize waiting for an exposé of the Tonkin Gulf hoax, but somebody else finally did it, "and by the time the facts came to light, it was too late to do much good." I suggested that our handling of American war crimes "may reflect a reluctance to believe them and, worse, perhaps the feeling that people don't want to hear about them anymore." Several times that week, I said, the Vietnam war had not even made Page One, but that morning, December 26, 1969, the front page did carry a sympathetic account of the arrival in Paris of a planeload of wives and children of American POWs and MIAs, a maneuver staged by Ross Perot to prop up support for Nixon's war—thus lengthening, ironically, the prisoners' ordeal.

Abe replied that he was stunned at my "tone of condescension and lecturing" and at my ignorance of the sterling work the *Times* was actually doing. Backhandedly, he confirmed my supposition that My-lai had been knocking on his door: "The fact of the matter is that the *Times* got into this story, not knowing that [Seymour] Hersh also was on it and that in a week of effort—and I mean effort—we were able not only to catch up with him, but to break the story on the day that he did and to keep ahead of the whole American press." (In fact, the *Times* was behind the American and world press in the play it gave the story when it broke. Reston wrote on November 30, 1969, that the government had managed to keep My-lai quiet "until it was forced into national attention by press and television," but it was no thanks to the *Times* or the *Washington Post*.) Abe asked me why, if My-lai had been available in Paris back in 1968, we hadn't reported it. I replied that in passing up the Sartre hearing, Tony and Rick "followed what was then and remains the policy of the *Times*," and I suggested that if they had covered it, the story might have met the same treatment as mine had. I concluded that I had expected him to be angry at me, but not that his conscience would be so clear. "I was not condescending," I said. "I was only trying to be a good German." That would be a good line to close on, but much more needs to be said.

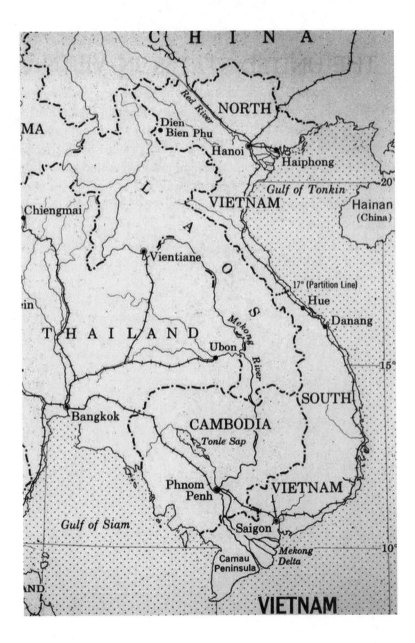

CHAPTER NINE

Aftermath

I must point out that many Americans, and many *Times* colleagues, shared my sense of guilt. (It was said of the Germans that only the innocent felt guilty.) Gloria Emerson has written that once in Saigon:

> I got so desperate—the Americans had started bombing Hanoi—I ran to the National Press Center, where they give the briefings... a forty-year-old woman running through the streets in the middle of the night... and I wrote on the wall in Magic Marker, "Father, forgive. They know not what they do." And I don't even believe in God... If they found out it was me they would have sent me home. *New York Times* correspondents must not go running around at two o'clock in the morning writing "Father forgive. They know not what they do." But afterward I thought how there's no way... no one, no one to whom you can say we're sorry.*

---

*Much of our cable traffic with Saigon was relayed through Paris. Gloria's copy was brilliant, her battles with editors stormy. A desk man passed me with a smile a request by the hawkish Ambassador Ellsworth Bunker for tearsheets and glossy photos from a puff piece by the Saigon bureau chief, Al Shuster. The foreign editor, James Greenfield, told Shuster that he, too, loved the piece. Shuster, Greenfield, and deputy editor Seymour Topping were examples of Rosenthal's preference for loyal mediocrity. (Regarding his recent promotion, Topping mentioned that at age twenty-one he was already a second lieutenant. Gloria exclaimed, "I'm SO sorry!") Abe has been quoted as saying that when a police official tipped him off to the slaying of a woman in Brooklyn, he deliberately picked the weakest reporter available to cover it, because he intended to make the story his own. His dilemma was that being excelled by other media made him look bad, forcing him to tolerate reporters—even Hersh, later on— whose outlook he hated . . . As noted, the *Times* is a battlefield.

In the same sense of guilt and frustration, I told the first minister of
the U.S. Embassy in Paris one day that my wife was out front
demonstrating against the war, and that that was where I ought to
be. But a hawkish spokesman for the U.S. delegation at the talks,
Stephen Ledogar, thought he was paying a compliment when he told
me that in spite of my feelings, he found my copy quite objective.
That hurt.

Now, Abe's claim of balance may be discounted as the delusion
of a notoriously unbalanced man. There is no end to accounts of his
bizarre partisanship.* A police car chauffeured Abe to the recapture
of the Columbia campus, site of the sit-in that touched off the student uprisings of 1968, and Abe filed an inflamed report. I have mentioned his bowdlerizing of the news from Chicago. Later, in another
war, Abe would visit El Salvador and yank Ray Bonner home in disgrace for reporting a massacre that the embassy falsely denied. He
blazoned screeds accusing the KGB of plots to slander Jerzy Kosin-
ski and to assassinate the Pope. But that's Abe. The trouble is that his
letter to me was different only in tone from those of two friendly, liberal editors, to whom I also sent letters criticizing our war coverage.

Much as they loved my work, they said, they resented my impli-
cation of a double standard. The *Times* is a battlefield, and caution was
essential in handling sensitive material. I told them they had no problem with the party line out of Washington and Saigon, even printing
as fact the body counts of Vietcong slain, whereas every troubling
report, even by our own staff, was screened with suspicion. I reminded
them of my having been required, back in 1963, to rewrite David
Halberstam (I of course made no substantive change). I recalled how
Rosenthal's deputy, Seymour Topping, snapped at a compliment on
Salisbury's eye-opening report from Hanoi, "We sanitized it."

One of those friendly editors replied that Halberstam "had guts
and instincts and a highly developed bullshit detector, and con-

---

*See Max Frankel's *The Times of My Life and My Life with the* Times, p. 414; Harrison
Salisbury's *Without Fear or Favor,* p. 394; and Tifft and Jones's *The Trust.*

science" but was also illiterate and a "horse's ass" whose copy had to be fixed to be fit to print—and it *was* printed, so there. As for Salisbury, he'd been "stupid"—an allusion to his failure to specify the Communist source of casualty estimates in Hanoi (on which ground the Pulitzer board vetoed a well-earned award; Topping, incidentally, later served as director of the Pulitzer program). As for me, he said, I did more harm than good to our common cause by challenging my colleagues' integrity. I replied, "I do indeed mean to attack integrity—yours, mine, everybody's. Who the hell do you think you are, an angel?... You reproach me with being ineffectual. Hell, we each fight in our own way. You, for example, know how to be effective, since you're now [an executive]. We're still bombing Vietnam."

"THE CAUSE OF THE WAR IS PLAIN ENOUGH"

That last exchange came in April, 1972, shortly before my return to New York. We were again facing a presidential election. Again, the peace talks were suspended, and again, the *Times* was getting it wrong. The head of the American delegation, Bill Porter, had told Sulzberger "we are refusing to sit down and negotiate with the Communist side until they are ready to discuss and negotiate in a meaningful way." But our Washington bureau reported as fact Kissinger's bald-faced lie that the North Vietnamese had snubbed him in Paris. A corrective letter by me drew a reply from Frankel dated April 17 to the effect that he was simply reporting the White House view of the situation, adding, amazingly, "I think it is an absurd view." I was not the only reader to misunderstand him, from what he was printing. A letter to the editor that week thanked the *Times* for a Frankel analysis that "helped me better to see the basic rightness of our present position in Indochina and the basic wrongness of the war protesters." In the following weeks, Terence Smith of the Washington bureau would write that the Communists were trying "to shift the onus on the United States" and Nixon was escalating in a desperate effort to "bring the Communists to the negotiating table"; Bob

Semple said they'd humiliated us in Paris, and Frankel wrote that the Democrats were "crowing" about it. Humiliation weighed more heavily than peace or justice in our columns. America's most influential print journalist, Scotty Reston, worried about it a lot. He wrote me on May 14 that he believed from all available sources that Nixon was "covering his retreat, and is now, behind all this bravado, almost begging the Soviets, the Chinese, Fulbright and all the rest of the opposition to let him get out." (Nixon had just mined the port of Haiphong. In a taped rant with Kissinger on May 9, he said, "I cannot emphasize too strongly that I have determined that we should go for broke.") In what I identified as a conscience letter, I had chided Reston for, among other things, defending Nixon's demand that Hanoi release our POWs. "You yourself," I reminded him, "observed to me recently that an amnesty for our deserters would have to wait until after the war." He replied that Hanoi's "holding the POWs—though this is the normal thing to do until there is a political settlement—is the last thing that enables the President to have any solid support.

"I find it very odd," he went on, "to say anything to a colleague in support of the American position in this war. I have fought it ever since I went there first, straight from Panmunjom, in 1953, so much so that I have virtually been banned from the White House and have not been able to get at Nixon since the Oregon primary of 1968, but the all-or-nothing argument is very dangerous with this man, and very likely both to prolong the war and assure his re-election, and I think this is not the objective you and I have in mind."

Well.

I do not question Scotty's sincerity. He now actually believed that he had been fighting American policy when our government was propping up the French, contemplating using atomic bombs at Dien Bien Phu, sabotaging the Geneva peace agreement, imposing the regime of Ngo Dinh Diem in the south, rejecting the promised national elections because the Vietminh would have won, and promoting repression in the south and covert action in the north and in

Laos. He believed that he had fought American policy while JFK built our military contingent up to 15,000 and terminated Diem with prejudice, and that he had fought it while LBJ carried on with napalm and Agent Orange and Operation Phoenix and eventually 550,000 U.S. servicemen. That is how Scotty remembered it now. Scotty's writings contradict his recollection. He did occasionally express misgivings about escalation (who didn't?), he was supportive of Halberstam, and he favored publication of the Pentagon Papers. But he was a sucker for the national interest, as defined from on high. For example, Scotty famously complied with Kennedy's request in 1961 that the *Times* play down the imminent assault on Cuba. On 43d Street, we followed the Bay of Pigs debacle by shortwave radio. Shock and anger gripped the city room—not in the main because our government had committed a criminal aggression and had lied to the world about it but because it had been crushed, exposed. A determination not to be thus humiliated again shaped policy toward Vietnam to the end.

Its passion was evident in a column by Reston on February 14, 1965, responding to worldwide concern about our escalation: "The cause of the war is plain enough. The North Vietnamese Communists, with the aid of Red China and to a lesser extent the Soviet Union, have sent their guerrillas into South Vietnam in violation of the 1954 and 1962 Geneva agreements." One wonders who can have been feeding Reston this balderdash. Sulzberger was talking to the same people, including Eisenhower, Kennedy, and Johnson, and they were all quite aware that it was our side that had been flouting the Geneva agreements and that the guerrillas in the south were in the main southerners, who had taken up arms—mostly arms captured or purchased from our mercenaries—only after years of repression. Moscow and Beijing never controlled Hanoi, and Hanoi did not yet totally control the NLF. A dignified exit by the Americans was long available, one that would turn Saigon over to a coalition of the NLF and unaffiliated civilians. However that might have turned out in the end, it could not have been worse than what did happen. But Washington repeatedly responded to such proposals with escalation.

When Johnson withdrew in humiliation from the presidential race in 1968, Scotty's support went not to the antiwar candidate, Eugene McCarthy, but to Humphrey, whom even LBJ held in contempt. Scotty again backed Humphrey in 1972. The *Times* was a house divided. Iphigene Sulzberger, the dowager, and John Oakes, the editor of the editorial page, swung the *Times*'s endorsement to George McGovern. In his inarticulate manner, Punch Sulzberger, the publisher, leaned the other way; at the height of the campaign he hired as a columnist William Safire, the author of Nixon's and Spiro Agnew's jeremiads against the liberal press.

On the news side Editor Rosenthal said McGovern made him ill. He no doubt identified the senator with those longhaired vandals at Columbia. McGovern in fact could have sat for a portrait by Norman Rockwell. Son of a Methodist minister in South Dakota, he was as clean, attractive, and honorable a major candidate as our country has ever had. Too modest to flaunt his World War II medals, he promised to get us out of a dishonorable and unpopular war, and we could take him at his word. But when he called the Nixon administration the most corrupt in our history, the national press gang snickered at what it portrayed as a final example of McGovern's ineptitude.

Yet already in early 1972 Nixon was marked by the ITT and dairy scandals, gaudy and highly impeachable muddles. He was engaged in a visible effort to overthrow a democratic socialist government in Chile—another war crime story that the *Times* blew.* He departed from Republican orthodoxy for the duration of the cam-

---

*This plot, too, was discernible in Paris. Asked by the financial desk to check out a closed meeting of the Paris Club of ten creditor nations, I overheard delegates remonstrating with the Americans over their stalling on a routine extension of credit for Chile. During a break I asked one of the U.S. team why the squeeze on poor Chile, and he said something about a right to protect their investors. "Aren't you telling idealistic students in Latin America," I asked, "that the only way to reform the structure is with a gun?" After a pause he replied, "That's what keeps me awake at night." Then he went back to his work, as I did to mine. It was not a story I could write for the *Times*. Sulzberger was, at the same time, encouraging Nixon to keep up the pressure on Chile (*An Age of Mediocrity*, p. 756).

paign by freezing wages and prices and pumping money into the economy at a rate that would lead to a crash the following year. In June Nixon's plumbers were caught wiretapping the Democratic campaign headquarters in the Watergate. Cash and a notebook linked them to the president's campaign committee and to the White House. But it would be many, many months before the Washington bureau would acknowledge the appearance of a "smoking gun." (John Oakes, on the editorial page, was less naive. Iphigene Sulzberger also perceived the bugging as an assault on democracy, and said so under a pseudonym in a letter to the *Times*. She also suggested that the *Times* report how much the taxpayers were spending on Nixon's residences; Abe refused, on the ground that it would look as though we were biased against Nixon [see *The Trust*, p.501]).

NOBLESSE OBLIGE

Robert Redford and Dustin Hoffman, in the roles of Bob Woodward and Carl Bernstein, have fixed the image of 1972 as a glory year for American journalism. It was a disgraceful year. The campaign coverage was dominated not by Nixon's crimes but by McGovern's tactical missteps. Woodward and Bernstein and Watergate were viewed with disdain by the national press corps, except for Dan Schorr of CBS and a few others. Meanwhile, Frankel reveled in journalistic glory, for reporting Nixon's discovery of China. In his memoir Max remembers himself as putting one over on a spiteful president who had limited the *Times* to only one ticket to his party. For that, Max worked so hard that he won a Pulitzer Prize. I am sure he wrote well; I recall some business about the Chinese leaders feeding choice morsels to their guests with chopsticks. The trip established Nixon's stature as a statesman and Kissinger's as his brilliant vizier. Was not the real story the way the Chinese had finally reeled in the American fish?* In any event, the version we did read helped

---

*Just four years earlier Sulzberger had written in his diary: "Talked with [Ambassador Charles] Bohlen this morning. The shit has hit the electric fan. France has recognized China—and we are boiling mad. I must say, de Gaulle has a diabolical sense of mischief." When de Gaulle did it, it was diabolical; when Nixon did it, it was genius.

assure Nixon's overwhelming reelection. That, and a Kissinger tease about a peace deal reached in Paris weeks before the voting.

After the election Nixon reneged, out of spite or hope that Beijing and Moscow would finally force Hanoi to back down. Hence the "Christmas bombing." At the *Times*, some two hundred staff members, including several top executives, signed an unprecedented advertisement calling upon Congress to "end immediately all American involvement in the Indochinese war." (Management required that somebody be listed as "coordinator"; colleagues drafted me for that undeserved honor.) Many of us attended the large protest in Washington during Nixon's gaudy second inauguration. Semple mentioned us in the *Times* as "a sullen crowd," and the TV news zoomed in on a few hippies, turning an impressive march for peace into a parade for pot.

Actually we were bone-chilled, and sad. But our day was at hand. The peace agreement, essentially as reached in October, was signed in Paris at the end of January by Le Duc Tho and Kissinger, whose Nobel Peace award therefore was described by Tom Lehrer as the end of satire. Our POWs were freed at last, having served Nixon's purpose. By then, however, the Watergate scandal was in full eruption. One episode had a curious effect on the *Times*. On the day that Vice President Agnew pleaded no contest and resigned, a copy editor pointed out that the *Times* stylebook denied the honorific Mister to a convicted criminal. On the ground that we could not withhold it from a man who'd been that close to the presidency, Rosenthal amended the stylebook on the spot. From that moment on, every rapist, child molester and serial killer has been mistered in the *Times*. Noblesse oblige.

To spare the nation the humiliation of a war-crimes trial, Congress excluded Nixon's deeds in Indochina from the articles of impeachment. It could not spare us the humiliation of the scramble of Americans fleeing Saigon, abandoning their native allies. Nor could it avoid the collapse of our client regime in Cambodia, nor the new phase of horror there, which ended only when the Vietnamese chased the Khmer Rouge out in 1979. For some fifteen years thereafter, China, the U.S., and Thailand helped the defeated Khmer Rouge sustain a border war with Cambodia and occupy its seat at the United Nations. It was striking, then, to read Tony Lewis in the *Times* in 1997, describing himself as one who had opposed the Vietnam War, accusing Noam Chomsky of defending the Khmer Rouge.

During the years when Tony was hewing to the Harriman line, Chomsky was untangling it as master analyst of the antiwar movement. He did argue that the number of Cambodians killed by Nixon may have equaled or exceeded those killed by Pol Pot. Sulzberger's diary shows that as early as 1965 our commanders in Saigon were considering the overthrow of the neutralist Prince Sihanouk of Cambodia. Our press corps, including the *Times*, echoed their line, exaggerating the strategic importance of Cambodia as a supply pipeline and "privileged sanctuary" for the Vietcong and mocking the prince as a saxophone-playing clown; I retorted to a colleague that the Cambodians ought to build him a statue in ivory and pearls for his agile effort to keep them out of the war. Our coup came in 1970, our B-52s ravaged the country, and the Khmer Rouge grew into the monster that took over in 1975. Tony surely knows all that and yet, when Indochina comes to mind, he still resents the Bertie Russells and Noam Chomskys who presumed to judge our national leaders.

Mind you, Tony is a courageous liberal, who has defended civil justice against the authorities in America, South Africa, and Israel. Likewise Tom Wicker, who called lightning and thunder down on Nelson Rockefeller for the prison massacre at Attica. Yet Tom has since toiled to put Nixon in a kinder light, and he and Tony both swallowed, hook, line, and sinker the Establishment's hoax that Social Security was going broke in 1983. I tried to straighten them out on that, but they could not believe that Reagan, David Stockman, Alan Greenspan, Pat Moynihan, and Bob Dole could all be lying (though Moynihan acknowledged long afterward, with a wink, that they were).

And yes, of course they're ashamed of My-lai, when and if they think about it. Yet in the year 2000, as I've pointed out, Tony could moon over John McCain, who showed no remorse. The excuse during the war was that we were fighting to contain communism. The Soviet Union is long gone, and China is a valued trading partner. Now hark to Anthony Lewis, a world champion of due process, writing about Bill Clinton's wag-the-dog bombing of Afghanistan and the Sudan:

> With its special power and responsibility in the world, the United States has to be free to act unilaterally in urgent circumstances. We cannot wait for international approval before responding to terrorism. President Reagan was right to attack Colonel Qaddafi's headquarters after an apparent [!] act of Libyan terrorism. And President Clinton was right to strike at the Afghan operations of Osama bin Laden, reported mastermind of the bombing of U.S. embassies.

Yes, bomb at will, Caesar. The New Rome is cured of the Vietnam syndrome.

Paris, August 12, 1966: Dined last night with Chip [Ambassador Charles] Bohlen. He had a long argument with Walt Rostow… about bombing North Vietnam. Chip argued that if it was militarily desirable we should indeed go ahead and bomb but that it was lunacy if we thought that by bombing we could force Hanoi to parley… To my astonishment, Chip assures me that the French consider me a CIA agent… He says this is true of Couve, Pompidou and all the rest. I say Chip is full of you-know-what.

Cyrus L. Sulzberger, diary extract

CHAPTER TEN

Cyrus

Cyrus L. Sulzberger and I had the same office address in Paris for seven years, but it would be misleading to say we shared it. He would not even share our telegraphers; to evade the eyes of what he called "the cabal against me in our office," he filed by Western Union. Our only tête-à-tête in all that time occurred in Amman, Jordan, in 1970, during the troubles that Palestinians call Black September.

Cy's secretary had cabled us visiting firemen there, PLEASE TELL EMBASSY SULZBERGER ARRIVING TUESDAY MORNING ADVISE PALACE HE AVAILABLE. That was the message as I recall it; the cable flimsy circulated among reporters until it was lost. A man at the embassy said with a sympathetic chuckle that they had already received their instructions through channels. An embassy car met Cy at the airport and took him to King Hussein; the ambassador gave him lunch and a tour, and sent him to interview Arafat. With nothing more to do until his departure next morning, he invited my wife and me to dinner. I said it was a pity he could not stay longer. He barked, "Why?"

And he passed me the check.

He explained that he'd had no time or need to get Jordanian money. Long afterward, it dawned on me that by putting his meal on my expense account instead of his, he was sticking it to his cousin Punch, the publisher. Punch's adviser, Sydney Gruson, said, "Cy was terribly greedy and never spent a penny of his own money," but it was more than that. The authorized family history, *The Trust*, says

Punch hated Cy for having been held up to him as a model during his troubled boyhood and for snubbing him during his farcical apprenticeship as a reporter in Paris. Punch's coterie derided Cy's prose as reading like soporific State Department position papers. For his part Cy had reason to regard Punch as a usurper. After his rigorous and perilous service as a reporter during World War II, Cy had been dubbed by *Time* magazine the Crown Prince of the *Times*, heir apparent to his uncle Arthur, the publisher. He was passed over, twice—the second time in favor of his dyslectic cousin. In 1954 he was also stripped of his title of chief correspondent and of his authority over the foreign staff and elevated, or exiled, to a column on the editorial page. "Today," he told his diary, "I ceased being a reporter and became a journalist," and said he would begin by calling on "my old friends, President Eisenhower and Secretary of State Dulles." He did precisely that. Eisenhower bragged to him about the recent coups in Iran and Guatemala; it was off the record, but Cy understood that Ike wanted credit for them in the *Times*. Off the record, too, Dulles, who had just proposed to use the atomic bomb in Vietnam, told Cy, "It doesn't make any sense to use one hundred shots or bombs to do exactly the same job as one atomic weapon, and it is much more expensive."

The job title Cy was groping for was not so much reporter or journalist as player in the great game. His memoirs claim that he served as a backdoor channel for negotiators on Korea, Berlin, and Cyprus, and as an adviser to President Kennedy on dealing with de Gaulle and Khrushchev, to President Johnson on Cambodia, and to President Nixon on Chile. He boasted that Eisenhower and Nixon received him privately while they were snubbing Scotty Reston and Max Frankel, respectively. Having married a Greek of social rank, Cy meddled actively, though apparently ineffectually, in Greek affairs. He was gratified by the overthrow of the socialists in 1967 but embarrassed by the brutal junta that succeeded them; he favored a coup to install a constitutional, conservative monarchy.

He adored rank; his office walls were a sort of photographic almanac of personages he knew, which he kept rearranging, as their ratings rose and fell. When de Gaulle, at a dramatic moment, accorded Cy an off-the-record interview that was no doubt intended to be passed along to Washington, Cy's parting request was for a new photo. It was perhaps unkind of Ambassador Bohlen to try to disillusion Cy as to the reason for his easy access to French leaders. Foreign notables who considered him a CIA agent were not far off the mark; they knew their words would get through. Bohlen gave him the apt code name Fidelis in relaying his reports to the CIA in Washington. Cy, who controlled the *Times*'s foreign staff until late 1954, was surely a party to the arrangement his uncle Arthur had made to plant CIA agents in at least ten *Times* bureaus abroad.* When Carl Bernstein reported in 1977 that one Sulzberger column was a piece of CIA black propaganda concocted by E. Howard Hunt, Cy at first denied it, then said that the words, at any rate, would have been his own.

He conceded that he might, like his uncle, have signed a CIA secrecy pledge. If so, he strained it when he published a diary entry dated December 22, 1961, regarding an imminent effort to assassinate de Gaulle and seize the French government to forestall Algerian independence. Cy quoted a CIA informant: "X tells me 'Don't leave Paris in January. That is the month.' He says there is a new secret organization in the army—much more secret than OAS—which is trying to enlist American aid. But Washington has refused."

The memoir tells no more about the plot, which was one of several that failed or were aborted. But it clearly indicates that in 1961 a CIA operative could consider doing to de Gaulle what the agency was then trying to do to Fidel Castro and would succeed in doing to Ngo Dinh Diem two years later. It seems unlikely that Sulzberger warned de Gaulle about the threat; at the time he appeared to share the hostility that the Washington establishment had held toward de Gaulle since his break with Vichy in 1940. Later he would call himself a Gaullist. He

**The Trust,* p. 530.

and I were unusual in the Anglo-American press corps in that we wrote favorably about de Gaulle, though for opposite reasons, Cy admiring the authoritarian aristocrat and I admiring the champion of national independence—for France, for Poland, for Cambodia.

A corrective history of the American war in Vietnam may be assembled from shards buried in the vast Sulzberger memoirs, *A Long Row of Candles*. As early as 1954, when the U.S. took over from the defeated French in the South, Admiral Charles E. Radford, chairman of the Joint Chiefs of Staff, told Cy he wanted "to turn the Indochina conflict into an allout war with China." An embassy official in Paris said that the State Department was being purged of old Indochina hands, that backing Diem was "lunacy," and that the CIA had bought Diem the support of two armed sects but the communists were virtually certain to win. A few months later Sulzberger interviewed Diem in Saigon and found that he "seems to border on the fanatic and doesn't appear to be very bright." The British ambassador warned that if an election were held, as promised by the Geneva accord, the communist-led Vietminh would win. Over the years many foreign leaders warned Cy, and through him the policy makers in Washington, that it was folly to pretend there was a government in South Vietnam and that we ought to get out. But Washington was traumatized by the "loss" of China and the fear that dominoes would fall in Southeast Asia if we left. So for two decades our leaders pretended to be defending a government that did not exist.

Cy, who went along with their game, was nonetheless struck by their contempt for their native satraps. He recounted that Henry Cabot Lodge, after actively promoting the elimination of Diem, escorted one of his replacements, Nguyen Cao Ky, to a "summit" photo op with President Johnson in Hawaii; after inspecting the aircraft accommodations, Lodge transferred Ky to the rear and seized the forward berth for himself. As noted in Chapter Eight, when Ky sounded off imprudently about attacking North Vietnam, Defense

Secretary McNamara told Cy that Ky "had better shut up or they will find themselves with a new air force commander."

As Bohlen told Sulzberger in early 1965, the decision had already been made "to bomb North Vietnam if, when, and how we please, unrelated to Vietcong actions in the South—except for the Hanoi-Haiphong complex, which, for the present, we are leaving alone." Gen. Maxwell Taylor told Cy that bombing the North had been discussed in 1961 (when Kennedy sent him to Vietnam on his fateful mission), and that he had made up his mind in favor of it in 1964. Sent back to Saigon by LBJ the following year, he admitted to Cy that he no longer believed the dominoes would fall if South Vietnam did, but he said: "My job here is to get a government.... The military can throw out any government it wishes to. All you really need here is two men—an honest, capable prime minister and a loyal commander-in-chief. That would be the answer. But where are they? We are trying to get tension to rise...." A commander told Cy, "pacification is down the drain."

They never did find the two good men. In 1966 Cy heard from the CIA that $100 million a year of U.S. aid was being stolen and smuggled to France. In Washington he found Averell Harriman "bewildered by the foolish Bobby Kennedy statement on including communists in the Saigon government" and "irked at [Walter] Lippmann and *The New York Times*." In the same aggrieved mood LBJ told him, "Think back to when we assassinated Diem," implying that we had done it to appease the liberal press.

"IT IS APPALLING TO CONTEMPLATE"

In those years a major effort at damage control was under way. Scores of selected journalists were being taken on junkets to Vietnam at government expense; leading ones got star treatment. General William C. Westmoreland took Cy in a swarm of aircraft on a thrilling overnight tour of hostile country along the Cambodian border and pointed across it to what he called the headquarters and main supply base of the Vietcong. On his return to Washington, Cy was shocked to learn that the CIA and Defense Secretary Robert McNamara considered the supply traffic through Cambodia to be marginal. He told LBJ and Walt Rostow that McNamara was all wet.

It is chilling to read the penultimate entry of the third and last volume of Cy's memoirs. It is December 28, 1971. Cy's friend Bill Porter, now envoy to the Paris peace talks, is triumphant. "Although Moscow has been screaming about our resumption of bombing of North Vietnam, there hasn't been one solitary peep out of Peking.... [T]he North Vietnamese depend upon China for a considerable amount of their food. Since they lost control by the Vietcong of the South Vietnamese delta and access via Sihanoukville of rice through lower Cambodia, they have been on short rations.... Bill said the new [sic] American tactic is that we are refusing to sit down and negotiate with the communist side here until they are ready to discuss and negotiate in a meaningful way" (*An Age of Mediocrity*, p.804).

In the months that followed, Washington told the world that it was the communists who were refusing to negotiate. The claim was that the communists wouldn't receive Henry Kissinger when he came to Paris to see them. That falsehood, repeated by the *Times*, was among several that caused me to send a flurry of corrective letters to colleagues in New York and Washington. It did not occur to me to approach Sulzberger—it never had, in seven years. Which may, after all, have been an error, for as I was packing to go home, I was surprised to hear through the secretarial grapevine that Sulzberger had expressed regret that I appeared to have avoided him. Then in a brief note he bade me "God's speed and good luck," and closed, "I respect you as a man of principle."

There is no indication that he was at that moment reexamining his own principles; he was still preening about expressions of regard for him by Nixon and Kissinger and Richard Helms of the CIA, and he was encouraging the squeeze on Chile that led to the Pinochet coup. But he must have been depressed by its savagery, by the disgrace of Nixon, by our ignominious departure from Saigon, and by his own impending forced retirement. Shortly after the death of his wife, Marina, in August, 1976, he wrote in his diary: "I realized with horror that in all my long life I had never done a single thing of which I could genuinely be proud: no act of true courage, generosity, sacrifice, or even pure kindness. It is appalling to contemplate."

SORTIE

I suppose I should explain here my decision to leave Paris. If Dick Eder had arrived on schedule, I might still be there. He'd been held over in Madrid because the Franco regime had ordered him out and relented only after a démarche by the State Department. So the *Times* kept him on with little to do but wait for the aging dictator to depart; Dick wrote me that Franco was waiting for him to die. In early 1972 the Paris staff was pleased to learn that New York had finally realized it was wasting his talent and was about to make him our bureau chief. Then one morning in May I arrived to find the secretary in tears. She pointed to a letter on my desk. James Greenfield, the foreign editor, was pleased to announce that Flora Lewis would join the *Times* as our boss.

I seized a phone to tell Greenfield I could not work with her. I had advised his predecessor, Seymour Topping, as much in 1967. She was writing a column for *Newsday* then, while her husband, Sydney Gruson, was liquidating the international edition. A Danish correspondent who was a valuable subtenant of ours was evicted to make room for her. Not a *Times* employee, she read our dispatches, dictated copy to our desk, and noisily dispatched our staff on errands. The grapevine had it that Flora was lobbying to replace our bureau chief, Henry Tanner, who was on home leave. When I found her receiving visitors in Tanner's office, I had a lock installed on his door and pocketed the key until his return. From New York, Topping commended my management of the bureau, agreed with me about the Flora problem, and promised to deal with it quietly. (He also gave me a merit raise and promised more.) On her appointment nearly five years later, *Time* magazine ran Flora's picture with the caption, "Opening the lock." The piece recalled the Tanner incident (which it did not learn from me) along with gossip that the Paris bureau was part of Flora's divorce settlement with Gruson, who had become Punch's right-hand man.

I reminded Greenfield that only a few months earlier he had expressed interest in my request that I, like Henry Kamm, be freed from bureau chores to travel and do features, responding directly to the foreign desk. He now replied that that would not do. In that case, I said, I'd come home.

What decided the issue no doubt was our difference in politics— Greenfield, Kamm, and Lewis supported the party line on Vietnam et al. and I opposed it—but our personalities were obviously a key factor. Greenfield, a career attaché now attached to Rosenthal, was not pleased by my kindly suggestion that he was not to blame for the appointment of Flora; he insisted that it was his own idea. (He showed his spite a few weeks later by turning down my offer of a rare interview with André Malraux that fell my way; I sold it to the *Times*'s Sunday magazine and, if memory serves, it drew attention in the French press.)

Reviewing my clips for those final six months, I am astonished at the range of history that I presumed to cover: interviews with Levi-Strauss, Jacques Monod, Jean Piaget, Arthur Koestler, Ignazio Silone, the economist Jacques Rueff; the stalled peace talks in Paris, a troubled Easter Week in Ireland, a grim last visit to Beirut. It was not dull. On reflection, I could no doubt have stayed with the bureau indefinitely, as an anonymous colleague pleaded in this note from New York, from which he inked out the signature and an identifying number:

2 June 1972
Dear John: DON'T DON'T DON'T!
Dear Mrs. Hess: DON'T LET HIM!

Seriously, the rue Scribe can't be any worse than West 43d Street under the current regime. Why not give it a try for three months, or six months. You might find that the problem has solved itself. She may be a bitch, but there's only one of her, while here we have layer on layer of them, ostensibly adult males. For example, there are more vice presidents than there are rim men on the foreign copy desk; there are more backfield executives, all at least "assistants to" or other Group O supervisors than there are rim men. Secrecy is the order of the day (Byzantium West); we learned of the new Paris bureau chief only through an item in Times Talk. New York, except for elegant neighborhoods, is filthy. Inflation continues at a pace more than apace. And as the price of food goes up the quality goes down. YOU WON'T LIKE IT HERE! Personally, I'm just gritting my teeth and serving out my time— [deleted] years [deleted] months to the day—till I can get that tiny pension.

Yes, after all, I would continue to work under Abe Rosenthal, and Flora's politics were not materially different from his.* But the relationship between the No. 1 and No. 2 jobs in a bureau is a delicate one. Roy Reed, one of the best writers on the staff, quit the *Times* rather than stay on in London under Johnny Apple. Andreas Freund, a fine trilingual journalist who had been the bulwark of the Paris bureau under half a dozen chiefs, found Flora intolerable; in the end she dis-

---

*Although movies were not her beat, Abe gave Flora half a page of the Arts & Leisure section to savage the about-to-be-released film *Missing* as a libel on U. S. diplomats in Chile. She said the film's director, Constantine Costa-Gavras, "is so sure of his suspicions, seems to feel so little need of specific evidence to support his deductions from the general iniquity of power, that one is driven to ask whether his attitudes derive from the fact that he is Greek." Sadly, *Times* critics followed her lead. The accuracy of the film, and the guilty knowledge of American officials about the crimes of Pinochet, have since been amply confirmed (see, for example, Fairness & Accuracy in Reporting's *Extra!* May/June 2000).

charged him for insubordination, and he sued and won a substantial indemnity. In hindsight I believe it was well for me to come home.

The selection of Flora Lewis in place of Richard Eder typified the eternal dilemma of the *Times,* which yearns for distinction but requires conformity. It radically reshaped Dick's career, and mine. He left the foreign staff, became a brilliant drama critic for the *Times,* and was demoted by Rosenthal because he would not write down to the market's standards. He then belatedly accepted the Paris bureau assignment but, still deeply hurt, he soon quit the paper and became literary critic of the *Los Angeles Times,* where he won a Pulitzer Prize. Finally, he returned to *The New York Times* as a book critic. Meanwhile I spent six exciting, exasperating, fruitful, and frustrating years, pushing at the limits of what the *Times* would permit in covering New York.

Corrections

Because of an editing error, a front-page dispatch on June 17 bore the headline "BUDGET CUT LIKELY FOR INTELLIGENCE." As noted in the second paragraph, the so-called intelligence agencies are to spend the same amount next year as this year.

Because of an editing error, a dispatch on June 18 was headed "DU PONT PLANS INQUIRY ON PESTICIDE CROP DAMAGE." This assertion was made in a company handout, but as noted in the second paragraph, the actual news was that Du Pont said it would defy a subpoena ordering it to testify on complaints that one of its products damaged crops.

Because of an editing error, a Page One headline on May 18 read "ADMINISTRATION TO FREEZE GROWTH OF HAZARDOUS WASTE INCINERATORS." The dispatch reported that the Administration planned to freeze enforcement of the law against two incinerators that have already been built, while promising not to approve any more illegal ones for the time being.

Because of an editing error, a dispatch on May 15 was captioned "ACCORD ON L.I. TO SHIELD PINE BARRENS FROM BUILDERS." The news was that half of the surviving 100,000 acres of the Pine Barrens nature preserve had been declared open to developers while sparing the other half for now.

Because of an editing error, none of the foregoing corrections appeared in *The New York Times.*

John L. Hess, in The Nation,
October 11, 1993

CHAPTER ELEVEN

Sin City

When I came home in the late summer of 1972, the *Times* was downplaying the corruption in Washington and ignoring—effectively covering up—the corruption in New York that would bring the city to virtual bankruptcy by 1975. It was abuzz, instead, with Abe Rosenthal's effort to match the glitter that he perceived in the style section of the *Washingon Post* and in *New York* magazine. His sidekick, Arthur Gelb, shared Abe's enthusiasm without the meanness. As metropolitan editor, he welcomed me on my return and continued to be supportive, in his erratic and forgetful way, to the end.

For shelter I made a beeline back to the Upper West Side, still affordable because unfashionable, and still unfashionable because of irrational fear of the Other. The *Times* stirred this fear both by commission and by omission. It blindly encouraged the devastation wreaked by Robert Moses, the revered builder of lovely parks, parkways, and beaches. That tale is told in Robert Caro's classic, *The Power Broker: Robert Moses and the Fall of New York*. Never elected to anything, Moses controlled planning, construction, highways, bridges, parks, and sanitation in the state and city from 1934 to 1968. He believed in automobiles and the white middle class, and he despised mass transit and the minorities—thus he located nearly all his swimming pools and playgrounds in white neighborhoods, and he designed highway underpasses too low for buses to reach Jones Beach. And he was, as the eminent Washington journalist Morton Mintz put it, our "Sacredest Cow."

"The *Times* fell down on its knees before him and stayed there, year after year after year," Mintz wrote, in reviewing Caro. "The *Times* and other papers printed Moses' handouts as if they were gospel, fawned on him in thousands of editorials, brushed aside citizens with evidence and even proof of wrongdoing, and chilled and put down those few on their staffs who itched to investigate what he really was doing."

When my generation returned from World War II, the city was in basically sound shape except for a shortage of housing. Armed with GI and FHA mortgages, many headed for the suburbs. Their traffic clogged highways faster than Moses could build them, and that suited him fine. Caro wrote: "When Robert Moses came to power in 1934, the city's mass transportation was probably the finest in the world. When he left power in 1968, it was quite possibly the worst." That's because the New York establishment did not believe in public transit. A long campaign supported by the *Times* finally succeeded in cracking the five-cent subway and bus fare and in turning the system over to authorities that were not accountable to the public. Fares rose and service went to pot; ridership declined; and traffic worsened—justifying further investment in highways and bridges, subsidized by the federal government.

In 1949 a disaster hit: Congress voted to finance "slum clearance." Moses seized upon it to ravage a dozen sectors of the city. He cut a terrible swathe across the Bronx, joined with the Rockefeller brothers in destroying the richly diversified Washington Street Market area of the Lower West Side (site of the World Trade Center), and would have devastated Greenwich Village and Lower Manhattan with a crosstown superhighway but for the resistance led by Jane Jacobs.

Uptown, the plain between Central Park and Broadway was blue-collar country. Its brownstones and small tenements sheltered Irish and German and, increasingly, Hispanic working people. Moses declared it a slum, and overnight he made it one. He condemned one six-block area for $15 million and turned it over to a promoter for $1 million. He gave a larger sector, gratis, to another prospective developer. Eventually the spaces were to be replaced by a bleak range of high rises, including subsidized middle-class apartments and one of the last low-cost public housing projects. But Moses' entrepreneurs took their time. While ostensibly planning construction and seeking capital, they abandoned maintenance of the low-rises but continued to collect rents. Their abuses and corruption were exposed during the 1950's by Joe Kahn and Bill Haddad of the *Post* and Fred Cook and Gene Gleason of the *World-Telegram*. They had to conspire to scoop one another, to hornswoggle their editors into printing stories that reflected on the sainted Moses. The *Times* would not let a reporter touch the scandal until 1959. Even then, it declared in an editorial: "Our confidence in Mr. Moses as an honest, incomparably able public servant is unshaken. His resignation from office would be an irreparable loss. Where is his equal?"

When we returned, to say that one lived on the Upper West Side would arouse amazement and pity. A slow and painful recovery was under way; luxury apartment houses on both flanks were being reconverted from noxious SROs to studio apartments and co-ops, but many of the former welfare tenants lingered, sleeping in doorways and the parks and begging on Broadway, marring what Mayor Rudolph Giuliani would later call the quality of life.

Fear of the Other was stoked by the media. One damaging example was the coverage of one of the blackouts inflicted on the city by Consolidated Edison in 1977. The *Times* city room rose to the occasion and by candlelight pounded out a thrilling, terrifying tale of looters who, as Francis X. Clines reported, "scattered roachlike" upon the arrival of the police. In contrast, a sidebar reported how eminent bankers responded: "City Power Crisis Musters/Executive Grit and Muscle." The *Times* said nothing about the negligence that had caused the blackout; instead it accorded Con Ed's CEO a profile headed "Cool Man on a Hot Spot." (Con Ed, on whose board sat a member of the Sulzberger Family, had saddled New York with notoriously unreliable service at the highest rates in the country. With the support of the *Times*, it acquired the power stations of the New York subways and two state nuclear plants and ran them badly, too.)

The looting that night, and its media coverage, fed the fear that Ed Koch was then exploiting in his successful run for mayor.

In a front-page series, the *Times* purported to discover "The Worst Block in Town" on West 84th Street. It surely had its share of crime, misery, and neglect, but it also, as I had occasion to learn, had some hardworking, talented, and feature-worthy people. The *Times*, of course, was not alone in its prejudice; I recall a mention in the *New Yorker* of the "menacing laughter" of Latinos on their West Side doorsteps. In my neighborhood I once saw a young cop brandish his club to break up what was actually a friendly debate in Spanish about the date of Columbus' voyages.

In an effort to show the Other in a different light, I did some features about ethnic communities that were enriching what Mayor David Dinkins later called the gorgeous mosaic of our town. I found immigrants who were working hard, shunning welfare, transforming neighborhoods, planting gardens in vacant lots. Those articles received a Meyer Berger Award from the Columbia School of Journalism, but they were like sprinkling a few drops of water on a bonfire. The metaphor is suggested by Tom Wolfe's fictional assault on the black community in *The Bonfire of the Vanities*, which the *Times* helped to make a bestseller—as it did also the pseudoscientific libel of black intelligence and morality by Charles Murray called *The Bell Curve*. A villain in *Bonfire* is a black minister-agitator, who was widely interpreted as based on the Rev. Al Sharpton. During the 1982 Democratic primary campaign, in which Sharpton ran up a surprisingly strong tally against the otherwise unopposed Senator Moynihan, a front-page analysis by Clines declared:

> Mr. Sharpton talks passionately of bearding Mr. Moynihan on behalf of all blacks and sympathizers ever rankled by some of the Senator's oft misunderstood but never forgotten allusions to "benign neglect" in the Nixon years and, lately, "speciation," or formalization of out-of-wedlock social problems.

Early on at 43d Street. [In-house photo]

Off to Paris. Official foreign correspondent photo, early sixties. [NYT staff photo]

BERGMAN PLEADS GUILTY TO A FRAUD IN MEDICAID AND BRIBING BLUMENTHAL

LEGISLATOR IRATE

Nursing-Home Owner Pledges Cooperation And Gets Immunity

By JOHN L. HESS

Bernard Bergman, the nursing-home promoter, pleaded guilty yesterday to a $1.2 million Medicaid fraud and to a new charge—the bribery of Albert H. Blumenthal, the Assembly majority leader.

Mr. Blumenthal, who was indicted last Dec. 5 on charges of perjury regarding his use of influence in behalf of Mr. Bergman, was arraigned on a superseding indictment that alleged receipt of bribes and misconduct, as well. He pleaded

The New York Times/Tyrone Dukes

Bernard Bergman, the nursing home promoter, rushing past newsmen as he arrived at courthouse yesterday.

Prairie fire burning.
[*The New York Times*, March 12, 1976]

Karen Hess with Jean Troisgros. [Author's collection]

With war history guide, Cambodia, 1993. [Martha Hess]

It was Clines who misunderstood, totally. Moynihan did not *allude* to "benign neglect," he *recommended* it, in a secret memo to Nixon (which ultimately leaked) that foreshadowed Nixon's Southern strategy; it was part of a neoconservative counterattack on the gains for civil rights and social justice of the preceding years. And Moynihan's suggestion that out-of-wedlock pregnancies might produce a new biological species —"speciation"—did not refer to formalizing social problems; it plainly spelled out the racist, genetic Malthusianism that he had been preaching, usually more allusively, for thirty years.

Moynihan, now, was a man who could truly say "I got my job through *The New York Times.*" Soon after his appointment as ambassador to the United Nations in late 1975 he said on *Face the Nation:* "I would consider it dishonorable to leave this post and run for any office, and I hope it would be understood, if I do, the people would consider me as having said in advance that I am a man of no personal honor." After seven months of bashing Communists, Arabs, and neutralists at the UN, he announced his candidacy for the Senate. The *Times* gave him fulsome coverage; his opponent, the militant feminist and peacenik Bella Abzug, received harsh treatment, including a memorable Sunday magazine cover photo taken from below with her legs apart. Moynihan won by a margin of a few hundred votes. The *Times* has served him as a house organ ever since.

A fellow Malthusian was Roger Starr, who dominated municipal policy on the *Times* editorial page in the 1970s and 1980s. In a memoir, *The Rise and Fall of New York City,* he declaimed that a "major influence contributing to the achievement of order in the nineteenth-century city was the lack of a system of public assistance.

"The improvement of medical care has had unexpectedly bad side effects on urban life," he wrote. "If health care has the effect of increasing the number... of dangerously uncivil people in the population, the cost of trying to impose moral order on them must rise significantly" (p.151).

The Rev. Dr. Thomas Malthus made precisely the same point two centuries ago: "Instead of recommending cleanliness to the poor, we should encourage contrary habits... make the streets narrower, crowd more people in their houses, and court return of the plague... build our villages near stagnant pools.... But above all, we should reprobate specific remedies for ravaging diseases."* Malthus did not, however, characterize the poor as genetically inferior. That was the contribution of his modern followers.

A BALANCED REPORT

Racism has been intrinsic to the American experience since the first colonial settlements, and the *Times* could not but reflect it. As noted, it was candidly racist regarding the troubles that immediately followed World War I. It was a detached and wary witness to battles against ethnic prejudice that engaged a growing sector of its readership: Sacco and Vanzetti, the Scottsboro Boys, the rise of Nazism, appeasement, isolationism, the internment of Japanese Americans. The color line was broken in baseball before it was broken at the *Times*; no doubt the former event helped along the latter. It was a difficult transition on 43d Street, not yet completed. White males continued for many years to question the competence and reliability of women and minorities. In a job interview an applicant was asked, "Do you think of yourself first as a journalist, or first as an Hispanic?" An editor of notorious inadequacy blamed his shortcomings on his being saddled with black reporters—several of whom left to make distinguished careers elsewhere. None could feel comfortable on 43d Street.

The *Times*, as I have recalled, covered the civil-rights struggle in the South with distinction. New York was another matter. For the staff as for its readers, race determined where one lived, where one felt safe, where one's children went to school. The newspaper's conduct was affected not only by fear but also by interest. A department store chief was said to have explained to Rupert Murdoch why he did not adver-

---

*From the 1803 edition of *On Population*. In her introduction to a reedition of the book in 1960, Gertrude Himmelfarb (wife of Irving Kristol) says Malthus had "a genuine sympathy for the unfortunates who were the victims of nature's relentless laws." In an op-ed piece in the *Times* on July 28, 1999, Himmelfarb boasted of her long dedication to the theme of "compassionate conservatism" being sounded by Gov. George W. Bush.

tise in the *Post*: "Your readers are our shoplifters." Our advertisers sought readers in Manhattan (below 96th Street) and in the suburbs. One day in my final investigation for the *Times*, a man at the Bronx Courthouse told me I was the first *Times*man he'd seen in a year. At the next staff meeting I asked why we had two correspondents in Suffolk County and none in the Bronx. Deputy managing editor Seymour Topping looked at metropolitan editor Mitchell Levitas, and Levitas looked at Topping. Then Topping said, "We have more readers in Suffolk." I checked. It was not quite true. Nor did it make journalistic sense. We had few readers in Africa, but we had four reporters there to cover the fires. It was commonplace to say that the Bronx was burning—Howard Cosell exclaimed it on CBS, and Wolfe located his bonfire there. Three of the *Times*'s heroes fed the blaze: Robert Moses by bulldozing a ruinous swath across the borough, Robert Wagner, Jr., by preaching abandonment under the euphemism "planned shrinkage," and Daniel Patrick Moynihan by jibing repeatedly that "People don't want housing in the South Bronx, or they wouldn't burn it down" (for example see *The New York Times*, December 20, 1978).

The myth that the poor were setting fire to their tenement apartments in order to get better ones at taxpayers' expense was doubly damaging because it helped to destroy the public-housing program while denigrating the people who needed it. It was doubly disgraceful of the *Times* in that the paper circulated a cruel falsehood while it missed what should have leaped to the eye of any reporter. Obviously, many fires were and are caused by kerosene stoves, makeshift heaters, and bad wiring, and some by negligent tenants (smoking, drinking); others are set by landlords as a means of summary eviction (still occasionally practiced, spurred by rent legislation that was welcomed by the *Times*). But the big story begging to be told was that syndicates were buying up slum properties, insuring them, burning them, and sharing the loot with lenders, insurance adjusters, and fire marshals. The arson racket was exposed by an alternative weekly in Boston. That set off similar inquiries with similar results elsewhere, including the Bronx. Yet I imagine that the reader today is more familiar with the myth that Moynihan and the *Times* helped to purvey than with the reality. Our editors shared the vision of the Bronx portrayed in Wolfe's novel and in TV police shows; they had no desire to poke in the embers. After my complaint at that staff meeting, they substantially beefed up coverage of the suburbs; they never did work up a sustained interest in the outer boroughs. Years later, when a *Times* dispatch from Mount Vernon identified it as a town "on the border of Manhattan," I displayed an unmarked map on TV showing the land between Mount Vernon and Manhattan (the Bronx) as terra truly incognita and invited the paper to explore it. When Reagan conquered Grenada, the *Times* described it as an island the size of Martha's Vineyard; I pointed out that it was also the size of the borough of Queens.

Ed Koch once said that to visit Queens gave him a nosebleed. That was singularly ungrateful, because racial prejudice there was and remains a bulwark to politicians willing to exploit it. The borough may boast having made Koch mayor. He was a Village Democrat who joined the liberal reformers in the sixties, did the civil rights bit including a trip to Mississippi, and got himself elected to Congress. There he was quick to draw the lesson of Nixon's Southern strategy. Although Queens was not in his district, he made his way to Forest Hills to stir up the natives in a protest against a housing project.*

Koch could get away with anything as long as he stoked the bonfire. He repeatedly accused the black community as a whole of being anti-Semitic (a thought earlier propounded by Moynihan and Nathan Glazer); he referred to people involved in welfare programs as "poverty pimps" (and, once elected, made alliances with several of the worst). He called Ronald Dellums, a tall, black congressman, "this Zulu warrior... a Watusi from Berkeley." He observed "an enormous backlash by the white middle class because they perceive crime as a

---

*Full disclosure: Koch circulated a letter signed by the New York congressional delegation nominating me for a Pulitzer Prize, for my work on nursing homes. (For reasons not worth examining here, Seymour Hersh and I, who were both nominated by the *Times* that year, were passed over.) Koch also sought me out for a private stroking. I told him I regretted his shift to the right. He knew better than to follow my advice.

black issue." He complained, "When a black is a victim, it's racist, and when a white is a victim, it's robbery." In a review of a book supporting a racist view of criminality he wrote: "An individual commits crime because of enduring personal characteristics. These include level of intelligence, genetic inheritance, anatomical configuration, gender, age, and early developmental pressures rooted in the nature of parental influence.... The people who try to blame civilization for criminal behavior look pretty foolish."

Early on Koch learned that to be accused of racism was political money in the bank. When a preacher in a black church in Brooklyn mentioned Koch's bias in a sermon, the mayor held a news conference to broadcast it, thus scoring points both with candid racists and with many whites living in denial. In polite circles, such as the *Times*, it was sometimes permissible to acknowledge that Koch, and later Mayor Giuliani, may have been a mite "insensitive" toward the delicate feelings of our brown citizenry. It was a fault, like "ethical impairment" (a euphemism for corruption), that the *Times* could actually mention in editorials endorsing Koch, Giuliani, and Senator Al D'Amato against liberal opponents.

Logic had nothing to do with it. Koch reduced the police force by one-fourth, and crime increased sharply during his twelve years as mayor. David Dinkins, the first black mayor of New York, restored the force to its previous strength and a bit more and moved it into the streets. Midway in his four-year term crime began a substantial decline that continued through the Giuliani administrations. Yet the *Times* treats it as unquestionable fact that Koch was tough on crime and Dinkins soft, and that Giuliani was responsible for the turnabout.

This has not, need I say, been a balanced report. I have passed over the evident effort of the new regime at the *Times* to address bias. It remains nonetheless the elephant in the city room. Not racism, perish forbid, but insensitivity. For further illustration of its persistence refer to the Appendix (item two) for my recent essay, "Statistical Bias."

Euphronios, Black-figured calyx krater: *The Death of Sarpe-don*, Greek vase VI century B.C. The Metropolitan Museum of Art, Bequest of Joseph H. Durkee, Gift of Darius Ogden Mills and Gift of C. Ruxton Love, by exchange.

CHAPTER TWELVE

Kerfuffle at the Met

One day in early 1972 an art historian and the president of the Art Dealers Association came calling on the *Times*'s critic John Canaday with troubling news: important paintings owned by the Metropolitan Museum were being hawked along Madison Avenue. Canaday passed the tip to the culture news reporter, Grace Glueck; she called the museum's director, Tom Hoving, who denied it, and other sources, who confirmed it but declined to be quoted. So she put it on hold. On reflection Canaday decided that he was obliged to weigh in. In a Sunday column headed "Very Quiet and Very Dangerous" he identified ten pictures that were "rumored" to be on offer: a famous early Picasso, a Cezanne, a Manet, a Gauguin, and so on. He recalled notorious past "deaccessionings" by the Met and other museums and questioned the wisdom and morality of such arbitrary disposals of public treasure. The following week the culture section was held back at the request of Punch Sulzberger—who happened to be a member of the trustees' committee that had "deaccessioned" the paintings Canaday had named and scores more that he did not yet know about—to carry a rebuttal by Hoving headed, "Very Inaccurate and Very Dangerous." It was, I would later write, "as violent an attack on a journalist as ever to appear in his own paper."

Actually Canaday had rescued the paintings he identified. They were hastily "reaccessioned," but Hoving scoured the museum's holdings for scores of other paintings which he sold secretly to selected dealers at bargain prices (the easier to unload them) in order to pay record prices for acquisitions that would draw front-page headlines.

Canaday got wind of the sale by the Met of a Van Gogh and a Douanier Rousseau of world class. (The dealer was asking three times what he had paid the Met for them.) Again Canaday sounded off, and again he was abused, in a rebuttal signed by C. Douglas Dillon, the banker-statesman who was president of the Met. At this point the *Times* faced a challenge to its judgment, its intelligence and its veracity. Since Canaday was fully engaged as a critic, and since Hilton Kramer, the culture news editor, and Glueck were otherwise disposed, Arthur Gelb asked me to look into the matter, without prejudice.

It soon transpired that the museum's dealings had been even more extensive and more scandalous than Canaday had reported. I made clandestine contact with a few brave Met employees, who justifiably feared dismissal and mistrusted the *Times*. Their tips were supported by anomalies in the museum's index cards, which were declared off limits after my first visit. Thus armed, I confronted Hoving. I've related the episodes that followed in a book, *The Grand Acquisitors* (Morrow: 1974), whose title I lifted from Hoving's flattering description of the museum trustees. I called the story, I hope not too breathlessly, "a series of scandals [that] set the art world on its ear" and "a rattling good yarn... about secret and peculiar deals involving millions of dollars in art, about the wooing and betrayal of an eccentric spinster heiress, about masterpieces called fakes and fakes called masterpieces, about stolen treasures, elusive dealers, tomb robbers, a chair mender in Zurich and a coin trader in Beirut... a cast of characters to make a novelist dream." It was also about morality and about the *Times*.

Years later Hoving turned to muckraking, too. In a series of books he heaped shovelfuls on his former patrons and in passing confirmed our reporting. My review of his *Making the Mummies Dance: Inside the Metropolitan Museum of Art* began:

Digging wearily through this middenheap of mendacity, I was struck by how much Tom Hoving has in common with Donald Trump. Their tales about the art of the deal and the deal in the art can teach us a lot about the times we live in, provided we don't believe a word they say.

In a preliminary volume of his auto-hagiography, *King of the Confessors* (1981), Hoving, former director of the Met, boasted about lying "smoothly and amiably" to get his first job there. "I had always been able to lie convincingly and without hesitation," he explained. Convincingly? Compulsively would be better, as illustrated by an incident that he now recounts this way:

"The *Times*, in a stunningly good piece of investigative reporting, rooted out the half-forgotten Ingres *Odalisque* in Paris and cast our on-and-off deal with [art dealer] Wildenstein as a classic case of clandestine art shenanigans. The painting was rushed back to the museum—to dead storage" (*The Nation*, February 8, 1993).

The truth is less flattering, but more amusing. The *Odalisque* was one of the Met's best-known objects. Acting on a tip (or should I say, following a stunning investigation?), I asked Hoving where it was. He replied, smoothly and amiably, "It's none of your business." When I demurred, he became abusive about the *Times*, Canaday, and me, said the painting had suddenly looked dubious and been sent to an expert for study, and finally, "We believe that the painting is not by the master."

The story in the *Times* next morning hit the Wildensteins like a bombshell. The Ingres had an impeccable pedigree, and they already had, so I heard, found a Japanese buyer. Now it was tainted and they were forced to return it to the Met, where it went, not to dead storage, but back on the wall, pusillanimously labeled "Ingres and Workshop."

The museum did not recover a Van Gogh, a Douanier Rousseau, and many other works that Hoving had secretly sold to selected parties at prices often far below the market—not to mention two irreplaceable collections of ancient coins that were dispersed at auction to finance the purchase of the million-dollar Euphronios krater. Nicholas Gage of the *Times* revealed that the vase had come from an illegal dig in Italy. Now, nearly twenty years later, Hoving says he never doubted that, and he mocks the fantastic story that the Met and its accomplices tried to peddle at the time about the vase lying forgotten, in pieces, in the private collection of the seller's father.

All that was fun and games, and nobody cared much, except archeologists. They considered that the Met's display of ruthless greed and the record price it had paid—many times more than had ever been paid before for a Greek vase—would be a huge incitement to more plundering. But buying dear was central to Hoving's policy. He describes an epiphany at a meeting of the Acquisitions Committee. Members dozed as curators presented small items they wanted to buy. "Why bother? I thought. Then a $100,000 acquisition was proposed. The trustees beamed. So did I. I had suddenly experienced a minor revelation. The hell with dribs and drabs.... From then on I'd acquire only the rare, fantastic pieces, the expensive ones, the ones that would cause a splash."

Later in *Making the Mummies Dance* Hoving recounts a story about Norton Simon, the billionaire collector, bidding against himself at an auction but not quite topping the record price for a Rembrandt, which had been set by the Met. Elsewhere Hoving says that he himself doubled, and doubled again, his own offer for a church lectern, each of which offers had enchanted the seller. His motive, so he says, was to jack up the price to forestall a possible British effort to keep the piece in England. "My collecting style was pure piracy," he boasts, "and I got a reputation as a shark."

One of his early splashes as director was his purchase of a Monet at a then-record price of $1.4 million. "I had stumbled on the masterpiece in 1960," he cannot help saying, though it was shown that year at the Museum of Modern Art. His account of his surreptitious discovery of the picture and the rapture he underwent echoes the fable of the ivory cross. He first peddled the yarn to John McPhee for *The New Yorker*, then told a different version in *King of the Confessors*, and then embroidered in new detail in *Mummies*. The banal truth is that young Hoving had been sent with a chaperone to buy a fine bit of medieval carving that had been widely offered but spurned because it was almost certainly Nazi war loot. Also, scholars question Hoving's identification of it. But it made a good yarn, or yarns, and the price was right: $600,000. The British Museum had just turned it down at $500,000.

For the Met's trustees, who were a cross-section of the pinnacle of the financial establishment, high prices were a confirmation of quality, and the shady origin of acquisitions lent a sense of romance and imperial potency. Hoving boasted here of smuggling, of buying stolen treasures, of bribing foreign custodians, of complicity in tax frauds by donors of art at artificially inflated prices. Safely covered by the statute of limitations, he brags in *Mummies* of faking missions abroad to justify luxury travel by himself and a crony, and of other indulgences, including the services of museum staff women and "pricey call girls." Since he had just fired a curator (whom he names) for embezzlement, he admits this was "naked hypocrisy" but says it was "glorious fun." (He was and is married, but among the better orders the rules seem to be different. In the circles where his wealthy parents lived, he remarks in passing, "wifeswapping was the game of choice.")

During the days when Donald Trump's *Art of the Deal* topped the bestseller list, its author was widely viewed as an admirable symbol of the go-go eighties; bankers and pretty women were eager to serve him, and he was mentioned as a likely prospect for high office. Hoving in his heyday at the Met was a symbol of the go-go seventies and could seriously consider a future in politics. We have seen less gifted practitioners of hype than those two go farther.

To finance a vast campaign of splash, Hoving and his trustees sold art, misappropriated bequests, imposed admission fees, and cut the number of the wretchedly paid staff by nearly 10 percent. Hoving writes that he won his appointment as director in 1967 by scaring the trustees about the threat of unionization and an impending prosecution for sex discrimination. Actually those crises arose years later. He crushed the union effort, in part by firing two leaders. He says he knew it was illegal and he would have to take them back, but it was "excellent business." The women's suit was settled out of court.

Squeezing bucks from the near-bankrupt City of New York appears to have been a breeze for these mendicants. Hoving says that as he was ending his brief tenure as Parks Commissioner to rejoin the Met, he arranged to beef up the city's contribution. Warned that this looked like a conflict of interest, he retorted, "Who'll stop me?" Or so he says. In any case, city officials staunchly defended him during the scandals that marked his tenure at the Met, notably his seizure of a swatch of Central Park for expansion on what he now gleefully calls spurious legal grounds.

Especially vocal in Hoving's defense was his successor as parks commissioner, August Heckscher, whom Hoving now characterizes as a "putz." Hardly anybody who ever befriended Hoving escapes such recompense. This is more tedious in *Mummies* than it may sound in summary here, and it is likely to be more meaningful to psychiatrists than to lay readers, but it is perhaps significant that Hoving devotes a chapter to describing himself as a "toady," spending months aboard the yacht of the trustee Charles Wrightsman, whom he now calls "a nasty son of a bitch" and "a drunken, foulmouthed roughneck," who cheated at polo besides.

Hoving has described his sponsor, former Met director James Rorimer, as a pompous, stuffy, arrogant, jealous, conniving man. Now he adds that Rorimer's death was hastened by the criticism of "crazy" and "evil" Roland Redmond, who was the only trustee to stand forthrightly for law and restraint during Hoving's reign. Nabobs who supported Hoving are described as "vapid," "cheap," "a vulgar bastard," "slightly scatterbrained" and "strictly an opportunist." One of them made his private curator trim his toenails. And so on. Hoving is just as hard on his staff supporters—but enough.

Any overview of the goings-on at the Met in that era is perforce obscured by the magnificence of its collections, the scope of its expansion and the dazzle of its blockbuster exhibitions. There is much to criticize and much left to admire. Judging all that is beyond my scope and, rather oddly, does not seem to interest Hoving very much anymore. If it ever did, that is. "I wanted to be accepted into the prestige and power of the Metropolitan far more than I really cared about the institution," he says early on in *Mummies*. He'd have done well to end his book there.

A PRAGMATIC VIEW

I believe readers of *The Grand Acquisitors* will still find the story "a rattling good yarn," and our work a credit to the *Times*. That calls for a few observations. Consider, again, that Punch Sulzberger was a member of the Met's acquisitions committee, which had to approve all the shady transactions we were exposing and others we never got around to. So he knew, or should have known, that Hoving was lying. Yet he allowed Hoving and Dillon to blackguard his staff in our columns. We heard that at one point Hoving assured trustees that our "vendetta" would end forthwith; Punch may have given him that impression, but he did not pass the word along to us.

It was argued that as a trustee Punch was bound by the confidentiality of the board's proceedings—the very curtain of secrecy that we reporters were working so hard to crack. That in turn raised the question of whether Punch had any business serving on that board. Most journalists, including our editors, agreed that he did not. But it proved irresistible. He, the undistinguished grandson of a Jewish printer from Tennessee, had been named a member and eventually would become—*mirabile dictu*—chairman of the most prestigious club of the American financial elite. The WASP supremacy persisted, however. Two heirs expressed outrage to me at the breach of faith

in the sale of paintings donated by their mothers, but they declined
to protest publicly. The banker Robert Lehman quit the board after
a humiliating snub, but in the end endowed a museum within the
museum to bear his name.

The entire board was humiliated repeatedly during the Hoving
era, and there was occasional public speculation that he would be
dismissed at the next board meeting. It never happened. I theorized
that the trustees did not want to acknowledge an error in judgment
by firing him, but some were doubtless charmed by his rascality—
they were, after all, grand acquisitors, heirs of robber barons, with
names like Rockefeller, Morgan, Gilpatric and Houghton. They took
a pragmatic view of the law, including international law; shipowners
who flew the Liberian flag employed Dillon as their wire puller.
Some trustees enjoyed the help of the museum in enhancing their
own collections and reducing their taxes (though they also made
substantial donations). So the game went on. The city's ex officio
representatives on the board said they would not dream of second-
guessing the director. The state attorney general and the district
attorney were forced by our disclosures to consider the apparently
lawless and imprudent disposal of public property and traffic in
stolen goods, but in the end settled for pledges by the perpetrator to
mend its ways—pledges it violated even as it made them. U.S. Customs, the New York Police Department, and foreign authorities
looked into the museum's acquisition of archeological treasures but
never quite closed a case. Resolutions were adopted, international
conventions were drafted, but little loot was ever returned. Even as
we were reporting his abuses, Hoving boasted the acquisition of an
overrated and overpriced collection of Asian art, paid for with
untraceable funds (a transaction that I described eventually in *New
York* magazine). And he left under his own steam. When, long afterward, he turned muckraker, he expressed greater contempt for the
trustees than ever I could in the *Times*, and hinted at more revela-

tions to come. The museum, incidentally, would not allow us reviewers to consult even the old files he had cited.

Hoving had another advantage: he did not have to cope with *Times* editing. In a disastrous experiment, Grace Glueck, the culture reporter, was assigned to sift the flow of news, reviews, handouts, and wire-service copy from all sectors of Culture Gulch. She tried to edit it. It piled up on her desk in a hopeless muddle until her final deadline, when she dumped it on the next substation. As a result, though I would file early and in short takes, I was obliged to hang around for hours to wrestle my copy past three levels of second-guessing. So it was less fun than it should have been. And it came to a depressing end.

I was digging into the looting of the estate of Adelaide de Groot, which had been in the custody of a bank represented on the museum's board. An artist's wife called on a different matter. She wanted me to expose what she described as a common abuse: a curator and critics helping themselves to gifts from artists' studios. We set a date to meet. Then she called to beg off; she said the critic Thomas Hess had warned them that to make an issue of it would ruin her husband's career. In all naiveté I asked Hilton Kramer whether he had any suggestions about my pursuing the matter. He exploded, sputtered something about my intruding on his beat, and complained to Gelb that I was spreading slander. Embarrassed, Gelb explained to me that Kramer thought I was alluding to a passage in *The Art Crowd* by Sophy Burnham—a worthy book that I had not yet read. It said that Kramer, scraping by at an art magazine before he came to the *Times*, would solicit advertisements for shows he would write up and had received a gift from a grateful artist.* What

---

*This was far more common than I knew. Long afterward, the *Times* obituaries of Clement Greenberg, Harold Rosenberg, and Thomas Hess would mention that they left collections valued in millions of dollars. But at the time they were picking up these examples of the new art they were promoting, it was not a story for the *Times*. More generally, there would be no further interest in pursuing the underside of the art market.

Gelb did not tell me was that Canaday was to be replaced by Kramer. It was a triumph for the Art Crowd. Canaday, a fine writer, had incurred its noisy enmity because of his dislike for abstract expressionism and the trends that followed. At the time I thought of it as an esthetic dispute, also affected by fashion and market considerations. It was not until I read Frances Stonor Saunders's *The Cultural Cold War* (1999) that I learned to what extent politics was involved. The CIA was subsidizing magazines and exhibitions to display the freedom and daring of our artists, in contrast to the weariness of Europe and the dreariness behind the Iron Curtain. The agency's role had to be clandestine, because Congress could not easily be persuaded to support shocking art and because our artists and intelligentsia were mostly of the left and critical of U.S. foreign policy. Not Kramer, of course. Aside from the moribund Stalinists, I know of no critic who was more class conscious. Early on he proclaimed New York the art capital of the world—which made the *Times* critic its imperial judge. Ever suspicious of the loyalty of artists and curators, he was actively hostile to reporting that reflected poorly on the master class. In the course of time, he appears to have found the graphic arts too limited a field and the *Times*'s tradition of objectivity too inhibiting, for he obtained rightwing funding to establish his own organ of cultural counterrevolution. And increasingly he spewed hatred for the *Times* as a hotbed of subversion.

The myth of a liberal media has served the Right well. Some on the far right no doubt believe it; everything, after all, is to their left. A few, like William Kristol, acknowledge that it's hype. But repetition has persuaded even mainstream journalists. Consider a recent *Times* magazine cover article reporting with awe the success of Rupert Murdoch's Fox TV News. The magazine concluded that Fox actually was a mite slanted but that that was a wholesome counterbalance to CNN's tilt to the left. When I caught my breath, I concluded that the news itself is subversive, so any messenger who purports to deliver the news seriously is likely to be blamed for it.

I detest the linkage, but one might think of Kramer and Hess as demonstrating the breadth of the *Times*'s tolerance. In my observation, however, conservative bias never had trouble getting into the paper, whereas reporting that reflected on the establishment—including reporting by the nonpolitical Canaday and the conservative Gage—made editors nervous. At the end of our adventure, Kramer, who opposed it, was promoted, Canaday was removed from the field and I had to threaten to quit to get that last de Groot story into print. I believe Gelb was relieved when I asked to return to general assignment.

What, then, did we accomplish? Well, we recovered the *Odalisque*, we salvaged part of a great collection of ancient coins the Met was dispersing by auction, and for a season we shed light on dark corners of the art market. But the light flickered out. Nothing basically changed. From time to time whistle-blowers would come up with stories about fakery, fraud, and the looting of archeological treasure—"rattling good yarns"—and the *Times* would mention some of them, but it never again led the way.

House ad, 1974.

CHAPTER THIRTEEN

Dining On the Times

Scotty told me a little while ago that I should have bid to replace Craig Claiborne; the idea horrified me. For one thing, I can't cook; for another, I like to eat too well, and for a third, I'd soon have all the food purveyors in America on your back.

I wrote that in a letter to Abe Rosenthal on May 25, 1973. Eleven months later he named me food critic of the *Times*.

There was talk that he did it to get me away from serious business. I don't believe it. True, I had just been exposing shenanigans in the art world, and true, I had been bugging Scotty and Abe about our coverage of Vietnam and had put my name down as coordinator of an unprecedented peace appeal by the *Times* staff. But they had no need to be devious. They believed that dining was serious business indeed.

As of course it was. But it was not the decline in the quality of our food that concerned them; I doubt they were aware of it. What newly affluent Americans like them craved was instruction in classy living. Scotty would write one day that Craig Claiborne, the quintessential snob, author of the $4,000 dinner for two in Paris, was one of the best things that ever happened to the *Times*. What among us we still called the women's page had not yet metastasized into Style, and the Travel section had not yet spawned The Sophisticated Traveler, but we were on the way. Abe emphatically agreed with an interviewer that he was trying to emulate Clay Felker of *New York* magazine, who was emulating *Women's Wear Daily* in advising readers which foods and feeding places were in and which were out this season.

What caused them to think of me as a promising guide was copy I had filed from time to time about food and wine in France. Otherwise one might say that I qualified by marriage to write about food. *Newsweek* once referred to my wife, Karen, as the finest American cook in Paris. She had learned to cook as a child in Nebraska, cooked for her board as a student and preserved an intense interest in the craft and its history. Even as the quality of produce declined, she managed to feed her family well. Then we moved to Paris—the only place, I once told her, where I could contemplate living without her cooking. There were never enough mealtimes for us to cope with the pleasures offered by our markets and by the bistros and the starred temples of gastronomy. We made friends with chefs and restaurateurs and toured vineyards with them every year to choose our wines. We dined with them *en famille*, we visited humble homes they came from (one of them a cave, another a dirt-floor hut), and we remarked on the ambiguity of their situation as caterers to the wealthy—and of the ambiguity of ours as well. We observed the birth of nouvelle cuisine with its mix of talent and hype and we directed attention to the passion of its creators for produce of old-time quality. Karen spent many hours in their kitchens, haunted bookstalls, and accumulated a serious library.

For more than half a century now I have shared my bed with cookbooks (on Karen's side, not mine) and have heard her exclaim at the pleasures of some and the absurdities of others. One night in Paris she broke into laughter as she leafed through a new Time-Life book on provincial French cooking by M.F.K. Fisher, Julia Child, and Michael Field. The editors had had the effrontery to have it translated into French, hired Robert Courtine of *Le Monde* to check the galleys, and unaccountably printed his often disparaging comments as footnotes (e.g., of a favorite Child recipe: "It's a lot of work for such a meager result! It's the sort of dish to dazzle and beguile foreign women, but it is false grand cuisine, and as antigastronomic as can be ").* Next day I filed a dispatch on the self-roasting cookbook, which caused a good deal of malicious amusement in New York, though it did not visibly reduce the flood of culinary pretension. (It was in reporting the discomfiture of *Time* that *Newsweek* mentioned Karen's role, and her expertise.)

Anyway, dining in France and around the Mediterranean, tasting, sipping, smelling, listening, and occasionally writing about it was indeed a moveable feast. I hated to leave it. But as I told Abe, the idea of serving as a professional diner and judge back home horrified me. To do it conscientiously, I would often have to eat badly, and I'd be writing for an audience that enjoyed eating badly; I put it that anyone who wanted that job shouldn't have it. When Charlotte Curtis asked me to take it on, I declined, firmly. But Abe found the right button. Alluding to the never-explained departure of his food critic, he said the paper was in a jam, and he appealed to me to be "a good soldier." The upshot was that I agreed to serve, for not less than six months or more than twelve, to give him time to find a successor.

As it happened, it was nine months before I reminded him of our deal and held him to it. On reflection, I think that was just about the right duration. It gave birth to Karen and my book *The Taste of America* (which recently found its fourth publisher; it is cause at once for pride and humility that we felt no need to change a word—indeed, from time to time we see published as news in the *Times* revelations that we reported in its pages twenty-five years ago).

We—I kept trying to alert readers to the fact that we were a pair, though usually we drew only one byline and one paycheck—*we*, then, may not have got "all the food purveyors in America" on Rosenthal's back, but we certainly ruffled feathers. That began with our very first article. Some called it a manifesto for its declaration that Americans

---

*And more: "Classic mayonnaise does not contain mustard.... There is no cream in 'true' hollandaise.... You must *not* put garlic in onion soup.... Nobody would *dream* of adding croutons to tripe." See *The Taste of America* by John and Karen Hess, p.183.

would never eat well until they regarded gourmet as a dirty word. The piece was my notion of a polite critique of the pseudo-French menu of a banquet prepared at the Waldorf for a New York food and wine society (see the Appendix of *Taste* for the text). Briefly, we said it was a fancy meal, but not a very good one. We suggested that the society turn its effort toward reviving the best of traditional American cooking and seek out and honor farmers and bakers who still produce what that requires. No "gourmet" group ever took up that idea, as far as I know.

When asked to suspend diced apple in a soufflé, the Waldorf chef said it could not be done. In a sidebar Karen told him how to do it and explained the structure of a soufflé in terms that caused a visiting French patissier, on being introduced to us by James Beard, to exclaim his appreciation. She contributed other recipes that sought to restore the simplicity and excellence of earlier cookery. To this day readers tell us that Karen's Thanksgiving turkey brightened their lives. Until then all popular cookbooks called for baking roasts for long hours at low temperatures and for boiling the flavor out of vegetables—both crimes propagated by home economists.

In a column we titled "De Gustibus" we hooted at the recipes on packages and in popular cookbooks and magazines, and we quoted the absurd, contradictory, and neurotic advice peddled by home economists in government publications and in the public schools. We disclosed that Home Ec courses in college did not include cooking, so that the presumed expertise of graduates was a commercial hoax. Some in the trade resented the revelation; others thanked us.

Karen traced this folly back to the exclusion of women from serious education. Schools for ladies taught homemaking, later euphemized as domestic science, then as home economics and even human ecology. An understandable feminist reaction was to expel cooking and sewing from the Home Ec curriculum, but graduates continued to be steered into food and fashions. Meanwhile these topics were excluded from feminist discourse—try and sell an article about cooking to *Ms.* magazine. This exclusion had the unfortunate effect of denying women credit for arts they had created. Claiborne amusedly repeated in the *Times* the boorish jape of Chef Paul Bocuse that women belonged in bed and that genius in cuisine was masculine. From Paris I filed a rebuttal. It was accepted by the Sunday magazine and handed to a new food editor, who gushed how thrilled she was to be working with me. I had to send back the galley proofs with a letter advising her among other things that a Paris restaurant was not necessarily located on the Left Bank and that I would never, never write that a friend recalled her mother's spinach "with Proustian recollection." She replied huffily that I could have it my way—but the article never ran. Ten years later Frenchwomen restaurant cooks teed off against the bocusards (they called them *phallocrats*) who excluded them from the benefits of professional recognition; once again I sold their story to the *Times* magazine. This time Mimi Sheraton, then the *Times*'s restaurant critic, learned about my project during a visit to Paris and beat me into print with a dispatch declaring that French restaurants with women cooks were indeed inferior.* The magazine decided not to contradict her and killed my report.

"THE BEST AMERICAN FOOD IS CHINESE"

Nine months was quite enough for a fair survey of public dining in America in 1973. Checking out the half-dozen restaurants most highly rated by major guides and magazines, we reported that Top of the Sixes did no cooking at all but instead reheated airline gunk frozen in Ohio; that we ate poorly at a celebrated caravanserai in Connecticut and worse at The Bakery in Chicago; that Trader Vic was a joke and that Ernie's in San Francisco made no visible effort to serve the fresh seafood and produce that should have been at hand. (Our sermon anticipated by years the crusade of Alice Waters.)

---

*Mimi also reported that Bocuse was serving veal liver as foie gras, a foolish libel that caused her and the *Times* to be ridiculed in the French media. As if she'd know. In a review I cite elsewhere, she wrote that "the calf's liver was so good it could have passed as something other than liver." When John McPhee discovered "the greatest restaurant in the world" for the *New Yorker*, Mimi hastened there to trash it; among other things she found the pancetta (raw-cured pork) insufficiently cooked. I may as well here identify her as the oxymoronic critic of the column reprinted on p. 155.

We summarized a crosscountry jaunt with a Sunday magazine cover piece headed "The Best American Food Is Chinese."

From coast to coast we found scarcely any decent bread, or coffee, or beer, or wine. A famous steakhouse in Kansas City served cinnamon buns with its beef; during that season the Four Seasons, though a serious house, provided sweet croissants with its main dishes. Many restaurants of pretension served, and sold, "fresh" loaves that we disclosed were made from packaged frozen dough popped in the oven. What all these, and store breads, had in common was large doses of sugar, an ingredient absent from honest bread since antiquity. Thereon Karen performed a feat of research that foreshadowed her brilliant career in American culinary history, transforming it from "fakelore" to a serious discipline. (Lately she has been highlighting the enormous African contribution in a series of pathfinding books.) First she traced the introduction of sugar to the industrial revolution in milling and baking; sugar was needed to replace lost flavor and to feed the yeast. Through the mid-nineteenth century cookbooks reflected disapproval of the use of sugar and other additives in bread, until writers came along who defended it. Leader among them was the revered Fannie Farmer, the first of a series of enormously successful American cookbook authors who began their careers as poor cooks. (Irma Rombauer's biography confirms it, and Julia Child's biography boasts of it.) An anniversary edition of Fannie's *Boston Cooking-School Cook Book* drew salaams from the foodie establishment. In a landmark piece in the *Times Book Review*, Karen showed how the sugar content increased edition by edition, decade by decade, in Fannie Farmer recipes where, often, no sugar at all appeared in older and better cookbooks.

Karen dubbed Fannie the maiden aunt of home economics. She cited her pseudo-scientific table of the chemical compositions of different species of fish. That was in 1896; about a century later the *Times* food section began to specify the chemical composition of every recipe, to the milligram. In my column in the *New York Observer* I noted that this was neurotic, inaccurate and pointless (How big was the portion? How much sodium was there in "salt to taste"? Who cares?) and that the figures were guesses based on a chart that itself was wildly inaccurate. The *Times* editors first added the word "approximate" to the measurements, then silently did away with them.

During our tenure we derided the diet phobias that colleagues were helping to spread; we begged for common sense and defended the flavor of salt, of butter, of olive oil. (We pointed out, for example, that there was good cholesterol as well as bad.) Evidently we did not get very far. The recycling of nutritional fads remains a staple of the food section.

There was a happier outcome to our defense of the city's vanishing markets. We went to Syracuse and reported how a market there was saving small farms and bringing a spark of life to a ravaged city center. The piece helped to inspire Barry Benepe, an architect and urbanist, to launch Greenmarkets, which became a cherished New York institution. A revolt by fish dealers saved the Fulton Fish Market (which is now again, however, apparently doomed by developers). During a predawn visit there I recorded that a large number of the buyers were Asians and that they were visibly grumpy about freshness and quality. I followed the Chinese to live poultry markets and into the fields where some of them were growing greens for Chinatown. And of course I linked that to the superiority of the food one could find there.

Contrary to a reputation we developed, Karen and I worked hard to find things to commend: chefs who knew the metier and had perceptions to share; little restaurants that tried; ethnic ones that kept the faith. We could not persuade the brass to abandon the silly custom of grading restaurants by stars (note that today the *Times* confers stars only on expensive restaurants; the modest-priced ones that it came reluctantly to review at the bottom of the page do not so qualify). But we awarded four stars only to Chinatown as a whole.

Reader response was frequently heartwarming. There was a bit of sniping from the fashion-foodie set, but none from the *Times* brass, except for one suggestion that we needed more "service" copy. "Service" assuredly did not mean that new branch of journalism inspired by Ralph Nader and Consumers Union. Our chiefs did not want us to tell our readers they were being taken for suckers, they wanted us to tell them how to be chic. When Richard Severo and Frances Cerra tried to practice consumer reporting at the *Times*, they were brutally silenced. I was not, but when an article of mine about Chinese truck farming was held back indefinitely on the ground that we'd had enough about that sort of thing for a while, I decided it was time for me to go back to home cooking.

I reminded Rosenthal of our deal. A few days later he told me complacently that he had solved the problem: he had persuaded Craig Claiborne to return. A reader commented, "It's the dawn of an old era." So it was. Silently, I concluded that we had not taught the Rosenthals a thing. Evidence, as I write, is the candid remark of the manager of a fashionable Chinese restaurant in midtown to a *Times* reporter that he served farm chicken to Asian clients and factory chicken to Occidentals, and both were satisfied.★

Claiborne, who described himself as a gourmet cook and graduate of the greatest culinary school in the world, brought with him as partner Pierre Franey, the executive chef of Howard Johnson's. They told readers how to fix a Howard Johnson-style gourmet meal in sixty minutes, most often featuring rolled-up chicken breasts (and got in a plug for Howard Johnson's canned bouillon). In other venues, including *The Taste of America*, we criticized their approach. As a result, the *Times*'s book subsidiary backed out of its contract to publish the work. Claiborne managed a small revenge by volunteering to review the American edition of Elizabeth David's classic *English Bread and Yeast Cookery*—annotated by Karen Hess. A nasty bit of work, his review called the American version even worse than the English; it

---

★Later, a writer in the Sunday magazine remarked that his guests found free-range chicken tough, or chewy, or something. Fresh orange juice tasted funny to their parents' generation, according to the *WSJ* . A letter recently complained that Velveeta processed cheese wasn't as good as it used to be. *Eheu fugace.*

was in fact a facsimile copy. It surely damaged sales of a valuable book, but David was philosophic about it. She had low expectations regarding our food-writing establishment. She gave no interviews, and was amused when one of the *Times*'s guest food writers faked one; David told Karen that the cat mentioned and illustrated in the article had died years before.

Enough. Now, during the generation that followed our hitch on the food beat, many things changed, some for the better, but if anything, the *Times* dedicated its food coverage more than ever to "sophistication," which is to say, pretension. The $100 dinner and the $100 wine, at first mentioned as sinful, became commonplace. From time to time after I left the *Times*, I found a need to remark on its work. Here is "The Oxymoronic Critic," a syndicated column I filed in late 1982:*

A new restaurant opened in my neighborhood, and our local weekly gave it a classy review. It said the service was "polite but could be more attentive," the scallops were "good, but overcooked," and the puff pastry was "good, but too doughy."

Now, each of those phrases is what the trendies would call an oxymoron: a contradiction in terms. That's not quite the right usage, but I'm talking trends, and I think I've spotted one.

Listen to that trend-setting publication known as the Good Gray Lady of 43d Street, dining out: One high-tone restaurant is "glowing and plush, if undistinguished"; another is also "undistinguished" but "bright and felicitous." A third is "colorful and refreshing but head-splittingly noisy," while a fourth is "pleasant, comfortable and unprepossessing!" In a fifth, the beef is "fine if served rare but dull if overcooked," while in a sixth it's the pasta that's fine, "provided it is not undercooked or overcooked," although the sauces with the pastas "often taste scorched."

*For more of the same see "Our Hungry Critics," Appendix item three.

Praise and blame are always tempered: "Like main courses, appetizers are decent, if less than breath-taking." "The food is far from brilliant, but it is pleasantly serviceable."

Reading these even-handed reviews is a little like watching a tennis match from mid-court; it's hard on the neck. Sometimes, the calls seem a bit inscrutable.

"Kidneys should have been more crunchy" and the texture of a terrine could have been "more sophisticated." Crunchy kidneys? Sophisticated textures?

At a three-star oasis, "drinks are large, so wine is superfluous, which is just as well because the selection is mundane."

I dig that the cocktails are generously portioned, but what in the world is a mundane wine list? I haven't a clue, but then I can't often afford to dine where the Good Gray Lady belts her booze. At the bottom of a list of recommended places, she adds one where "prices are low"—main courses $6.75 to $11.25. (This was 1982, mind you. The cost-of-living index roughly doubled by 2003.)

For those who do follow her advice, the beauty of this style of criticism is that if the customer is pleased, she can say, "I told you so," and if not she can say, "I warned you."

When a contradiction is uttered on purpose to make a sharp point, like calling somebody a smart fool, you have a proper oxymoron. I am not sure that the samples above fit that definition.

On the other hand—now I'm doing it—life is complicated and expensive meals are unlikely to be either perfect or totally bad.

A public figure I admire said at a news conference the other day, "The truth is always in the middle." None of the reporters raised an eyebrow because we are trained to believe this, but it is of course nonsense.

When Galileo said the earth moves around the sun and the church fathers said it didn't, the truth was not in the middle. Yet when Galileo came up for retrial two years ago, the Good Gray Lady ran a piece about it that was beautifully even-handed. It suggested that maybe he was properly punished. The pope ruled otherwise.

We are so conditioned to believe that the truth is in the middle that we reach for it. On the day after the [1982] election, most of the pundits pundited with approval that Americans had voted for the middle way.

That sounds like the objective truth, doesn't it? In fact, we voted every which way. Maybe the average was in the middle, but that's where the average usually is found, isn't it?

Politicians and journalists can stay out of trouble by intoning at every turn, "on the one hand, and then again, on the other." But it's not necessarily true, and it's nearly always boring. What we need, to borrow an old jest, is more one-armed critics. (United Feature Syndicate, November 15, 1982.)

Did I say in 1982 that I can't often afford to dine where the Good Gray Lady belts her booze? Here is a casual phrase from a *Times* review on April 24, 2002: "My instructions to the chef were simple: do what you like with a target price of $200." Presumably, plus wine and tip. Draw your own inflation chart, with lines down below for wages and benefits of the lower orders.

To close this chapter on an upbeat note, it is gratifying to mention the birth and extraordinary growth of an international movement called SLOW, as opposed to fast foods. Beginning in the mid-1990s in, of all places, the far left in Italy, it distinguished itself from other movements concerned with agribusiness and additives and the environment and world poverty by its love for good eating. Its restaurant guides have attained the status in Italy of Michelin in France, its expositions promote the revival of vanishing crafts and varieties of plants and animals, and its slick magazine has been spreading the message around Western Europe. SLOW boldly invites us to spend more on our food, so that we and our providers may live better—a message far different from that long purveyed by the *Times*.

This man used to write stories about a local nursing home scandal in New York.
Now he's writing about a national disgrace.

Like Watergate, the current nursing home scandal simply will not go away. And among the main reasons are the stories on nursing home abuses by John L. Hess in The New York Times.

When John Hess started writing about nursing homes in September, 1974, he assumed it would be a temporary assignment. He was wrong. This was a story that couldn't be dropped, and he's still at it.

Something was wrong. Hess could see that from the start. Something was wrong when a home could remain open—and receive Medicaid payments, despite flagrant violations of Federal fire safety codes. Something was wrong when there were vermin in homes, when patients were left lying in their own body wastes, when patients were drugged into apathy. But that something that was wrong turned out to be far bigger than the isolated horror stories Hess documented.

As Hess followed the trail he uncovered a pattern of corruption: payroll padding, real estate manipulations, inflated Medicaid payments and widespread political influence.

At the root of what was wrong was the system. Hess puts it this way:

"The problem was to replace a system that relegates the elderly to commercial depositories, sometimes summarized as 'No deposit, no return,' with a system of dignified care."

For months, and in more than 100 articles, John Hess has been bucking the system. It's a system he describes as a "license to steal," a system that spawns massive fraud and invites the use of political influence. It's that system that is now under investigation by Federal, state and city governments.

John Hess really started something.

The New York Times
"All the News That's Fit to Print"

Ad in Editor & Publisher, *March 1975.*

CHAPTER FOURTEEN

Setting a Prairie Fire

L ong afterward, at a dinner where I was receiving an award for investigating nursing homes, Arthur Gelb told me how it came to pass. His mother, after visiting a sick friend, had told him, "Artie, you've got to do something about nursing homes." A day or two later he called me to the Metro desk and asked me to do something about nursing homes. I reminded him that he had just granted me two months off, in lieu of accumulated overtime, to work on a book. He said please, just one piece.

I pulled the clips and found that nursing-home scandals had been a perennial for decades. They were all pretty much the same: patients ridden with bedsores, lying in their own waste, ignored or abused by overworked and unsupervised attendants. Public officials express shock and promise reform. Then silence until the next scandal. There had been such an exposé in New York media only a few months before.

I returned to Gelb. Artie, I said, we do not need another one-day shocker telling how bad things are. We need to tell why they're so bad, why the laws aren't enforced, why they've never been enforced, and who is to blame. Look, there's a hell of a story here. Give me two or three rookies; I'll point them the way and be off. I promise they'll win you a Pulitzer.* In his ineffable way, Artie said he'd think

---

*I had previously urged Abe and Artie, in a memo, to set up an investigative group like those that had been winning Pulitzers for the *Philadelphia Inquirer* and the *Boston Globe*. They never responded; as I have mentioned before and will repeat, muckraking in New York tended to make the *Times* brass nervous. One editor sought to ban the phrase "investigative reporting" as redundant. As I've tried to show throughout these memoirs, truly investigative, questioning, skeptical reporting was practically un*Times*ian. That is why I asked for rookies: they would still be unspoiled.

about it. Meanwhile, he said, please give me one story. My book had to wait. He never did, of course, assign me any help. But we made his mother proud.

A preliminary article caught the attention of some dedicated health inspectors, auditors, and social workers who had been seething in frustration for years. They laid out the picture for me, and I was able to lay it out in a four-part series in October 1974. It was virtually all there.

Corruption and abuse were built into the system. The American Medical Association and its allies had staved off national health insurance until 1965, when Medicare and Medicaid were enacted as a compromise. This released a torrent of money, and entrepreneurs (read: hustlers) came running. The result was inevitable: many people now received care who could not otherwise afford it, but cost and waste and mistreatment soared. Providers had an irresistible incentive; the less they spent on patients, the more profit they earned. There was but one payer, the government (federal or state), and politicians could be subverted out of petty cash. So everywhere that anybody cared to look there was scandal.

But New York was special. A thriving cartel of profit-making nursing homes already existed, tapping city welfare funds and effectively controlling the licensing of new homes. Properties were sold back and forth at a dizzying rate, to conceal ownership, evade taxes and inflate costs—an important inducement in the rating structure. Shares were sold to investors in units of beds, and their prices were booming, at a time when the stock market was going down. The cartel originated among, and preyed upon, Orthodox Jews from East Europe. Members of the community told spine-chilling tales about its chieftains, which turned out to be true: The don of this mafia, a titular rabbi named Bernard Bergman, had been involved with his parents before the war in importing heroin bound into prayer books. An associate, Eugene Hollander, was implicated in a major scandal in 1960, involving patients being locked in and abandoned at night to avoid paying wages to the nurses whose names appeared on his logbooks. (Later he would bill Medicaid full price for damaged canned goods for his nursing homes and a Renoir for his wall; he told a physician who complained about neglect, "What is a nursing home but a waiting room for a funeral parlor?" They made money on funerals as well, and old-timers swore that Bergman once kept bodies in a coolroom to continue collecting their welfare checks.) After the raids in 1960, the city's investigation commissioner sent a devastating report to the Manhattan district attorney. The cartel collected a large slush fund, the report disappeared, and welfare payments to the nursing homes were sharply increased, on the stated ground that it was poverty that had led them to crime.

Now multimillionaires, Bergman and Hollander were able to buy heavy clout by well-placed donations and by persuading top political figures that they were authentic representatives of the Orthodox voting bloc. They delivered its blessings to Governor Rockefeller and President Nixon. They bought insurance from a firm owned by the Speaker of the Assembly and the Democratic boss of Brooklyn and hired the leader of the Reform Democrats to defend a notorious nursing home from a troublesome inspector. (I observed that the difference between a Reform Democrat and a regular in New York was that one could buy a reformer cheaper.) With active input from key figures of both parties, violations were caused to vanish, waivers and variances were granted, troublesome audits were buried, fees were adjusted upward.

As noted, most of the foregoing was laid out in my four-part series in October. Now the problem was to keep the story from dying, like every nursing-home scandal in the past. To avoid that, I had to set a prairie fire. And along came a carton of matches. I was approached by an aide to Andrew Stein, a young assemblyman who was identified in every reference by the *Times* as ambitious and publicity-seeking— which was obviously biased, though obviously true. Those qualities are scarcely unique among politicians, but Stein had been so indiscreet as to acknowledge a dream of becoming president. Like Dan Quayle, he was the lightweight son of a powerfully connected publisher, who had generously financed his election to the Assembly and had arranged his appointment by Governor (now Vice President) Rockefeller as chairman of a special state commission on the cost of living. Stretching that job description to its limits, Andy would turn up in a variety of venues where abuses had been reported. The preceding winter he had appeared on local newscasts, pushing into the doorways of a nursing home where foul conditions had been reported. Ignored by the authorities, he and the lively TV reporters involved had then moved on to other fields. Now, suddenly, the *Times* was interested in that one. Could we help each other? Could we ever!

Stein had available the research staff that the *Times* would never provide me, plus a weapon that a journalist could only dream of: the power to subpoena, to open records that were abusively sealed and to require testimony under oath. I sat down with Stein's eager helpers and pointed the way: Follow the money trail. Explore the real estate dealings. Exhume the audits. Scan officials' appointment records. They did, staging photo ops and hearings as they went. I sought no exclusivity; rather, I was glad to proffer the occasional match to a competing reporter to keep the fire going. On one occasion a conscience-stricken nursing-home operator told me he would go on the record only if he were subpoenaed. I got Stein to summon him to a hearing, but before it opened, his devastating account of the cynical conduct of the nursing-home association was on the front page of the *New York Post.* I had been scooped by my own story.

Stein was apologetic. I was reproachful but amused. My editors would have been outraged. They took a proprietary approach to news. It was about then that Abe Rosenthal fired Denny Walsh for offering to a magazine an exposé that Abe had been withholding for months because of the threat of a lawsuit. In my case a request by a nursing-home lawyer for more time to comment was enough to cause the desk to delay publication of an exclusive for days. To keep the fire going, it was better that the story not be exclusive. I did what I could to keep it from being so.

In a monograph in 1989 titled "Objectivity and the New Muckraking: John L. Hess and the Nursing Home Scandal,"* Robert Miraldi, a professor of journalism at SUNY New Paltz, was highly admiring of my work—even of my "objectivity"—but uneasy about my relationship with "a news source," namely, Stein. But I was not objective, and I was rather more of a news source to Stein than he was to me.

Miraldi had been a reporter for the *Staten Island Advance*. "In early November," he wrote, "my editor gave me a copy of a Hess story on a Staten Island nursing home which, in one year, had seventeen changes of ownership, resulting in a huge increase in reimbursement. The editor told me to drop all other stories: 'We've got to play catch up on nursing homes.' For the next eight months, I had to write dozens of nursing home stories. It was typical of what was happening in all the city's media. I attended hearings and press conferences where as many as fifty reporters covered events."

That was the prairie fire. It crackled in the press and TV for months on end, sent sparks that set fires in other states, brought Congressional attention. Bergman helped by fleeing to escape a subpoena, with me pursuing him by telephone to Vienna and Jerusalem. He returned and sued me and several others for conspiring to deprive him of his rights. (An absurd charge, but a dangerous ploy that could have forced me to face questioning about my news sources, under penalty of contempt of court. Fortunately the suit was dismissed.) Revelations of skullduggery popped like strings of firecrackers. They were inexhaustible. It seemed that every transaction in this industry was corrupt, from the fictitious trimming of toenails at $75 a patient to the construction of a $24 million private nursing home on public land with public funds. Annoyed by complaints from a city health official, its promoter

---

*Reprinted in Miraldi's book, *Muckraking and Objectivity* (Greenwood Press, 1990).

quietly arranged passage of a law transferring supervision of nursing homes to the state. There, provoked by our disclosures, a top health official tossed us his diaries, filled with improper advances by politicians and lobbyists. The Democratic governor-elect, Hugh Carey, promised that his first official actions would be to name a special commission to explore the situation in nursing homes and hospitals and to propose reforms and a special prosecutor to punish violators. Which he did. At the same time he disposed of a loose cannon by permitting the charter of Stein's commission to expire.

To head the new commission Carey chose Morris Abram, a prominent civic leader who as a lawyer and lobbyist had represented private hospitals and a shady health insurance promoter. The appointment marked a limit to what our crusade would achieve. As much as I could, I had emphasized that the abuses stemmed from the operation of a welfare program for private profit. I reported that conditions were generally better in nonprofit homes, and although abuses could and did occur there, they were curable, whereas those in the profit-making sector were not. Under my prodding Stein took the same position. At one of his hearings, a patient transferred from a Bergman nursing home to a nonprofit one testified that it was like moving from hell to heaven. In his final report Stein again called for providing public funds only to nonprofit nursing homes. Abram opposed that. He was nonetheless obliged to preside over televised hearings that perforce stoked the fire. They tended to direct blame at the previous Republican state administration, which richly deserved its share. In a remarkable but valuable digression Vice President Rockefeller was questioned on the stand about the eviction by state hospitals of tens of thousands of mental patients with no provision for their subsequent care. He replied that it was necessary to create the problem to force communities to solve it. (That cruel neglect, which persists to this day, was actually bipartisan, as was all the corruption we exposed.) The Democrat Abram, his career much enhanced by his role in those hearings, went on to campaign for Reagan in 1980 and became an ambassador and a conservative spokesman for major Jewish organizations. As for Stein, he rode his new fame to a citywide election as council president, a ceremonial job, but failed in bids for the mayoralty and eventually abandoned a political career for which he was evidently not endowed. As the nursing-home crusade was ending, I had gently warned him that the political establishment might never forgive him but said there were few public officials who could say they had achieved as much.

TO THIS DAY

M iraldi analyzed nearly 150 stories I had done in ten months, "often working twelve hours a day, seven days a week." He summarized the results as "a nationwide inquiry... a scandal that implicated a score of high-ranking New York officials and Vice President Rockefeller, the criminal indictment of two hundred nursing home owners [or aides] for stealing millions and billing taxpayers for items ranging from a Renoir to trips to Europe, the return to the public of millions of dollars... the revamping of New York's nursing home reimbursement system and the establishment in New York of a permanent special prosecutor to deal with nursing-home [and health care] violations."

Does it sound exhilarating? Miraldi surely could not imagine how much of my twelve-hour days had to be spent in combat with multiple editors. In a despairing memo to Gelb one morning I told him I'd had to spend three hours the evening before, "fighting to keep the story together." It was "Get it all up high," and then the stuff that had been in the third graf earlier was suddenly too low. I had to rewrite the *summary*, for God's sake. As a result I had no time to tell the reader who the politically powerful Shea Gould firm is, nor to fill out the picture of Hollander as a client. I begged Gelb to get the editors together to agree on what they wanted, or play with the story as they chose but take my byline off.

With respect to what we accomplished, I must first point out that many people were engaged in this crusade, notably a state auditor whose advice was priceless and who was never forgiven by the bureaucracy. I accept that nothing would have occurred but for the fire I set in the *Times*, so one might call Gelb's mother the original spark. Among achievements I would add as most gratifying was the closing of a number of old-law pesthouses. I was not elated by the convictions of Bergman and Hollander. Bergman served a brief prison term, Hollander a nominal one in a midtown hotel, and they were barred from operating nursing homes, but their real property was held inviolate. I later learned that Hollander was still drawing well over a million dollars in net rent on one of his former nursing homes. (I also found that his attendance log at that halfway house had been crudely rigged, like his nursing records back in 1960, but by then I was too tired to pursue the story.) In other words nothing had fundamentally changed. In a moment of cynical candor, Abram predicted that there would be need for another show like ours in five or ten years. It never happened, but scandals persist to this day. Check the Web.

Although we did indeed implicate "a score of high-ranking officials" and ended the careers of two of them, none was ever convicted. I will discuss in another chapter how hard it is to prosecute a politician in New York. The naming of a special prosecutor for nursing homes nonetheless established a motivation to continue the cleanup. Charles (Joe) Hynes, the appointee, was conscientious, energetic and likable. Miraldi recalls a news conference when Hynes, confronted by a technical question, suggested that the reporter ask me. I shared all I knew with Hynes, while as a matter of principle I never asked of him, and he never offered, any information he could not properly give. His only exclusive tip to me was a friendly word of advice: that anything I said in the city room of the *Times* would reach politicians downtown in fifteen minutes. My colleagues on political beats tended to think I was too rough on their favorite sources. Hynes also told me, not exclusively, that funds for his new agency had vanished from the budget just delivered to Carey's desk.

I wrote a story, and the funds were restored. Our Albany bureau assured readers that it had been a clerical error. A young AP man in Albany did what my colleagues there should have been doing. He dug into the files we had opened and tied the Republican boss of the State Senate to a nursing-home finagle in Binghamton. I begged the desk to give the AP story a play, because it demonstrated the bipartisan and nonsectarian nature of the evil; it was buried in a late city edition. It wasn't "our" story. This outlook helped provoke an annoying incident. Jack Newfield of the *Village Voice*, who had jumped on the Bergman story in November, sought a Mafia angle and ran with it. (It proved to be small change; Bergman was paying off a petty labor racketeer.) When a congressman announced an investigation, I was obliged to report it, but I was careful to mention the source. Gelb struck the reference. I insisted, and he allowed me to credit the *Voice* but not Newfield. I foolishly apologized to Newfield, and he went berserk. He loudly accused the *Times* of stealing his news and filed a formal complaint with a news council, which stupidly circulated the charge in a press release before dismissing it as groundless. Newfield went on to advertise that it was he who had first exposed Bergman (a month after my October series, but Newfield was, to be sure, more shrill). There is no way to know whether Newfield's tantrum affected the judgment of the Pulitzer board. Representative Ed Koch had enlisted the entire New York congressional delegation to nominate my work for an award, and the *Times* entered it as well, but it was passed over. The board that year also passed over Seymour Hersh's terrific exposé in the *Times* of the CIA's unlawful domestic espionage, which also, to be sure, ran into nasty sniping from within the media.

Amusing thought: my obituary will not read "Pulitzer prize-winning journalist." A better cause for modesty that sticks in my mind came up in a news conference by Joe Hynes. It was about a sting that nailed a nursing-home operator. There we were on the front pages, and had been for months, hurling bolts of lightning at corruption in the industry, and yet this operator was blandly talking terms about kickbacks with a hustler he'd never met. That's the way business was always done, and we hadn't really changed it. Indeed, in May, 2002, the *Times* published an exposé of the dreadful neglect of mental patients in profit-making warehouses, which had been mentioned in our hearings and followed the same scenario of official misfeasance and of racketeering, down to the toenail cutting. The *Times* had given Clifford Levy a full year for the investigation and would no doubt put in for a Pulitzer, which the story deserved. But there was no prairie fire, no proposal for fundamental reform, perhaps in part because over the past decades privatization had become a religion and tax-cutting a sacrament.

The repeated scandals have obscured the great needs that produced these reforms and the great relief they provided. By now it is a commonplace, even among many liberals, to say, "You can't solve a problem by throwing money at it." What the scandals suggest, however, is that a lot of money was thrown, not at the problems, but at the politicians.

John L. Hess, The New York Times, *August 15, 1976*

CHAPTER FIFTEEN

Exit

D uring the months when I was feeding the fire of the nursing-home scandals, I paid little attention to the signal of an historic crisis. The *Times* brushed it aside. When Standard & Poor posted a warning about New York's solvency in November 1974, our man on the beat, Michael Stern, declared, "There are no doubts that the city can and will pay its debts" (November 7, 1974). Wall Street was less trusting. The following April it declined to underwrite an issue of new city bonds to pay off old ones that were falling due. Stern responded valiantly, "Can New York City default on its debt and go bankrupt? The answer is no, and it can be given without qualification, according to city and private financial experts" (April 11, 1975).

Not all the experts, surely. Indeed, that prior November an internal memo in one of the city's banks warned of "possible criminal liabilities" if they continued to peddle the city's bonds under the kinds of assurances the *Times* was endorsing. But they went on unloading their own holdings on an unsuspecting public, until the showdown in April.*

By law the city has to balance its operating budget (including interest on its capital debt) every fiscal year. Always running short by the final quarter, its money managers took to selling tax anticipation notes—that is, collecting revenue in advance, at a discount. They would, so to speak, balance the budget retroactively. The actual deficit would be pushed forward into the following year, when the operation

---

*See Martin Mayer's account in the *Columbia Journalism Review* (January/February 1976) headed "Default at the *Times.*"

would be repeated, on a larger scale, the figures being doctored as needed. When the alarm was finally sounded, Mayor Beame—an accountant by trade, as the *Times* pointed out, reassuringly—bought $50,000 worth of city paper for his own account.*

Nonetheless, underwriters refused to go along with the refunding issue in April, and the crisis could no longer be denied.

The *Times* might call bankruptcy unthinkable, but the city already *was* bankrupt; the question was which of its creditors it would stiff. When the federal government refused to bail it out (as the *News* famously put it, "FORD TO CITY: DROP DEAD"), City Hall chose to hold back paychecks to public servants, welsh on their contractual wage increases, and dip into their pension funds, so as to pay off the bonds due. Since the city's credit remained shaky, its budget and notably its sales tax revenues were placed under a state trusteeship called the Municipal Assistance Corporation, headed by the banker Felix Rohatyn of Lazard Freres—a receiver in bankruptcy who would thenceforth be canonized as the man who saved New York from bankruptcy. In frequent essays in the *Times* and the *New York Review of Books,* Rohatyn insisted on sharing the credit with all sectors, on the grounds that all had shared the sacrifices. Well, the sacrifices of the public sector were visible enough: wages and hiring frozen, schools stripped of amenities like music and art, the police force reduced by one-third, the parks by far more, housing and social programs canceled. But I am unable to identify a penny of sacrifice by the mayor, the comptroller, or the six major banks that engendered the crisis. (Incidentally, inspired by Rohatyn's new eminence in municipal finance, his firm, Lazard Freres, entered that lucrative field for the first time, comanaging a huge bond issue for the Javits Center.)

On the day that the SEC got around to accusing city officials and the banks of criminally deceiving investors, Steven Weisman, then

---

*In a similar effort to reassure the public about a looming disaster, Governor Hugh Carey offered to drink a glass full of PCBs. There is no record that he actually did, but with the *Times*'s approval he made a sweetheart deal with General Electric that left the PCBs in the Hudson to this day.

our bureau chief at City Hall, responded: "But the most unanswerable question of the entire report is: What would have happened if the Mayor, the Comptroller, and everybody else did fully disclose the facts as the SEC said they should have? The answer, in the view of everyone interviewed yesterday, was simple. The city would have gone bankrupt."

In other words, the answer to the unanswerable question was that they lied to save the city. It followed that in purveying their lies as the truth, the *Times* had helped to save the city. And Rohatyn continued to save it by his dedicated insistence on more sacrifice.

According to Rohatyn and the *Times*, the fiscal disaster had its roots in the indulgence that former Mayor John V. Lindsay had shown toward the city's greedy employees, and its cure lay in keeping them on short rations while reducing taxes to encourage business. That prescription continues to dominate the *Times*'s outlook. I have mentioned in Chapter Four how the *Times* berated Mayor Dinkins for awarding teachers a modest cost-of-living catch-up and then more recently blamed our mean pay scale for an alarming shortage of teachers. The writer responsible, Joyce Purnick, soon reverted to the party line; in a book review in mid-July 2001 she agreed with a rightist author that the teachers and subway workers had "eaten Lindsay's lunch."

THE MUNICIPAL STABLE

Occupied as I was with nursing homes during the winter of 1974–75, I had no idea that the city was cooking its books, but I was painfully aware of how awful our fiscal coverage was. In a memo to Arthur Gelb pleading for relief from harassment by subeditors, I mentioned a fresh example of their dimwittedness. The lead headline that Sunday (August 25, 1975) had reported the mayor's confession that the city's debt would hit $2.8 billion. The figure actually referred to the (unlawful) budget *deficit*, not the far larger (but lawful) capital *debt*. Obviously the reporter did not know the difference, nor did the copy editors, for in a late edition they took the trouble to clutter up his readable, though erroneous, lead with a pointless internal clause, which I suppose was intended to bring something up high. I asked a deputy city editor how such a thing could happen. He replied, complacently, that he was not on duty that night.

Anyway, I was struck by the figure given for the budget gap. I told Gelb it would be easy to account for it by outright theft and blatant waste. In 1969 a grand jury reported that a billion dollars had been stolen from Medicaid in New York in its first three years. In 1974 thefts by nursing homes were conservatively estimated at $300 million a year. A noble federal effort to subsidize day care for working mothers was being looted of another $300 million or so. The law shrewdly barred use of that money for construction, but politically connected hustlers audaciously diverted virtually all of it into long-term leases on day-care centers yet unbuilt. In a splendid example of investigative journalism by amateurs, day-care workers exposed the racket and identified the perpetrators. Three mayors successively expressed shock and promised reform but actually signed new leases and raised the rents. When I asked the commissioner in charge why he had more than thirty personal bank accounts, he replied that his wife collected the gift fountain pens that they awarded. (See Appendix item four, "The Scandal of Day Care: How Sharp Operators Cheat Your Children.")

The city's leasing, construction, and maintenance of buildings have always been rife with corruption. Fifty years ago a bookkeeper for a school building contractor described to me the rigging of contracts and the bribery of officials. Those scandals never cease; as I was writing these lines in 2001, the Board of Education has had to cancel starts on new schools and repairs of old ones because of cost overruns in the billions. School janitorship was notorious then, as it is today. The bribery of inspectors was endemic, and continues to be. Nothing involving money was immune.

During the fiscal crisis a contractor was caught serving spoiled food to poor children, and not for the first time. At my desk one day, I exclaimed that we worked in an Augean stable, and that anybody who did not turn up an occasional turd was no reporter. It was a gaffe. My neighbor looked grim; he must have thought the remark was aimed at him. He was a rising star of the metropolitan political staff, which never looked for turds and seldom recognized them as such. When I reported how the Democratic boss Stanley Steingut had lobbied officials on behalf of the nursing-home racketeer Eugene Hollander, the editor in charge of local political coverage, Sheldon Binn, asked me, "What did Stanley do that was wrong?"

Binn was making the distinction between honest graft and dishonest graft that has long infected American journalism, but he moved beyond it. At the time, Congress members were expressing shock at revelations of bribery by U.S. corporations doing business overseas. Binn sent me, with an approving note, a response by Irving Kristol, the guru of neoconservatism, in the *Wall Street Journal*. Spurning the myth that bribery was un-American, Kristol declared that graft was the lubricant of democracy. So for Binn, when Steingut approached state officials to ease the rules for a supporter's nursing homes, he was lubricating democracy.

Clearly, Binn's staff was not about to clean the municipal stable. That is why I renewed my appeal to Rosenthal and Gelb to set up a team of fresh young reporters to investigate local corruption (as a counterweight, I thought but did not say, to a staff that was shielding corruption). There were grounds for hope. Our editors were proud of the honor they had earned by publication of the Pentagon Papers, and embarrassed at having been beaten on Watergate. Rosenthal had engaged Seymour Hersh to dig for dirt in Washington and Denny Walsh in San Francisco. Gelb confided that Abe had acknowledged that my nursing-home investigation had turned into a pretty good story. I told Gelb there were lots more out there. I specified that I was not a candidate to run an investigative unit—anyhow, my wife and I were busy promoting *The Taste of America*. But the city's crisis clamored for a response. I brandished a copy of the Green Book, the city government directory, and invited Gelb to poke a pin into it; I assured him that wherever it landed, he could find a scandal. Once again, he temporized. He implied that Abe was open to persuasion on approving an investigative unit. Meanwhile, he invited me to pick a scandal and prove my point.

Thus began, if you will permit a grim pun, my terminal investigation for the *Times*. As food critic I had deplored City Hall's effort to close the Bronx Terminal Market, and had got a strong whiff of the corrupt deal that followed. So that was the scandal I chose. It was a swindle of medium size, costing the city about $100 million, but would offer breathtaking examples of mismanagement, theft, and lawlessness infecting our political structure. Before my inquiry ended, I could identify the motel room in Madison, Wisconsin, where a promoter delivered $30,000 in cash—the city's own money, as it happened—to Mayor John V. Lindsay as a campaign contribution, in exchange for a ninety-nine-year lease under terms that the city's lawyers warned would spell disaster.

Not long ago I found reason to retell the story as a soap opera, involving "money, love, hate, jealousy, deceit, betrayal, adultery, addiction, attempted suicide, forgery, bribery, theft, wiretapping, hysterics, tragedy and farce [with] unflattering walk-on roles for mayors, shoals of political sharks, platoons of lawyers and a sprinkling of prosecutors, movie people and multinational executives," with the terminal serving as a "cash cow, … a striking example of public-private partnership, wherein the public pays the feed bill and the private partner gets the milk."* Here, I need to address it as a small episode in the history of the *Times*.

We had as usual passed on to the public the official version: the city said it was incapable of managing the Terminal Market and was

---

*See *The Free Press*, July 1998.

losing money on it, so it would lease its thirty-two acres and its build-ings to a seasoned developer named David Buntzman, who would rehabilitate it at no cost to us, and create 2,000 new jobs. In fact, as I would later disclose, the city had been making a modest profit on the market and began losing money and jobs there only when it brought Buntzman in. He doubled and tripled the merchants' rents and paid the city nothing—indeed, he held that, under the terms of his lease, the city owed *him* money. As for his experience as a devel-oper, the old pirate's only previous success had been in selling the city a tract near Hunts Point for not quite three times its assessed value, for urban development. There he promised to create three thousand jobs. Unfortunately, the title to the land was under a cloud of bankruptcy, which made it useless for development and illegal for purchase by the city. The city's corporation counsel bypassed that obstacle by holding $260,000 of the price in escrow. When Buntz-man was pressing to lease the Bronx Terminal Market, he was advised that Lindsay's campaign for the presidency was short of funds. He pointed out that the city was still holding money due him—and obtained a check for $125,000. His donation came out of that escrow (even there, he pocketed the lion's share), and the lease was promptly signed, which is why I could report that the city had been suborned with its own money. (As for the Hunts Point devel-opment zone, rather than create three thousand new jobs, it resulted in the loss of at least six hundred; the last time I looked, twenty-five years later, no more than four men were at work there. There had also been dealings there involving the Mafia and the Bronx Demo-cratic machine. It is interesting to reflect that the site adjoined the crime scene of Tom Wolfe's *Bonfire of the Vanities*, with rather a dif-ferent cast of villains. But I digress.)

When Buntzman took over the market and began doubling and tripling rents, some merchants sought to organize resistance. The old pirate told them they would lose; he boasted of his political clout, including his delivery of cash to Lindsay and his ties with Democratic bosses. Some tenants left, some made deals, some were evicted. When I took up the story, one of the larger surviving tenants, Goodie Brands, was suing to avert eviction and to nullify Buntzman's lease as corruptly obtained. The suit was doomed to fail, because the city was defending the lease and supporting the eviction, before judges beholden to party bosses, but Goodie was glad to share its affidavits with a reporter.

My first published stories caused the city to suspend its defense of the lease and announce an investigation. Officials said they could no longer comment because the matter was in litigation. Nicholas Scoppetta, the investigations commissioner, seized the germane files of the Department of Ports and Terminals and refused to let me inspect them because they were under investigation—I could not even read the market lease, he said. Fortunately he was no more efficient at concealing evidence than his colleagues were at managing the city's property. Copies of much that I was looking for had been submitted to the Board of Estimate for routine approval and had routinely been buried in the archives. A couple of days in the dusty old coal cellar of the Municipal Building turned up enough clues to keep a grand jury busy for months.

Among the many objections that had been raised by city employees to the preposterous draft lease was that it conflicted with the city's commitment of some of the same space to the Yankees, for parking. The lease was signed anyway, on Buntzman's word that he would consider that problem when the time came. When the time came, he held the city up for a redraft of the lease that cost the city an additional $10 million.*

---

*Speaking of the Yankees, I came up with memoranda that showed that Lindsay's aides were lying about the cost of the stadium overhaul. Their first public estimate was $24 million; their private estimates were several times that. I proved that they spent well over $100 million—perhaps three times that, counting incidentals and interest on bonds. I pointed out that the city could have bought the Yankees club itself for $10 million, which is what George Steinbrenner paid for it. My lead on the story was "They'll never call it the House that Truth built." The city desk killed the line as too flippant for Page One. When I appealed, it was restored, to the end of the piece—where it was spotted nonetheless by another writer and appropriated as his own.

Every loose thread in the Terminal story led to another scandal. Every contract was dirty, every politician seemed to be connected, to one degree or another. When I asked Buntzman to comment, he referred me to one of his lawyers, Pat Cunningham, the Democratic state and county chairman, who would for a time head the Yankees. Cunningham referred me to Buntzman's new press agent, John Scanlon. I phoned the number Cunningham had given me, and a receptionist answered: "Municipal Assistance Corporation." It transpired that Scanlon, a protégé of the Brooklyn waterfront gangster-politician Anthony Scotto, had been hired as publicist for Rohatyn's rescue of the city's finances and was using his office there to flack for at least three of the city's substantial looters—Scotto, who pretty much controlled the Department of Ports and Terminals, Buntzman, and a nursing home trafficker. Small world. Scanlon asked me, as one moonlighter to another, to ignore his conflict of interest, but I found it newsworthy. In a matter of hours he lost his office, his secretary, his car, and his MAC credit card, and I gained a formidable enemy.

I suspect that Scanlon was the author of Scotto's boast to Murray Kempton, "I can buy any reporter in town for a cup of coffee." Scanlon bought drinks. He was a regular at hangouts of the press gang in the Village and the Hamptons, and helped organize their softball games. By and large they overlooked his services to crooked politicians, strikebreaking publishers, and tobacco companies. In the person of Scotto, the heir to a murderous mafia family, they cultivated the image of a college-bred Don Corleone who had seen the light; in sarcastic response I called him St. Anthony of the Docks. When the Feds finally nailed Scotto for swindling his longshore union members, Kempton led some of our most popular journalists in denouncing the prosecution.

Kempton, whom I had known for decades, liked to shock us romantics by writing admiringly about the likes of Frank Costello, Westbrook Pegler, and Roy Cohn. He also shared the addiction of American journalism to the mythical boss who despises WASP hypocrisy, defends the people's interest as well as his own, and is always good for a great quote. Such men long dominated New York politics and the affections of those who covered them. One favorite was Councilman Matty Troy, the Democratic party chairman of Queens. When the flag above City Hall was lowered to half staff in a Vietnam war protest, Matty hoisted it back up. That was Matty, always colorful. When the Feds nailed him for tax evasion, press rooms were devastated. One of our finest reporters exclaimed to me, "Doesn't everybody cheat on taxes?" No doubt, said I, but what was the nature of the income that Matty had failed to report? It was loot from the estates of modest citizens, for which Troy had had himself named executor. He could not be prosecuted for theft because that is a state crime, and he controlled the district attorney and the judges. Just so, Al Capone could not be prosecuted for murder in Illinois, so the Feds had to get him for tax evasion. When they got Troy, the *Times* ran two sob stories about the pain it caused him and his father, but not one word about the widows and orphans he had robbed. Judges, politicians, and reporters en masse attended a banquet to honor Matty on his departure for prison.

THE MERRY-GO-ROUND

I repeat that reporters tend to be at once more naive and more cynical than the general public. If I were to stand at the bar in Gough's across the street and grumble that politicians were crooks, printers would shrug at the banality of the observation, but fellow journalists would wince. In exposing politicians to prosecution, I was attacking their friends, men who partied with them, who literally played ball with them, and who kept them informed about what they needed to know.

In a house organ of the *Times*, our senior metropolitan political reporter, Frank Lynn, explained how he had kept his sanity after a lifetime covering politics and politicians:

It was easy. It just takes a Machiavellian skepticism, a deaf ear, a Laurel and Hardy-like sense of humor, the patience of Job and, when Job fails, which is frequent, a handy 2-by-4 for getting attention and encouraging humility.

I know what most people think of politicians, but they are really not all that bad. For one thing, how many of us would endure the scrutiny, the second-guessing, the questioning of their actions and motives . . .

And so on. A really hardbitten journalist, Frank was.

What was missing from my pursuit of the Buntzman scandal was an ally like Andrew Stein who commanded the power of subpoena. Enter Maurice Nadjari. A Republican, he had been named special prosecutor for the criminal justice system in the wake of the police corruption scandals sparked by Frank Serpico and David Duke and the Knapp Commission. (I was abroad then and missed that show, which is why this memoir has scanted the exemplary role and the travails of David Burnham of the *Times*.) Nadjari was a pet of the media when he went after bad apples in the precincts. Then he took aim at higher police officials and judges and politicians, and the climate changed. One by one his cases were dismissed with sharp rebukes, and his appeals were denied. Columnists and editorial writers questioned his competence and his regard for the rights of the accused. A decade later, under a Republican administration, the Justice Department took Nadjari's targets into federal courts and sent to prison, among others, the Democratic bosses Pat Cunningham, Stanley Friedman, Stanley Simon, and Anthony Scotto. Donald Manes, the borough president of Queens, committed suicide to avoid doing time. A U.S. attorney, Rudolph Giuliani, was launched on his political career by his role in these and other prosecutions, with the help of grateful members of the press corps. But in January 1976, when I was opening that can of worms in the Bronx, prosecution of crooked bosses was out of fashion. Nadjari was fighting a sentence of dismissal by Governor Carey. He nonetheless added the new evidence of corruption to his caseload.*

For me, it was a flash of hope. As far as I could tell, Scoppetta never began the investigation he had announced, and the city's lawyers claimed to be helpless to contest the market lease or pursue the sundry abuses now coming to light. It seemed to me that criminal prosecution offered the only prospect for the city to recover its property. As a good citizen, I called on Nadjari with an armful of data and laid out what I knew. He assigned a pair of young assistants, and I saved them weeks of work by showing them in a few hours what to look for in the files of the Department of Ports and Terminals, which Nadjari had taken over. Nadjari called up a special grand jury, and I returned to my digging. That was the sum total of our dealings. It should go without saying that, unlike the apparent relationship between Giuliani and favored reporters, I never requested of Nadjari and he never leaked any information about his grand jury investigation.

On my own I kept coming up with newsworthy additions: the fake development zone at Hunts Point, an apparent arson at the Bronx Terminal Market, more evidence of official negligence, details about the campaign contribution to Lindsay. In a Bronx courtroom one day, a judge declined to recuse himself for accepting cartons of Zsa Zsa Gabor cosmetics from Buntzman and went on to reject a

---

*This was a time of passionate discussion about the role of journalism. Alarm was being expressed by the media establishment—and not only the establishment. Gary Wills, Nat Hentoff, and on occasion such other good souls as Kempton and Pete Hamill accused us of convicting public figures without due process. The pack made much of Nadjari's poor batting average. I asked: Compared with whom? Who else had been prosecuting judges and politicians? I pointed out that Nadjari had to try his cases before state judges who were beholden to party bosses for their jobs; Mario Esposito, Steingut's partner in the title insurance racket and a man precious to reporters for his colorful candor, bragged that he had "made" thirty-two Brooklyn judges—that is, nearly all of them. But even in the alternative media, few defended Schorr or Nadjari. I somehow found time to write a dissenting piece, in the media review *MORE* (see Appendix item five).

plethora of more serious charges and to move forward the eviction of Goodie Brands. But the climate on 43d Street had changed. Mitchell Levitas, a neoconservative, was now metropolitan editor, and he did not care for the story—nor for the Bronx, for that matter (see Chapter Eleven). He rejected my report on the court session I had just attended but then, at the urging of Sidney Schanberg, who was deputy metropolitan editor at the time, he allowed an abbreviated version to appear on a back page. In an aside Schanberg told me that my trouble was that I was trying to cover New York as if I were still a foreign correspondent. When he was in Southeast Asia, he explained, he could write that a government was corrupt— "but you can't write that the government of New York is corrupt."

When I phoned Deputy Mayor Stanley Friedman with a question, he expressed amused surprise that I was still on the story; he said he looked for me on the ship news page, and hadn't found me. He was clearly well cued in on the situation on 43d Street. The word was that Abe Rosenthal had profanely suggested in a staff meeting that the story was going nowhere. I have since thought that he was uncomfortable with the revelations about Lindsay. Abe's relationship with the mayor during his first term had been a scandal in the trade; Harrison Salisbury called it a "blazing infatuation." Abe reportedly allowed a Lindsay aide to vet copy about the mayor before it appeared. That passion had cooled, almost surely for political reasons. Abe had moved distinctly to the right, while Lindsay remained a classic liberal, on civil rights and on Vietnam. Indeed he was resented, and finally defeated, on those grounds. I do not believe that Lindsay was personally corrupt; he simply let a corrupt structure stand while he pursued a presidential ambition. I never got his side of the local stories because he never replied to my phone calls, though he was in occasional touch with *Times* political reporters at their desks near mine.

Early every afternoon, Levitas' assistant, Martin Arnold, would roam the city room with a fistful of handouts about routine events. Canny reporters made themselves scarce during that hour. Like as not I'd be there, on the phone, or studying documents, or writing. He took to asking me to suspend whatever I was doing to cover a nothing story.* I appealed to Levitas: "We are *that* close to an indictment!" The word "we" visibly shocked the desk: except in matters of national security, objective journalists are not parties to events, they only gather facts—preferably uncontroversial ones.

It was not until many years later, during the trial of *Buntzman* v. *Buntzman*, that I learned how close we actually were to indictments and to the recovery of the city's stolen property. Terrified at the likelihood of prosecution for bribery, tax evasion, and other offenses, David Buntzman had checked into a Washington hospital with a purported breakdown and had begun seeking a plea bargain. In return for immunity he proposed to surrender the market lease, pay some of the rent he owed the city, and testify against officials he had dealt with. Nadjari let David simmer while David's son Arol testified before the grand jury. The delay may have been fatal for the People. Nadjari's dismissal took effect on June 24, 1976. Carey's appointee in his place, John Keenan, buried all Nadjari's cases. He told the Buntzmans there would be no indictments; two years later he quietly issued a grand jury finding that, although Buntzman's cash contributions had "the appearance of impropriety," it could not be determined "whether the contributions had been made for favorable consideration."

Two news analyses I managed to get into the paper late in the summer of 1976 reflect my discouragement, anger, and disgust. The first, on August 15, reviewed the looting of poverty programs,

---

*I could not refuse them all. One handout said that to reduce expenses, the botanical gardens in the Bronx would be closed to the public during January. My lead read, "The begonias will bloom unseen at the New York Botanical Gardens next month." As I was leaving, an old sidekick, George Barrett, now acting night city editor, stopped me and asked me apologetically to change my lead. The night news editor, Lew Jordan, did not like begonias, he explained. I located a garden employee, who confirmed that nothing would be on display but begonias, and a few poinsettias. George wondered if I couldn't squeeze them in. I asked permission to go over his head, and explained the situation to Jordan, who shrugged and said okay. I returned to George and told him begonias were okay, and went home, depressed by the knowledge that I had humiliated an old friend.

notably the day-care centers, to make the point that we were throwing money not at problems but at politicians. The second, on September 20, addressed a "merry-go-round succession of new scandals that are really old scandals" and the repeated failure of officials to correct known abuses. Reading them now I marvel, like Homer Bigart, that they got past the desk. But they did not address the culpability of the media, and of the *Times* in particular. (For doing just that at a later date, Schanberg's column was killed, and he left the paper.) At this time, I found the situation becoming intolerable. The SEC was charging City Hall and its bankers with fraud and deceit, and the *Times* was saying they had lied to save the city. Municipal services were being cut, scandals were going down the drain, and Levitas was spiking my contributions. After one more installment of the Buntzman saga was rejected, I announced that I would not work for an editor who would not print that story.

"News is something someone wants to suppress. Everything else is advertising."

Lord Northcliffe

"A journalist whose writing does not stir up either a duel or a lawsuit is a bad journalist."

Hippolyte de Villemessant, founder of Le Figaro

CHAPTER SIXTEEN

Death Watch

M y crusading at the *Times* had come to an end. I should have made the break neatly and moved out. Once again Gelb fudged, and so did I. He asked me to take the night off, then offered me the post of obituary editor. For lack of an immediate job option, I took it.★

It could be interesting and even amusing. It was Alden Whitman who turned the writing of death notices for living celebrities into an honored branch of our craft. Before him, it was a chore nobody wanted. This was not because reporters were notably squeamish—indeed, during the Depression the staff of the *Times* maintained a Ghoul Pool, or lottery, based on the list of advance obituaries. Whenever one appeared in print, the pool would be awarded to the player who had drawn that name and a new lottery would be organized.

A shortcoming was that the date of each payoff was unpredictable. This was even more annoying to the authors of those lives. Accustomed to seeing their daily work appear in print within hours, they found it frustrating to toil on a biographical sketch that might not appear for years, or might never appear, for while death is certain, a life forever changes. I myself recall writing the fourth *Times* obituary of Orson Welles in as many decades. If memory serves, the first obit in the file recounted the untimely demise of a boy wonder of stage and radio who had failed in Hollywood; the second, of a bright hope of stage, radio, and Hollywood who had failed in Europe; the third of

---

★The following originally appeared in similar form in *Grand Street*.

a star of stage, radio, Hollywood, and the European cinema who had failed again. The authors of all three lives had themselves passed on. Their subject now had extended his reach to television with apparent zest, though he had not yet emerged as an aficionado of California wine. My own pressing of the life had, I should like to think, less acid and more fruit than its predecessors, but like them it could not be sold before its time; by now it may well have gone flat. The moralist in me says *Viva Welles*. The writer in me would as lief have been more productively occupied.

Furthermore, when an obituary did appear in those pre-Whitman days, it could cast little credit upon its author, for the editors would no more identify him than they would the embalmer. This anonymity was in fact one reason Whitman got the job. A copy editor on the national desk, he was one of those I mentioned in Chapter Three who were subpoenaed by the Senate subcommittee in 1956 and ordered to name former colleagues who had been Communists. Like Mel Barnet, the classicist and cheese enthusiast, Whitman declined to testify. But unlike Barnet, who took the Fifth and was fired, Whitman cited the First Amendment. He was indicted, but the case was finally dismissed on technical grounds in 1966. Meanwhile, the paper kept him on, but, as he later would write, "the *Times* was not about to confer a byline on someone in contempt of Congress."

Bored with editing, he said, he was happy to take over the obituary beat in 1965 "for the real emotional satisfaction that comes from creative writing." Whitman was in fact very good, and good writing stands out remarkably in the *Times*. An obit of T. S. Eliot that he had to write on deadline showed what an intelligent and cultivated reporter could do. As his reputation in the trade grew, editors gradually accorded him more time and space, then a byline and even a travel allowance, for Whitman persuaded them that his work would be enhanced if he could interview his subjects. This was no doubt true but gave rise to some romantic speculation. There were hints in the shop about shocking secrets locked up in the *Times* morgue, to be opened only after death. Another legend was that it took untold resources of tact to set up an obituary interview. As I learned when I succeeded Whitman for a spell, nearly all subjects were only too willing to burnish their images for posterity; the disappointment was that they said nothing they would not have said for the next morning's paper. Men and women in the public eye spend their lives developing a persona they may finally believe to be real; they are not about to destroy it for a stranger, alas.

Advance obituaries were locked up in the morgue, not to protect any secrets but, I suppose, to keep other reporters from cannibalizing them for feature articles on deadline. Secrecy also served to avoid embarrassing confrontations. During my tenure, I received a call one day from an emissary of Rudolf Bing, the Metropolitan Opera impresario, who advised me that Sir Rudolf deigned to check his advance obit for accuracy and, presumably, to see if it was up to its subject. I asked him to convey our excuses to Sir Rudolf and say that the *Times* could not show him the article in advance but would be happy to sell him a posthumous subscription.

After Whitman retired in 1976 with some five hundred obits in his file, he said his object had been in each case "to fashion a true and honest portrait, one that would be valid and readable and go beyond a once-over-lightly that characterizes so many newspaper obits." He succeeded better, no doubt, than any other who held that job, but was his goal not a mirage? Has anyone ever drawn a true portrait? We are forever rewriting those of our forebears going back to Socrates, and seldom does one of them emerge the handsomer for such a reexamination. For the *Times*, the assumption has always been that our statesmen, warriors, business tycoons, and civic leaders achieve their eminence by talent and virtue. (In my years on rewrite, seldom was a corporate executive exposed in crime or other folly but that his clip file would yield an adoring profile.) An obituary is the last place one would look for a corrective.

This rule was tested harshly by the death *in flagrante* of Nelson Rockefeller. His courtiers and the authorities sought to falsify the circumstances. To its eternal credit, the *Times* rewrite bank would not go along. As a result, the *Times*'s account of Rockefeller's death was accurate, while its account of his life was pretty much the official portrait. It was only in another forum a few weeks later that I could observe that Rockefeller had lived as he died.

Nil nisi bonum would seem to be a safe precaution, but it depends on who is *mortuis*. When one poor obit writer followed it in the case of Wladyslaw Gomulka, the Polish Communist chief, Executive Editor A.M. Rosenthal apologized publicly to *Times* readers.

The normal inhibition of the *Times* has to be shared by any obituary writer, to some degree. His portrait will appear before the funeral rites and likely will have been read by the mourners. If during the lifetime of the defunct the *Times* has not advised its readers that the general was a butcher, the statesman a fool, the executive a tyrant and the poet a nasty bit of goods, the obituary is not quite the time or place to correct the record.

A solution for the writer is to avoid when possible those subjects whose official personas are radically out of line with his own perceptions. Thus, after a dreary week of study of the oeuvre of Saul Bellow, I decided I was the wrong man to write his obit. On the other hand, I found it rewarding to review the careers of men like Saroyan and Algren who I thought had been unjustly mauled by the critical academy. Incidentally, when those obituaries appeared, my byline was stricken from the prepared texts. The same has since occurred to Alden Whitman, who like me had the maladdress to criticize the regime of Rosenthal in public. Anonymous we entered his world, anonymous we left it. No matter. We are still there in that morgue, along with our surviving subjects. Long may they live.

I am still bemused by the last coup of the legendary press agent Ben Sonnenberg. He died during the 1978 newspaper strike but managed to get his *Times* obituary into the *Congressional Record* the next day. It was, in fact, Senator Moynihan who placed it there. That, I believe, was my last *Times* byline. The next time one of my subjects died, Rosenthal struck my name from the obituary because I was no longer on the team (though Moynihan evidently was).

On the death watch I had felt like a slacker. History was being made every day, and being badly reported. Jimmy Carter was elected president in 1976, and began, with deregulation, the undoing of a century of social progress. His first year saw the first cutback in Social Security, disguised as a rescue. It was the beginning of a campaign that has been one of the most disgraceful episodes in the history of American journalism. Interested readers can find my account in the Epilogue.

Carter cleared his key appointments with David Rockefeller. He accepted fatal advice from Paul Volcker (double-digit interest rates plus inflation), James Schlesinger (gasoline foulup), and Rockefeller and Kissinger, who persuaded him to give shelter to the Shah of Iran, thus precipitating the occupation of the embassy in Tehran. At the State Department, Pat Derian made a noble effort to make civil rights a pillar of foreign policy, and was foiled by Richard Holbrooke, notably in the Philippines and Central America. The *Times* served, as usual, as the voice of the establishment. Upon Carter's election, Leslie Gelb, our man in the revolving door, returned to government service for a second hitch. His place as the *Times*'s poohbah on strategic affairs was taken by Richard Burt, of whom Hodding Carter remarked, "You don't have to read anything less juvenile than Richard Burt to see [National Security Director] Zbigniew Brzezinski's lips move." With Carter's defeat by Reagan, Gelb rejoined the *Times* with a bang—a Sunday magazine cover that cried in large type, "What this country wants and needs is not a board chairman or a passive President, but a strong one, even—yes, even—something approaching the old and besmirched Imperial Presidency." Meanwhile Burt formally joined the government.

In New York in 1976 the *Times* played a game worthy of Rupert Murdoch's *Post* in helping Moynihan edge out Bella Abzug. The following year the *Times* helped Ed Koch win election as mayor by attacking "poverty pimps" and party bosses with whom he was secretly allied.* And I was writing obituaries....

Then came the 1978 newspaper strike. Doing commentaries on TV and columns for an ad-hoc striketime daily, I found it exhilarating to be back in combat with live issues, and I decided not to return. I have never regretted it. Which is not to say that I was ever detached from the *Times*. For the next quarter century, as I contested conventional wisdom on TV and radio, in syndicated columns and in freelance articles, I often had to challenge the version of reality being presented by that organ of conventional wisdom.

Enough.

I have had to pass over many another historic battlefield. The reader may find some of my contemporary comments on the Web. For now I sign off as I used to in the age of telegraphy—

— 30 —

---

*See Appendix item six, "The Shame of the Urban Press."

On snakes, tea, and poll weevils

By John L. Hess

From Quill, 1982.

Epilogue

OBJECTIVE UNTRUTH

P eter Kihss died not long ago, and was properly honored as a non-pareil of our craft. His best and happiest years were on the *Herald Tribune,* but the *Times* gave him a fine obituary. I was struck by a note giving him credit for the phrase "because of an editing error" in corrections. I had long cherished the illusion that it was I who had inspired it—a bit of post-hoc reasoning, no doubt. The change came immediately after the publication of a prominent error that had been written into a dispatch by Tad Szulc. I protested to the brass, for the nth time, that people reporters dealt with would hardly believe that we were not responsible for what appeared under our names, unless the correction specifically said so. But of course Szulc himself must have thrown a fit. Many of us had raised the issue for years, but met resistance from "the clerks." None had better grounds than Kihss. He was the only reporter I know to have been the victim of deliberate sabotage. A spiteful copy editor, miffed at his complaints, doctored figures to turn an article of his into gibberish. Pete stormed out, sick at heart. After a few days, Frank Adams, the city editor, coaxed him back. He said the perpetrator had been disciplined, but he declined to identify him. "You'd kill him," Frank said. "I would," Pete agreed.

The incident was recounted to me by a copy editor boastfully, if you can imagine, and by Kihss as an act of rape that haunted his unhappy years on the *Times*. His fabled dedication to the accurate collection of facts was the peg for an essay I wrote for the professional journal *Quill* just after the elections of 1982:

I was reading my daily budget of poll analysis while my wife was clocking the 51st Psalm. By a natural progression, I got to thinking about Peter Kihss and the boa constrictor.

Pete is a legend in New York journalism, perhaps its most dedicated collector of facts, or call it objective truth. He began to establish that reputation as a cub reporter one day long ago when he was sent to cover the arrival at LaGuardia of a thirty-foot snake.

Never one to accept a press agent's word for anything, Pete assembled a crowd of bystanders, rolled the boa out on the tarmac, and measured it. That's the kind of reporter he was.

How long was that boa? How should I know? I'm not even sure it was LaGuardia—maybe it was Floyd Bennett Field.

My point is that the length of a snake is relative: it depends on its last meal, and how many men were holding it down, how hard they were pulling, things like that. But if it measured, say, twenty-four feet, then that press agent had been stretching the truth.

Now you want to know why my wife was timing the 51st Psalm. You'd never guess, so I'll tell you.

In researching the history of tea, the earliest reference she found on how it was brewed in England was in a paper by "the Eminently learned Sir Kenelme Digby, Knight," published in 1669. Sir Kenelme decreed: "The water is to remain upon [the tea leaves] no longer than whiles you can say the Miserere Psalm very leisurely."

So my wife read the King James version at a stately pace from "Have mercy upon me" to the promise of "bullocks upon thine altar." It took just two minutes. Allowing that the eminently learned knight might have been a slow reader, she concluded that he believed in steeping tea for no more than three minutes, at the outside. It was, for her purpose, a useful fact.

If it had been any more precise, it would have been less useful or, if you prefer, less true. To give the optimum brewing time of tea in milliseconds, or the length of a snake in millimeters, would give only the illusion of truth, a computer version of reality.

The correct time, my wife would say, depends on the condition of the leaves, the shape of the pot, and how you like your tea. Just so, she maintains that an old recipe that calls for "six to eight eggs" is more truthful than a modern update that would say seven.

In the golden age of economics—that is, before the computer—Adam Smith began his great work with the tale of the unskilled workman who "could scarce, perhaps, with his utmost industry, make one pin a day, and certainly could not make twenty." He contrasted this with a shop he had seen where ten men, by the division of labor, could make upwards of forty-eight thousand pins in a day.

In the first instance, old Adam allowed that he might be off by 1,900 percent, yet his point was valid. The computer has changed all that. Today we are drowning in figures brought down to thousandths of a point, adjusted for seasonal variations, and nearly always misleading.

Now the computer, in combination with the opinion poll, has taken over politics. It is ever so scientific. The little sidebar tells us that each random sample will, nineteen out of twenty times, respond like the total electorate, give or take three or 4 percent.

To be sure, they are often wrong. I have the unscientific impression that they have never been so wrong as they have been this year, when some rival scientific polls taken the same day have differed from each other by as much as ten points. And they change dizzily from day to day. This is called volatility. It means the voters are flighty.

In perhaps the most brilliant journalistic démarche of the campaign, Mike Royko of the *Chicago Tribune* called on voters to lie to pollsters. But of course they've been lying all along. Either they don't know how they're going to vote or they don't know why, or they don't think it's everybody's business.

When, inevitably, their actual vote differs from the poll-based forecasts, the poll weevils call it an upset. Then they order another poll to find out why.

Either they've forgotten how to cover elections any other way, or they're just plain lazy. If you treat a campaign as a battle over policy, as a struggle over the fate of the Republic, you've got your work cut out for you. First, you have to study issues, like the nuke, and then, when you've said where they stand on that, what are you going to tell your readers tomorrow?

Whereas, if the only issue is who's got the momentum, you get a new computer printout every day, and there's your story. Tomorrow, you'll explain what went wrong. With a scientific breakdown of the vote among Yuppies, Seventh Day Adventists, and folks who live on odd-numbered streets.

Besides, when you talk about things that matter, it's much harder to be objective. Like, when George McGovern bowed out, several media personalities blurted out loud, "There goes the class act of the campaign."

It was true, but it was hardly objective. Objective reporting had required them to treat McGovern's entry as absurd and to ignore him thereafter. Even though he did far better on the hustings than their polls had predicted, they never accorded him the momentum. Exit McGovern.

So we head on to November with nothing but scientific polls to guide us. Let us pray, beginning with the Miserere, very leisurely.

The reader may find quaint the foregoing tilt against the windmill of polling. The *Times* and other media became not less but more dependent on polls. A remarkable example, as I write, is the front page on August 16, 2001. In the opinion of the editors, the most significant news in the world that morning was an opinion poll—or rather, a non-opinion poll—which found that an overwhelming majority of voters in New York had no opinion about any of the candidates for mayor, and did not think the election would make any difference.

The *Times* put an upbeat spin on it. It concluded that New Yorkers were taking a rosier view of their town than they used to, and thanked Mayor Giuliani for it, but they thought things would get even rosier when he was gone. Within a margin of plus or minus 3 percent. One reason the *Times*'s canvassers found such good cheer may be that grouches tend to hang up on strangers who call them at all hours. Citizens who do respond are presumably people who don't mind answering foolish questions about things they hadn't thought about.

Anyway, it was a modest victory for reporters to get "Because of an editing error" into corrections. But as the "Corrections" I composed for *The Nation* illustrate (see the Chapter Eleven frontispiece), editors almost never confess truly important sins of judgment, as reflected in those four sample headlines that caught my eye in May and June, 1992. Each spun the truth to its opposite. Three concerned the environment, which the *Times* swathed in soiled plastic diapers later that year.

"The war over how to cover American baby bottoms has ended in a rout," Michael Specter exclaimed (*The New York Times*, October 23, 1992, p. A1). He said "exhausted" activists had been forced to confess that the disposable diaper was just too convenient to resist and, to their crushing embarrassment, might be less damaging to the environment than old-fashioned cotton. An accompanying scientific chart showed disposables to be dramatically less wasteful of water and energy, and less polluting.

Specter did not name the activists he claimed to have talked to, but a number of activists were not too exhausted to fire off letters to the *Times*. Two weeks later an "Editor's Note" acknowledged that the chart had been based on research paid for by Procter & Gamble, the dominant maker of disposables (Pampers and Luvs). In checking their files, the editors must have learned that the story itself had been recycled, having appeared on July 14, 1990. It had then been thoroughly rebutted by activists, though not in the *Times*.

Finally, on November 9, 1992, the *Times* published three of those reader letters. They not only challenged the research as bogus (not a first offense for P. & G.), but they rehabilitated the cloth diaper as easier on the environment, far cheaper, and even, where good diaper service was available, more convenient. So in the end, both sides were heard, weren't they? Well, let's see. A frontpage homerun for P. & G. that was doubtless discouraging to environmentalists in general, offset by a pettifogging "Editor's Note" two weeks later and three letters of rebuttal four days after that. P. & G.'s flacks might score it Pampers 98, Environment 2.

Incidentally, that research was concocted for P. & G. by Arthur Little of Boston. The same consulting firm was engaged by Philip Morris in 2001 to advise the Czech Republic that smoking was good for its fiscal health, because it killed so many people before they could collect pensions. That shocked the Czech government, but it should not have shocked *Times* readers. Peter Passell, among others, had been pushing the same "cost-benefit analysis" in his economics column. For example, he computed that proposed clean air regulation would cost industry $6 billion to $10 billion a year, to save no more than 500 lives. "Valuing these lives at $3 million each, the total benefits will fall short of $2 billion," he wrote, so "many environmentalists concede [that toxic emissions control] would be about as cost effective as the Pentagon's

$600 toilet seats" (*The New York Times*, August 15, 1990). Like the "exhausted activists" who conceded the diaper debate to Michael Specter, those "many environmentalists" were not further identified.

All these attitudes—a pseudo-objectivity, a naïve embrace of establishment spin, a disdain for dissent—marked a darker episode in the *Times*'s history. When the Long Island Lighting Company (Lilco) applied in the 1960s for a permit to build a nuclear power plant at Shoreham, the *Times* was of course enthusiastic. As the organ chosen by the government to relate to the world the development of the atomic bomb, it had sung the praise of a magic new source of energy that would make electricity so cheap it could be given away. It never, ever dawned on the *Times* that cheap energy was the last thing the utility industry would want. As a franchised monopoly, it operated on a cost-plus basis: the more it spent, the more it earned. As one scientist put it, a nuclear reactor was the most expensive device ever invented to boil water. Hence a utility in Louisiana, where oilfields burned natural gas to get rid of it, ordered up nuclear plants, and doubled and tripled its rates.

Long Islanders were promised that Shoreham would cost a mere $250 million or so, and would assure them a safe and cheap supply of electricity. As the years went by, the cost crept up, to a figure last reported at $5.5 billion. Utilities may not normally charge customers for plants not yet on stream, but New York State let Lilco pass along much of its outlay, until its rates vied with Con Edison as highest in the nation. *Newsday* reporters were doing yeoman work on cost overruns, dubious contracting, needless delays, and shoddy work that had to be torn up and redone, although their editorial page, like that of the *Times*, would remain loyal to Lilco to the end. Commenting on the affair from time to time in my column and on TV, I observed that the publishers were flouting their own interest as large users of electricity, as well as the interest of Long Island, in favor of the financiers downtown. It got worse, not better.

Chernobyl and Three Mile Island clinched the fate of Shoreham. Residents concerned about the impossibility of evacuating Long Island won the nominal support of local politicians, a criminal conviction of Lilco for fraud (which was thrown out by the federal judge who heard the case), and a state order barring the plant from opening. By 1982, it appeared that Lilco was virtually bankrupt, stuck with billions of dollars of debt on a plant that would never operate. In its news columns the *Wall Street Journal* was playing the story hard and straight. Lilco's stock fell to $3 a share; in a just world, it would have been zero. On New York Channel 5 I offered the only market advice I've ever given:

"Buy Lilco, sell Long Island."

I regret that an excess of scruple kept me from following my own advice; anybody who did would have multiplied his stake tenfold within a couple of years. I was predicting that Wall Street would manage to pass the cost of this debacle on to the public (as with the savings-and-loans et al.), and so it did. Lilco bought out local politicians, gave a key job to a leader of the consumer opposition, threatened power blackouts and, in defiance of state admonitions, loaded the reactor for testing, thus presenting a huge future bill for its decontamination. The *Times* applauded every step of the way, and berated its critics. Finally, in a reverse of the march toward privatization, Lilco was sold to the state at a cost to customers and taxpayers never honestly calculated—but well more than double the $5.5 billion mentioned. Typically, the deal was unveiled as a gift of the contaminated and useless Shoreham plant to the state for $1; in the small print, Lilco sold its entire distribution system and was guaranteed a 13 percent return on all the money it had borrowed and squandered. The *Times* lauded Lilco and berated its critics at every turn. Near the end, an editorial accused them of "bad faith" and "obstruction," and told Long Islanders to blame Governor Cuomo, Suffolk county, and themselves if they sweltered in blackouts that summer because they had blocked the opening of a reactor generously given to the state for $1 and falsely described as unsafe. (See *The New York Times*, March 11, 1989, "A Wiser Fate for Shoreham." The editorial was written by Nicholas Wade, who specialized in rebutting environmental and scientific alarmism. In an essay in the Sunday magazine, he offered as a model of skepticism and enterprise his own grandfather, who ignored instructions aboard the Titanic to clamber into a lifeboat restricted to woman and children.)

A journalistic martyr of this campaign was Frances Cerra. After six years of consumer reporting for *Newsday* (for which she earned a Polk award), she joined the *Times,* in the same capacity, in 1974. She learned (as I did at the same time and as Richard Severo would later) that, in her words, the *Times* "never wanted stories critical of consumer treatment by major corporations." Writing in the *Columbia Journalism Review* long afterward, she said that in 1980:

> I was finally demoted to Long Island reporter after I failed to produce enough service stories or, as I called them, "news-you-can-use" stories. These are the shopping hints, the how-to-get-a-better-bargain stories. They have their place, and whenever I did one I received compliments from my editors. But I was always far more interested in investigative stories, in seeing, for example, whether sky-rocketing insurance rates for malpractice, autos and so were truly justified. I did a series on these issues, noting along the way the revolving door between the regulators and the regulated, and the political ties of the powerful lawyers who represented the industry.
>
> These stories, and others like them, never earned me any compliments. In fact, I was called on the carpet for describing one such lawyer as "politically connected." ...I realized later that they truly had no interest in my work. By hiring me they had answered the criticism that the *Times* had been neglecting consumer coverage."

The reader will recognize my own experience on the food beat, as related in Chapter Thirteen. I moved on to the nursing-home scandal; in Long Island, Cerra naturally had to report on Shoreham: the cost overruns, the construction errors, the doubt that the population could be evacuated. Other reporters told her Lilco's top management was complaining to their bosses that they were biased.

"In mid-1982," she wrote, "I was assigned to do a 'status report' on Lilco. I dug around, looked at the finances... and wrote a story which said that Shoreham might drive Lilco into bankruptcy. The story never ran."

Cerra said she was called in by Abe Rosenthal's assistant, Peter Millones, who told her that her report was irremediable, that it threatened to harm Lilco's financial situation, and that in view of her bias she must henceforth strike Shoreham from her beat. She chose instead to return to New York. After a year in Coventry there, she quit the *Times* and, for a long time, was lost to journalism. Then she returned, as a coach to activists creating alternative media, which may well be our last best hope.

THE BIG WHITE LIE

"The only real whack ever taken at Social Security came a decade ago, when Congress hid behind the big white lie that the system was on the verge of bankruptcy." —Peter Passell, *The New York Times*, December 15, 1994.

That is the only forthright affirmation of the great hoax that I have seen in mainstream media, aside from my own vain cries. It cannot be called an admission, since Passell wrote of the deed with evident nostalgia. At the moment, he was lamenting the failure of President Clinton's Bipartisan Commission on Entitlements and Tax Reform to recommend further cuts in the safety net. He explained that the absence of an economic crisis "leaves policy makers without a convenient moment to rise above interest-group politics in the name of the greater good."

Aside from Passell's embrace of lying, note the now routine assignment of the term "special interest" to women, children, the elderly, the disabled, wage earners, and minorities, and the assumption that their interest differs with the national interest. Note also the assumption by many economic pundits, led by Alan Greenspan, that good news is bad news—that, for example, if unemployment fell below 6 percent it would call for a corrective tightening of the money supply.

In any case, Passell was wrong on his facts. Congress took its first real whack at Social Security not in 1982–83 but five years earlier—as I have good cause to know, since I was one of the first to be hit. The bean counters in Washington announced that they had made an error in the formula for computing individual pensions, threatening the system with imminent failure. They proposed to correct it by increasing the withholding tax and cutting future retirees' benefits by about one–fifth—a pretty real whack, wouldn't you say? They promised it would assure the system's solvency for at least the rest of the century. The "rescue" was approved during the holiday season of 1977. *Time* magazine cheered, incoherently, "Up, Up, and Away!" (November 7, 1977).

My stay at the *Times* ended soon afterward, but I cannot bring myself to close this memoir without pursuing the further history of that great hoax, which continues to this day. Most of us paid little notice to the first whack, because the hit was muffled. The withholding tax was ratcheted up in inconspicuous nips on payroll stubs, and the benefit cuts did not take effect until my class turned 65, in 1983. It was only then that we learned by word of mouth that our pensions would be substantially lower than those of our older siblings—hence, a notch on the charts. (Seldom mentioned was the fact that the average monthly check was less than $400.) Some "Notch Babies" complained for years. Their only recompense was a widely repeated tribute by the *New Republic*, which called them "spiteful,

singleminded, and, to the uninitiated, deeply baffling—a parody of
a special interest group." With a celebrated cover and cartoon, it gave
elderly Americans the sobriquet "Greedy Geezers." George Will in
Newsweek sneered, "The elderly are not more rapacious than the rest
of us, they are just better at being so."

The insults reflected a cliché often repeated in the *Times,* that
Social Security was a third rail for politicians or, in an alternate
metaphor, that retired Americans were an 800–pound gorilla that
kept the government in terror—"one of Washington's most fero-
cious lobbies," as a *Times* editorial would put it (February 5,
2003). The dimension of the monster often cited was the thirty-
two million (or sometimes thirty-three million, or thirty-four million) "members" of the American Association of Retired Persons.
They were the subscription list, actually, of a mail-order business
of tainted origin, which peddles insurance, pharmaceutical dis-
counts, and other services. Constantly in trouble with the IRS over
taxes and with the Postal Service over its attempts to use non-
commercial mail rates, the AARP strenuously avoids offending
the authorities, and it in fact took sides against its own "members"
in the dispute over catastrophic medical insurance. In a word, the
AARP has far more to fear from politicians than politicians have
to fear from the AARP. And if Social Security was a third rail, it
has been repeatedly short-circuited, with the unfailing support of
the media.

The "rescue" of 1977 did not for a moment halt its attacks. A
syndicated column of mine on April 4, 1980, quoted this from the
Times:

> Gray Panthers cheer [inflation] because they know Social
> Security payments are linked tight as mating dragonflies to the
> Consumer Price Index... [T]he index nowadays exaggerates
> inflation by calculating the cost of housing every month as
> though everybody bought a house that often. Most retirees,

of course, took care of their housing needs while they were salting away their World War II overtime.

Some dragonflies. Actually, the cost-of-living adjustment (COLA) lags six to twelve months behind the index. To assert that the elderly are immune from inflation was merely ignorant; to accuse them of welcoming it was unspeakable. The reporter borrowed that brickbat from Albert Kahn, who had persuaded President Carter that deregulation would conquer inflation, and was now blaming COLA for his spectacular failure. The *Wall Street Journal* and its echoes in the *Times* added that our cost of living actually did not rise at all, because common folk were forever shrewdly substituting cheap for dear, such as chicken for beef. My column responded that (A) war profiteering was not the only occupation of my contemporaries (whom Tom Brokaw would later gush over as the Greatest Generation) and (B) that to reduce inflation further, consumers might replace chicken with beans, and housing with park benches. (Moynihan led a clamor about substitution twenty years later, and the index was quietly throttled down by about half a percentage point—still another unheralded whack.)

The illusion that the elderly as a class were rich was a media construct. Reporters, TV crews, and cartoonists located them habitually in swimming pools and golf carts at sunkissed resorts that were affordable to no more than 2 percent or so. Actually, two-thirds of the elderly depend on Social Security for a major share of their income. Without it, half of them would fall below the poverty line; even with those modest checks, one out of eight still qualifies as poor. Meanwhile, as a result of stonyhearted government policy, the proportion of children in poverty climbed well above that—which those to blame for this policy cited as a further reason to cut benefits to the elderly.

The hateful talk about old people that became current in the media in the late 1970s would have been unthinkable in my youth. That was in the Great Depression, when the country was really hard up. We, most of us, greeted with enthusiasm a slew of New Deal legislation: public works, public housing, minimum wages, the 40-hour-week, paid vacations, the right to organize. The crown jewel was the Social Security Act of 1935, which promised a modest subsistence to retirees and the disabled and their dependents. The beauty part was that it would be a right, an entitlement—a word that the media would turn into an epithet. It meant not having to apply for welfare—another word that was turned into an epithet, often modifying nouns like cheats, bums, and pimps. It was liberating to think that our elders (and our disabled colleagues, and widows and orphans) could face the future with dignity. I worked at a variety of jobs for the next fifty years and do not recall hearing a fellow worker complain about our supporting the old, the disabled, the widows and orphans. So it was painful, when our turn came to receive benefits, to find ourselves castigated as parasites.

Blather about generations (what *is* a generation?) was a calculated weapon of the crusade against Social Security. A few twenty-somethings who had never held meaningful employment were recruited to complain that their elders were looting their heritage. They scored better with the media than with other young Americans. Another propaganda front, the Association for Generational Equity (AGE), was funded by major corporations (e.g., General Dynamics, U.S. Steel, ITT, Metropolitan Life, and the savings-and-loan lobby) and headed by Senator David Durenberger (R-MN) until he was exposed as a crook, and then by Richard Lamm, the former Democratic governor of Colorado, famous for having told the elderly sick, "You have a duty to die and get out of the way." AGE was frequently cited in the *Times* as a serious source. It reached something of a climax in an article in *Fortune* magazine in 1987, which predicted literal, bloody war between generations if baby boomers dared to claim their inflation-adjusted pensions when they reached sixty-five. An "expert on gerontology" suggested that the would-be retirees "could be sent on a five-day camping trip with two days' worth of food."

Nobody did more to make such talk acceptable in mainstream media than the investment banker Peter G. Peterson. During the Reagan and Clinton eras, one could rarely surf the airwaves or skim the print media, including the *Times*, without meeting him and his helpers, sounding the alarm. Or he would be amplifying it in costly ads by his austerity lobby, the Concord Coalition, when he was not presiding over the Council on Foreign Relations, or gracing the society page in black tie at important functions, sometimes as host. He may have done his most effective proselytizing in resort wear, though, hobnobbing in the Hamptons with such useful tablemates as Don Hewitt and Leslie Stahl of *60 Minutes,* Diane Sawyer, Peter Jennings and Barbara Walters of ABC News, Mort Zuckerman of the *Atlantic, U.S. News and World Report,* and the *New York Daily News,* Joseph and Barbara Epstein of the *New York Review of Books,* Ken Auletta, John Scanlon, et al.

Vanity Fair called on the great man at his spectacular beachside retreat one weekend for an admiring profile (August 1993), which touched on the themes of this memoir in several ways. The interview was interrupted by telephone calls arranging the appointment of Leslie Gelb (ex-*New York Times*) as president of the Council on Foreign Relations, of James Hoge (ex-*New York Daily News*) as its editor, and of former Senator Warren Rudman (R-N.H.) as a director of a foundation funded by the health-care giant Johnson & Johnson.

Peterson said he happened to be tackling health policy at that very moment, which was at the height of the popular movement for universal medical insurance. He referred to a chapter of his forthcoming book, *Facing Up: How to Rescue the American Economy From Crushing Debt and Restore the American Dream.* "The issue isn't whether these new [health] benefits would be nice to have," it said. "They would. The issue is whether we can afford it. We can't." The observation lends piquancy to his wife's explanation that Peterson commuted in a $2.5 million helicopter to safeguard his health. The issue was not whether it was a nice benefit to have. It was. The issue was whether he could afford it. He could.

While he was reticent about his finances, *Vanity Fair* put his take-home in 1992 at $7 million. His investment banking firm, the Blackstone Group, was then predicting returns of 25 to 30 percent a year for the rest of the decade. That lent piquancy, again, to his description of the cost-of-living adjustment to Social Security, then running at about 3 percent, as "one of the greatest fiscal tragedies in American history." Piquant? There is more, for Peterson was at President Nixon's side when that fiscal tragedy was enacted.

It happened in 1972, the year of Watergate. Peterson, the former head of the military contractor Bell & Howell, was Secretary of Commerce and a close economic adviser to Nixon. He was never indicted, but Congressional hearings found that he had engaged in secret dealings with ITT that spared it from antitrust prosecution, enriched Nixon's campaign coffers, and furthered the plot to overthrow the government of Chile. Meanwhile, Nixon was committing fiscal heresy by freezing wages and prices, easing credit, proposing a minimum income for everybody and raising Social Security benefits. At the same time, he tied future benefits to the consumer price index. As conservatives have ruefully explained, this was intended to keep Congress from awarding more generous increases in the future. In the event, they misjudged the political and economic outlook entirely.

Nixon won re-election handily but his monetary policy led to the collapse of the gold exchange standard and a recession in 1973. Inflation climbed to double digits. Except for Social Security, major elements of the safety net—the minimum wage, aid to families with dependent children, food stamps, unemployment insurance—were not indexed, so they declined sharply in real terms. Unions came under pressure, and givebacks and two-tier wage agreements (lower scales for the newly hired) became common. It is no coincidence that 1973 marks the year when the standard of living of a majority of Americans began to decline and the gap in incomes began to widen dramatically. It was then also that, returning from abroad, I remarked that we were beginning to resemble a third-world country. In the hard times of depression and war, a spirit of sharing had predominated; now it was devil take the hindmost.

Peterson has called what was going on in the business world a "mad, drunken bash." He should know. Abandoning Nixon to his fate in 1973, he headed for Wall Street to heist his share of the booze. There were mergers, hostile takeovers, leveraged buyouts financed by junk bonds, an orgy of looting by savings-and-loans, poison pills—all great stories that the *Times* covered badly, when it covered them at all. Recounting the criminal rigging of the Treasury bond market, Martin Meyer was amazed at how *Times* reporters swallowed the preposterous handouts of Goldman Sachs "hook, line and sinker."

Conventional wisdom went along with all that was happening, which is to say that the *Times* went along: Government was inefficient, private enterprise made the wheels turn. Unions were a drag, high wages and featherbedding and job tenure damaged our competitivity in the world market. A *Times* editorial declared: "The Right Minimum Wage: $0.00." Bigger was better, but downsizing was also good. Mergers, friendly or hostile, horizontal or vertical, were serendipitous. Conglomerates nurtured synergy. Good management was mean and lean, and was wisely rewarded by stock options and golden parachutes. Layoffs in the Rust Belt meant prosperity in the Sun Belt and lower prices for consumers, and if smokestack industry moved abroad, well fine, our future lay with the service economy. Japan was overtaking us because of its high rate of savings; it followed that a larger share of our national product should be assigned to those who would reinvest it—hence, taxes should be cut on high incomes and on corporate profits and capital gains, and be deferred on IRAs and 401(k)s. Zealots like Jack Kemp and Bill Bradley favored a flat tax or a form of national sales tax, and were praised by the media for their courage. But the existing tax that best served to redistribute wealth was FICA—the one withheld from low and medium wages. It had been enacted with Social Security, to assure the affluent that they would not have to pay for it. The revenue has more than covered the benefits ever since—so much more, in recent years, that it erased an enormous Federal deficit and carried the budget into surplus. The tax is so tilted against low-wage earners that Peterson expressed pleased surprise that there had been no serious movement to reduce it.

In his first year, 1981, Reagan obtained a huge cut in income taxes and a sharp buildup in military spending. Thus began the "crushing buildup" of the national debt that Peterson decried— though he continued to raise money for the Republicans. (It was only after the election of Bill Clinton that reducing the deficit became national policy. Peterson bragged to *Vanity Fair* that he had helped shape Clinton's decision to make it the theme of his first State of the Union address.) For his part, Reagan's opening program, which set off an explosion of the deficit, also called for a major cut in Social Security, which he had often publicly derided. Congress did sneak in a couple of nicks (benefit checks were rounded off to the next lower dollar figure, and orphaned students were disqualified) but the big whack was loudly voted down. The proposal was thought to have contributed to a Republican setback in the 1982 elections. Now the foes of Social Security set out instead to *rescue* it.

The groundwork was laid by a powerful campaign of disinformation. Cover articles and cartoons in the *Atlantic, The New Republic,* and the *Washington Monthly,* widely reproduced and quoted, fixed the image of the elderly American as an old sharper cheating the young, or riding their backs like the Old Man of the Sea, or as a hog rooting at the trough. A powerful rhetorical device was the assertion that the typical retiree got back all he had paid into Social Security: in nineteen months, according to one issue of the *Washington Monthly*; twelve months, according to Cokie Roberts on ABC News;

about two years, according to George Will; three-and-a-half years, according to David Gergen; and a generous four to six years, according to *Fortune*. In vain, I challenged Cokie to say whether, if her house burned down, she would be content to accept a refund of her insurance premiums. Playing the game, I suggested that allowing for the employers' share of the tax, for inflation, for interest foregone, for the enjoyment we might have had from spending that money when we earned it, for the benefits never collected by our contemporaries who died betimes, I could easily claim (as some of my readers did) that we were being shortchanged. It was no use; more than a decade later, a *Times* editorial would complain that retirees "get back from Social Security much more than they paid" (February 5, 1993). In a news column a few days later, Jason De Parle, who came to the *Times* from the *Washington Monthly*, agreed that retirees were taking out more than they had paid in, "leaving less to build housing, fight infant mortality, provide better schools, battle drug abuse and otherwise invest in the future" (February 11, 1993). In a word, we were baby killers. Also from the Washington bureau, Robert D. Hershey Jr. gave 3.5 years as the break-even point, although the Congressional Research Service put it then at 14.2 years. Hershey complained that retirees "often resent the suggestion, however correct, that their benefits include a portion that is a gift, or *to use the pejorative, welfare*" (my emphasis).

All the talk about the return on the withholding tax begs the issue. Social Security is not an insurance company, it is a social compact. It does not even handle the money; FICA taxes are paid to the Treasury and mingled with its accounts, and the benefit checks are issued by the Treasury. As I kept saying, it made no more sense to talk about Social Security going broke than it would to talk about national security going broke.

Another potent scare was whipped up by a series of articles in the *New York Review of Books* signed by Peterson, purporting to prove with tables of statistics that Social Security would devour the economy. It revived the argument raised by Malthus in England two centuries ago, that population multiplies geometrically while production grows arithmetically, so that it is criminal folly to feed the poor. In the event, production grew much faster than population, but Malthus achieved his goal, the repeal of the entitlement to home relief. With a similar aim, Peterson purported to demonstrate that within a couple of decades every worker would have to support two or more retirees. His analysis quite persuaded, and frightened, even such liberals as Tony Lewis and Tom Wicker of the *Times*. Tony opened one column by citing Leona Helmsley's sneer: "We don't pay taxes. Little people pay taxes." I remonstrated with Tony that Leona did not mean that old people did not pay taxes, she meant that rich people did not pay taxes. He replied that he still had to put the needs of children ahead of the elderly—as if this administration, or this Congress, would divert to children any funds they took from their grandparents!

Media people should have seen the flaw in Peterson's argument from our own trade, which was just then in the throes of a spectacular technological revolution. It was visible everywhere. A while ago, some of us maritime veterans were swapping yarns about World War II, and marveling at the comfort of life today aboard the dwindling number of ships that still fly the American flag. I did a rough calculation: as compared to a rustbucket I had sailed on, these floating palaces, with half the crew, haul twenty times as much cargo at more than three times the speed (and do even better in loading and unloading). So it was reasonable to conclude that modern seamen are one hundred times more productive than we were. And so are the butchers, the bakers and the CD makers. A hundred-odd years ago, four out of five Americans lived on farms; today, two million farmers grow more food than 260 million of us can eat. So it takes very few workers to feed, clothe and shelter us all; our problem is how to employ all the surplus energy of an incredibly rich society.

But Malthusianism dominated the media in 1982, as it would to this day. No critical eyebrows were raised when Reagan's merry prevaricator David Stockman (a protégé of Senator Moynihan who would later join Peterson's Blackstone Group) announced that Social Security faced bankruptcy; Reagan said the money would run out in August, 1983. It was a barefaced lie; benefits had always been roughly in balance with FICA revenues, Congress owed Social Security funds something like $30 billion in lieu of withholding taxes on Pentagon payrolls, and the Notch was about to kick in, supposedly guaranteeing solvency for decades to come. Ignoring these facts, Reagan named a bipartisan commission including Senators Moynihan and Bob Dole, headed by the Wall Street forecaster Alan Greenspan. In a short time, Greenspan whipped up a guess that Social Security might run a deficit of $150 billion to $200 billion by 1990. He achieved this figure by assuming rates of inflation, unemployment, and economic activity that were wildly more pessimistic than those he was forecasting for his private clients. The fictitious figure was the one featured in headlines and news bulletins ("A time-bomb is ticking," NBC News intoned). Soon they all proclaimed a savage whack as a rescue. And just about everyone applauded.

Although it was billed as a lifeline to the elderly, it was in fact an assault on our children and grandchildren—the very people we were supposed to be exploiting—because although it did trim our benefits by a few percentage points (and ultimately theirs, compounded), it raised payroll taxes and, most shockingly, ordered the retirement age raised from sixty-five to sixty-seven, in phases to begin in the year 2003. In return, Social Security was declared safe until the year 2075. Needless to say, this assurance would last not much longer than the one given in 1977.

In 1983, the trust funds—that is, the cumulative surplus of payroll taxes over benefits—began climbing toward the trillions, but so did the national debt. Personal income tax rates had been cut by more than half, corporations paid little or nothing, Cold War expenditures continued to rise. Inevitably, the establishment gazed greedily at the benefits consumed by the geezers. They were made partly taxable as income, in two successive whacks that got past the 800-pound gorilla. They actually affected quite modest incomes, and could be considered double taxation, but my chief objection was that they introduced the element of a needs test to our entitlement.

Nothing helped. The liberal economic columnist Leonard Salk wrote in the *Times* that the federal deficit was "overwhelmingly a consequence of America's military outlays and entitlement programs such as Social Security... together with the nation's unwillingness to pay the taxes needed to finance the expenditures" (January 27, 1988). He apologized manfully in his next column, after I pointed out to him that his pay stubs would show an increase that very month in the bite for Social Security, which had been running a huge surplus. That was in January, 1988, when the overwhelming favorite of the media and the least whelming favorite of the public for the Democratic Presidential nomination was Bruce Babbitt of Arizona. During his brief run, he won raves in *Time, Newsweek, The Washington Post, The New Republic*, the *Washington Monthly*, and *The New York Times* for his advocacy of a national sales tax and a cap on Social Security. In a front-page assessment that sneered at all the other candidates, the *Times* quoted a knowledgeable source as calling the COLA issue "a litmus test for political courage among political reporters." (In the next presidential election, Paul Tsongas passed the same litmus test with the same result; he had become by then a lobbyist for the insurance industry and a crusader for AGE and the Concord Coalition.)

But in that final year of the Reagan administration, a miracle occurred. The White House and Congress, which had been trimming social programs for more than a decade, suddenly voted to extend Medicare to cover pharmaceuticals and catastrophic illness. The *Times* had in fact just protested an assurance by Reagan that everything in the budget but Social Security was on the cutting table, with an editorial demanding "Social Security Cuts, Too." But it joined the rest of the media in preening at the evidence that we were, after all, a caring nation. Passage of the legislation no doubt helped elect George H. W. Bush.... And then—then came what was called, in those words, the revolt of the greedy geezers. It was almost entirely spontaneous and its motives were never accurately explained by the media, but it was powerful enough to cause Congress to repeal overwhelmingly in the autumn of 1989 what it had approved overwhelmingly in the summer of 1988.

Commentaries expressed bafflement, shock, shame, grief, and anger. The *Times* mourned, "Without the catastrophic health care program, the elderly poor will have trouble sleeping at night. For other reasons, so might the elderly affluent, who defeated it." In fact, the program did not affect the elderly poor, as defined by law, since all their needs were in principle covered by Medicaid. As for the elderly affluent, the editorial writer was apparently relying, as was much of the media, on the reporting of Martin Tolchin of the *Times*, who was mystified. One lesson he drew was that opinion polls "can be deceptive." He referred to those showing that 90 percent of the public had supported the bill in 1988, "giving lawmakers little warning of the ambush they would encounter this summer."

Well, how could the public have known what was in the bill? Not from Tolchin. Consider a dispatch of his on its passage that began: "The United States may be a youth culture, but the elderly seem to have cornered the market on political strength. On Capitol Hill there are increasing complaints that elderly are casting too large a shadow over the Congress, and getting more than their share of federal benefits at the expense of the middle-aged and young." He cited as evidence of the conflict between geezer power and Congressional resentment the passage by the Senate of catastrophic Medicare and, on the same day, rejection by the House of "longterm home health care for the elderly." Tolchin was, as it happens, mistaken on all counts. Geezer power was weak and demoralized after a decade of abuse and defeats. The bill beaten in the House called for home care not for the elderly as such but for the handicapped of any age

(Down's syndrome children, for example). And the catastrophic Medicare bill was a big white lie.

When I was tilting at corruption in New York, Tolchin had tried amiably to straighten me out on the decency of politicians and the value of the grease they apply to the gears of democracy. He took this faith to Washington, and it never flagged, through the saving-and-loan, Abscam, Iran-contra, and sundry other scandals. "Lawmakers are more honest and more ethical today than ever before," Martin and his wife, Susan, declare in a new book (*Glass Houses: Congressional Ethics and the Politics of Venom*, 2001). The venom in their subtitle is ascribed to muckrakers. At the climax of the Medicare fiasco, Tolchin was particularly offended by a group of old women in Chicago who were reported to have rocked the limousine of Dan Rostenkowski, the powerful, and totally corrupt, chairman of the House Ways and Means Committee. "Rusty" was what was called a "moderate" Democrat; he had been a key figure in passage of all the Reagan budgets, and he scored points with the media by calling for a cap on Social Security and a further increase in the retirement age. But he readily cleared the catastrophic Medicare bill, which had the approval of all the lobbyists in town, including the AARP.

It purported to meet an acute need. Alone among advanced countries, the United States lacks a national health program. Efforts to adopt one had been beaten back by the American Medical Association from 1936 to 1966, when a compromise was reached: Medicaid for the poor and Medicare for the elderly. They did much good, and some harm. Medicaid was welfare, run by the states, with matching Federal funds, a structure that guaranteed waste, parsimony, and corruption (see Chapter Fourteen). Medicare, financed by a payroll tax and premiums, offered very limited coverage to elderly or disabled people on Social Security. Its nigh fatal shortcomings were that it applied only to them, rather than to the population as a whole, and that it was supervised by care providers, who in the first years allowed doctors and hospitals to simply add the Medicare payments to their bills. Runaway inflation ensued. By 1984 the elderly were paying more out of pocket for health care than they did in 1966 ($2,394 a year, or 18.1 percent of income, on average, against $300 a year, or 15 percent, in 1966, according to the House Select Committee on Aging).

Everybody was hurting, the elderly more than other age groups because they tend to need more care. So when this plan to pay their catastrophic bills came along in 1988, everybody cheered. What nobody mentioned was that it wouldn't cost the government a penny; the elderly would pick up the whole tab, and then some. It was headlined as a plan for the affluent to help the needy. Nobody in the mainstream media seemed ever to have read its terms. They were these: for the first year, $4 was taken from every monthly Social Security check, however small, and all persons over 65 who paid $150 or more in income tax would pay a surtax of 15 percent, up to a maximum of $800. The flat fee and the surtax would go up sharply the following year, and continue to rise as needed. It was surely the world's first tax on age.

Who knew? A front-page analysis in the *Times* described the surtax as being levied on incomes above $35,000. Following a complaint by this geezer, a buried correction said it applied to incomes from $15,000 to $35,000. Nuance. But it was irrevocably fixed in the minds of the working media that the program was a gift by the rich to the most stricken elderly. So it was a shock to supposed beneficiaries to learn they were worse off than before. Many of us were already covered by retirement programs or by private so-called Medigap plans that paid much of what Medicare did not cover. (Robert Pear actually got this backward, explaining that Medicare covered what company plans did not.) In our case, the true beneficiaries would be our employers and insurance companies, who quietly but explicitly planned to reduce their contributions accordingly. And the elderly in general found themselves singled out to pay the soaring bills of the sickest among them.

When the first nicks were taken from Social Security checks and retirees began to study the program, outrage flared. They held teach-ins in community centers, bombarded officials with questions, and gathered petitions, ad hoc. Members of Congress found that they could not come home without facing anger. Hastily, they repealed Catastrophic Medicare before it paid for a single pill (though it did score a clear profit for the Treasury on that year's deduction of $4 a month). Pundits, even liberal ones, never did get it. Murray Kempton accused Democratic Congressmen of pandering to the rich and betraying the poor. Lars-Eric Nelson of the *New York Daily News* proposed, only half in jest, that people who drew Federal benefits be disenfranchised. John Chancellor, another nice guy, said on the air that the only Americans who "made out" in the Reagan years were the elderly, who "robbed the babies." This after salaries for talking heads in his own league had climbed to seven figures.

The bashing never let up. During the six months beginning in September, 1990, I counted no fewer than five op-ed articles in the *Times* traducing the elderly, including one by Peterson (complaining about "free medical care for millionaires"), one by Lamm (raising the ante to "hundreds of thousands of elderly millionaires"), and one by Peterson's actuary, Neil Howe, who blamed the elderly for everything from declining wages for the young to the national debt and the savings-and-loan crisis. When I mentioned this in a column, two writers advised me that they had been invited to comment on the generational divide and had submitted pieces that were sympathetic to the geezers, but they were not printed. The *Times* was by no means the most biased or shrill on the matter, only the most influential. In the historic battle that followed, it could aptly be described in the *Columbia Journalism Review* as the paper that stole the health care debate.

"DELICIOUS PROSPECT"

"The debate over health care reform is dead. Managed competition has won.... Congress now faces a delicious prospect:

come January, it can start with a managed competition blue-print, dot i's and send the President, whether his name is Clinton or Bush, a bill he'd be proud to sign."—*The New York Times,* October 10, 1992.

Conventional wisdom has it that Clinton won by pushing his party to the right. Actually, his share of the vote was a shade less than the feckless Dukakis had obtained four years earlier. Clinton squeaked through at least partly because late in the campaign he picked up the banner of universal health insurance. It was in direct conflict with the philosophy that Clinton and Al Gore had espoused in the Democratic Leadership Council, but they found that nothing roused audiences like a mention of the crisis in medical care.

A movement sparked by doctors and nurses in Boston had spread across the country. It called for replacing Medicare and Medicaid with a "single payer" plan, as in Canada and other countries. They argued that the cost of providing decent care for all, if it needed to be justified, would be largely offset by savings from preventive care and the reduction of red tape, waste, overhead and profit. (For comparison, the administrative cost of Medicare came to about 3 percent, that of private insurance plans about 30 percent.) Understandably, this was viewed with alarm by insurance, pharmaceutical, and private hospital companies, and by the conservative sector of the medical profession led by the A.M.A. At a secret meeting in Jackson Hole, Wyoming, their leaders met with a Clinton aide, Ira Magaziner, and sold him on a counterprogram devised by an eccentric professor named Allen Endhoven, who gave it the oxymoronic logo of managed competition. It called for local agencies to auction off franchises for the operation of competing health maintenance plans. That was the "delicious prospect" proclaimed in that editorial by Michael Weinstein, a disciple of Endhoven's who had joined the *Times*'s editorial board and, as he wrote on that October day, effectively closed the discussion. With one outstanding exception, *Times* reporters followed Weinstein's lead, denigrating socialized medicine abroad and ignoring its advocates at home. The exception was a report by Robin Toner, in the financial section, about the confabulation at Jackson Hole, under the telling headline, "Hillary Clinton's Potent Brain Trust on Health Reform" (February 28, 1993). On the front page five days later, Robert Pear ran what appeared to be a damage control piece strongly and wrongly implying that the A.M.A. was being ignored in planning for the health bill, as was an unidentified group of advocates of Canadian-style "single payer" care that was suing for admission to the hearings. Oddly, Pear's main source had been present at Jackson Hole.

President-elect Clinton had assigned the "delicious prospect" of drafting the bill to Hillary. Rebuffing the "single payer" advocates with contempt, she embraced Endhoven's program and set up an elaborate system of committees to work out its endless details. The meetings were secret; only some five hundred persons took part. The doctors and nurses who led the movement for universal care brought suit to open the proceedings under sunshine law; they failed because Hillary's office falsely advised the court that only government officials were being admitted (far too late, a judge angrily fined the government). In fact, the industries affected were well represented, which added to the irony when at the end they disowned their own misbegotten offspring.

In the year-and-a-half during which this farce went on, a variety of draft bills made their way into print. As a public service, the *Times* published an elaborate comparison of what it considered the four that were in contention. It omitted a fifth, the "single payer" bill, which then listed one hundred sponsors in Congress. It was a classic example of the *Times*'s allergy toward dissent from the left, if universal health care may be considered a leftist notion. By the time Hillary's monster was unveiled in mid-1994, it offered a comic prop for the Republicans. No health plan so much as came to the floor for a vote.

The way the *Times* covered the denouement deserves a bit of detail. On June 10, the lead headline said "Health Legislation Advances in Senate," with the drop head "Two Committees Take Steps on Proposals." Not true. Ted Kennedy's Senate Labor Committee had indeed approved a compromise bill (which then died), but Moynihan's Finance Committee had taken no step whatever. Instead, Moynihan, who had argued that there was no health-care crisis, only a welfare crisis, contemptuously disclosed the outline of a bipartisan proposal that he said his committee would *not* approve. In a passage that may stand as a monument to the *Times*'s passion for objectivity, Adam Clymer wrote:

> Mr. Moynihan's proposal eliminated several politically popular benefits in the Clinton bill, like prescription drugs and long-term care for the elderly and government insurance for early retirees. Mr. Moynihan's willingness to eliminate these provisions, in a year when he is running for re-election, made it clear that he was seriously pushing for health care legislation and not just acting for show.

In other words, Kennedy and anybody else who proposed "politically popular" reforms were showboating, while Moynihan, who had denied there was a health crisis and threatened to hold any bill hostage to his own crusade against welfare mothers, and who had promised that no bill would pass his committee without the support of Bob Dole, was proving that he really wanted reform.

Three days later, a *Times* editorial described the Moynihan proposal as, "in a word, odd." With a wink, it explained: "But Mr. Moynihan was playing politics, not health economics. And his touch appears deft. He offered a bill that, despite differences, borrows heavily from the Clinton plan because he knew it would fail—proving once and for all that the President's plan cannot win and that horse trading is essential."

The news department then took another look, and led the paper on June 16 with "Moynihan Bill a Political Enigma." So on June 10 it was serious, on June 13 it was a trick, and on June 16 it was a puzzle. Go figure.

A story that might well have led the paper on June 16 was relegated to the second section: Empire Blue Cross had been accused of stealing $200 million from Medicare. It exposed a structural flaw in Medicare. Its operation had been turned over to contractors like Blue Cross and Travelers, which sell their own Medigap and other health insurance. Inevitably, they were tempted to pass as much of the cost as possible to Medicare. The lesson might seem to be that it would be cheaper to turn the job over to Social Security. But readers would be hard put drawing any lesson at all from the *Times*'s news report. That was the one in which Robert Pear explained that Medicare was a supplementary program that paid some bills not fully covered by private insurance. It is, of course, the other way around.

In the event, no health care bill reached the floor for a vote in either house. The Clinton plan, a Rube Goldberg monstrosity disowned by its instigators, emerged in a huge pile of paper that Republicans used to demonstrate that government health insurance would be a terrible idea. The public, which had been enthusiastic about it two years earlier, was left confused and dispirited. Across the country that November, millions of Democrats stayed home, and the Republicans captured both houses of Congress.

Over the next six years, policy was effectively determined by agreement between them and Clinton, with the support of a bloc of "moderate" Democrats. The "special interests"—labor, liberals, feminists and the elderly and poor—were shunted aside. A fateful agreement was struck to cap spending and eventually to erase the national debt. Nafta was pushed through with the unanimous and enthusiastic support of the media, over warnings that it would undermine labor conditions and environmental protection. And that pillar of the Social Security system called Aid to Families With Dependent Children was repealed and replaced by an ill-designed system of cash grants to states.

Through it all, liberals defended Clinton as the lesser evil. The battle turned to farce during the Monica Lewinsky affair. There was indeed, as Hillary said, a conservative conspiracy to impeach her husband, but considering the damage he had done to liberalism, I was one of the few on the left who found the fuss amusing. Noting that the first mention of a president in the Constitution specifies how to impeach him, I suggested that there should be no great pother about firing an executive for being caught kanoodling with the office help. It was during that crisis that Clinton engaged in two fateful diversions: the bombing of Afghanistan and the Sudan, and the insertion in a State of the Union address of the slogan "Save Social Security first."

The phrase fixed in the public mind the belief that Social Security was in danger of going broke. It did not call for saving Social Security *as is*—on the contrary, Clinton had expressed sympathy with proposals to privatize it—but he promised that he would not raid the trust funds to reduce the national debt. Thus was born the "locked box" embraced by Gore and Bush in the fall of 2000. It made no sense at all, really, since the trust funds are an accounting myth, an imaginary piggybank stuffed with IOUs, but in any case the overall budget surplus began to vanish with the arrival of a recession six months later, and the notion of eliminating the national debt disappeared in the rubble of September 11. Also gone were bipartisan promises to reduce the cost of prescription drugs and to enact a patients' bill of rights. The drive to divert Social Security funds into the stock market had lost momentum with the collapse of the dot.com bubble and was now suspended, but its advocates nursed the dream, and continued to press for cuts in the COLA and a rise in the retirement age.

For further confessions of a Greedy Geezer, log onto www.seven stories.com. Also see the final Appendix item, "City to Elderly: Drop Dead."

Appendix

1.
A BLOOMING WONDERFUL CITY

Newsday, December 5, 1986

Visiting Paris this autumn, toward the end of the dahlias and the beginning of the chrysanthemums, I looked into a question that must bother every American who travels abroad: Why are *their* public spaces so much more lovingly tended than ours?

The answer, not to leave you in suspense, is that they care more—like, about one hundred times as much.

I didn't pluck that figure from the air. I talked with parks people in Paris and New York, and got these figures: The city of Paris, from its own tax funds, pays about 1,500 gardeners to tend 5,660 acres of parks. New York has fifty-nine gardeners and twelve horticulturists for 25,188 acres. I make that out to be about one skilled hand for 3.7 acres in Paris, and one for 370 acres in New York.

We are rather better off when it comes to trees. Paris' Department of Parks, Gardens and Green Spaces has only about twice as many *bucherons* and *élargueurs* (we call them climbers and pruners) as we do to care for about one-fifth as many trees in parks and along streets.

In an effort to learn why, I visited among other places the new Parc Floral in the Bois de Vincennes and the office of the park staff union, the Syndicat des Espaces Verts. The gardeners and tree trimmers were as friendly as could be, but clearly we were an ocean apart.

For instance, I mentioned Riverside Park, which stretches under my window in Manhattan. I said it was one of our finest, a lovely Olmstead design, and until this year the city had not planted a flower there for forty years or more.

I said volunteers did most of what gardening there was in Riverside and many other places, and tended the trees along our streets if they were tended at all.

I don't think they quite believed me, but they looked worried. They mentioned that Jacques Chirac, the mayor of Paris, who became Prime Minister as well last March, was a great admirer of the Reaganite philosophy of reducing services.

Maurice Pedinotti, a union official, used to head the gardeners who took care of cemeteries. "This time of year," he said, "we'd be setting out chrysanthemums for All Saints Day. It was magnificent. Now they've got a private contractor, comes around once in two or three months. It's sad."

The parks people said Paris did not get special treatment because it was the capital—in fact, many provincial towns did more gardening, in proportion. But allowing for the generally higher standards of public amenities in Europe, the same forces appear to be at work there as in America. For example, jobless youths are being hired to do park work at less than the minimum wage.

Back in New York, a spokesman for the Parks Department told me that in its "Golden Age," Commissioner Robert Moses commanded an army of 80,000 workers. That Golden Age was, of course, the Great Depression, when millions of the unemployed were hired by the federal government to, in the contemptuous phrase of the conservative media, rake leaves. Actually, they built many of our present parks and parkways, among other things.

Do we now need another depression to force us to hire people to improve our parks and restore our public services? Or can we come to see these as rights just as important as our private wants? A poet once wrote that if you have two loaves, you should sell one and "Buy hyacinths to feed thy soul." He no doubt had more than two loaves. So do we. Rather, let's consider whether we should not abandon a few private luxuries to pay for a few public necessities.

2.
STATISTICAL BIAS

EXTRA!, May/June, 2000

When New Yorkers went into shock over the 41 bullets fired at Amadou Diallo, journalist Elizabeth Kolbert found "comfort"—her word—by recalling the sodomizing of Abner Louima. The business with the broomstick, she explained in the *New Yorker* (March 29, 1999), was not what we hire the police to do, whereas we do pay them to accost characters like Diallo who fit a certain pattern. That fusillade, she said, "may not be racism at all but something new, a form of racial bias that is statistically driven and officially sanctioned."

She meant, of course, profiling, and it's hardly new. Nor was there anything new in the thought that bias backed by statistics is not racism. It was a notion that she shared with her former colleagues at *The New York Times*, such as Malcolm Browne and Peter Passell, whose reviews helped make a bestseller of *The Bell Curve*. It's not racism, stupid, it's the stats.

The Diallo shooting brought out a statistical pattern at the *Times*, which was visible one night on its cable TV panel show on New York 1. Two white Metro columnists, John Tierney and Clyde Haberman, urged viewers to grant the police the presumption of innocence (a presumption the police had denied to Diallo); while Bob Herbert and David Ramirez, black and Latino respectively, were critical.

When an appellate court later ruled that the policemen could not find a fair jury in New York City, Herbert was on vacation and Ramirez had been reassigned, so there was nobody to contest the view of four white columnists that the court was quite right. Joyce Purnick also thought it was excessive to accuse the nocturnal manhunters of the Street Crimes Unit ("We own the night") of murder by "depraved indifference" (*The New York Times*, February 17, 2000).

Early on, the *Times*'s Haberman charged Diallo protesters with a sort of depraved indifference to truth and justice (*The New York Times*, March 23, 1999). He said it was they who were stirring up racism, and practicing McCarthyism by applying that foul word to Mayor Giuliani, and he reminded them how soft New York's only black mayor, David Dinkins, had been on black racist crime. Haberman and Tierney alternated in the Metro column in warning that public safety would suffer if the hands of the police were tied.

Actually, stats occasionally published in the *Times* contradicted them. The steep decline in crime began midway through the Dinkins administration. A recent front-pager by Fox Butterfield reported, with stats, that other cities had obtained as good results as New York or better with community outreach and foot patrolling, as promoted by Dinkins (*The New York Times*, March 4, 2000).

Giuliani's statistically driven strategy was to sweep "high-crime" neighborhoods by paramilitary force, stopping and frisking every male deemed suspicious. A state audit of some forty thousand such accostings found that about one out of ten resulted in an arrest. Though it was not widely noted, the Diallo trial revealed a large flaw in this stat: the defendant cops, though required to report every stop-and-frisk, couldn't remember how many they had made even that night, and had no notes to refresh their recollection.

Further light was shed by one of those TV real-life cop shows, which was screened on Court TV during a pause in the trial. The cameras followed a chase through a suburb of three youths who had been waving a pistol and a rifle around. The perps were forced off the road, made to straddle prone, the works. Scary. It turned out that the weapons were toys and the youths were clean-cut and blond. They were let off with a scolding. If they had been black, they surely would have figured in the stats by getting shot or arrested, or both. But bias did not figure in the Diallo trial; the judge ruled it irrelevant.

Even kibitzers on Court TV who were sympathetic to the defense voiced astonishment at the laxity of the prosecution and at the judge's marathon instruction to the jury that it must acquit if the cops might have thought that Diallo was a criminal or that any of them was in danger. They were embarrassed after the verdict when his honor went calling on defense counsel for a farewell embrace.

A final statistic: A poll that weekend found that a majority of the public, upstate and down, thought the verdict was wrong. The editorialists for all three New York City dailies thought it was correct. But they all felt bad about Diallo.

3.
OUR HUNGRY CRITICS

The New York Observer, January 7, 1991

A restaurant consultant summed up the food scene for *Newsday* this way: "The good news is that it's no longer trendy to be trendy. We are beyond arugula...."

The second sentence contradicted the first. Arugula is a delicious green. The only reason to pass it by is that it is last season's green. Which confirms Sacha Guitry's great gibe that nothing is so out of fashion as fashion, and my own mournful footnote that even good fashions are no good, because they must soon perish.

In another life, I was once drafted for a hitch as the *New York Times* food critic. After exhausting the entertainment therein, I applied for my release and left with two parting comments: (1) that anybody who wanted the job should not have it, since nobody who loved to eat well could put up with it, and (2) that as long as food copy was controlled by fashion editors, the nation would eat badly. (The second comment was deleted by the fashion desk.)

Since then, these dyspeptic observations have been repeatedly confirmed. For example, on the weekend after *Newsday* readers were told that trendiness was no longer trendy, the Sunday *Times* magazine food page led off:

"Now that the initial euphoria over the arrival of Italian prosciutto has subsided, the question remains, what to do with it?"

The question remains, what the devil did the chap do with prosciutto when he was still euphoric about it—roll it with arugula and stick it in his ear?

Guest food writers in the *Times* magazine tend to the eccentric. One said she traveled with a bottle of jalapeno sauce to lend taste to her restaurant grub (it leaked in her suitcase). Another said that one Christmas she served "red-white-and-green lasagna, with layers of tomato, turkey and spinach," and confessed charmingly that "everybody seemed vaguely disappointed, including me," so, "I've returned to tradition—with a twist." The twist, which begins with serving curried zucchini soup beside the fireplace, is even weirder than that "lasagna" casserole. Trust me.

These are guest foodies, as the hideous trend-word calls them. The regulars, like the Paris fashions, can be a little odd, too. Consider a review of the Chefs and Cuisiniers Club, a newish restaurant that seems to be near the apex of trendiness. In what I call oxymoronic, on-the-one-hand-but-on-the-other-hand *Times* style, the review exclaims:

"The calf's liver, a special, was so good it could have passed for something other than liver...."

But—

"Osso buco was dark, rich and homey on only one of three tries."

One may deduce that the critic does not care for liver and is either remarkably forbearing or remarkably hungry. A week later, she was saying of another feeding station: "One night, the potato cake accompanying the chicken was soggy; another time it was dry."

Also, one supposes, the portions were too small....

I am perhaps not paying adequate honor to the critic's courage and dedication. Lecturing the manager of another restaurant where "sometimes [the mashed potatoes] are buttery and hot, sometimes neither," she advised that "it's not a good idea to serve aging mussels."

Yet she returned—and was rewarded. "Those spoiled baked mussels were transformed into mussels in a deliciously garlicky parsley sauce with bits of tomato concasse and bread crumbs."

Journalism has its martyrs, but who before would order bad shellfish a second time. Unless—*honni soit qui mal y pense*—the critic tries these out on her guest tasters?

The custom of passing judgment on every item on the menu, ordered not once but on several visits, began after my own hitch. To the naive, it may seem fair and scrupulous (should the drama critics adopt it?), but it is not necessarily conclusive. Witness: "I *think* the coffee ice cream is superb; I am not certain because one night it tasted as if it had been made from instant."

It all makes dining out seem like Russian roulette. If in my day the rule had been that the critical dog must return to his upchuck, I'd never have stomached it. Anyway, the Good Gray Lady would never have let me spend that much money. She had not yet arrived at the frenzy of pretension that characterized the yuppie era.

An example, from that Chefs Cuisiniers review: "The short wine list is good and very 'inside,' just what a group of chefs would select though the general public wouldn't recognize most of the choices."

The *Times* critic did not let the (sneer) general public in on the identity of those snooty "inside" wines, but a review of the same restaurant in the tabloid *Newsday* gave us a clue. It recommended as best buy a Long Island vintage, at only $18 the bottle.

One can go on and on, but that's like reordering bad food, isn't it? One should just note that, in general, poor taste is characteristic of much fashion gush, like that page layout in the *Times* on what the eminences of the rag trade were wearing to AIDS funerals.

Let us, then, leave the hungry critics and enjoy an overlapping category, the inscrutable ones. Join me in savoring the comment by one of my favorites, that the dancer Suzanne Farrell grew up "as an imaginative, rather undisciplined yet spunkily well-behaved little tomboy" and became "a true believer, capable of chilling degree of loyalty and yet staunchly sensible."

Not entirely changing the subject, the Left is often charged with lacking a sense of humor. Well sure, the real world must inspire anger and pity in all of good will, yet the charge overlooks many wonderfully funny artists and writers. Indeed, humor tends to be subversive, and what passes for humor in the Right is often just meanness. A propos, Paul Johnson writing in the right-wing British weekly *The Spectator* that "a woman would prefer to be raped by a man of her own race." One D.A. Roberts responded: "Well, I hadn't thought about the subject in quite those terms before, but I suppose my ideal rapist would be an Oxbridge man with at least a good Upper Second, a lover of early Baroque music, a keen gardener and a competent croquet player, but not an Anglican, a food and wine bore, or a habitual *Spectator* reader."

Peace, and a happy new year to nearly all.

4.
THE SCANDAL OF DAY CARE:
HOW SHARP OPERATORS CHEAT YOUR CHILDREN

Working Woman, May, 1977

For openers, let's leave No-Nose out of this. Day care has enough enemies as it is. Besides, there is no evidence that Fred (No-Nose) DeLucia, a late soldier in the Brooklyn Mafia family of Joseph Colombo, ever had anything to do with day-care centers. To be sure, No-Nose's brother Frank was a partner of John Gurino, who built at least six centers with money borrowed from a Mafia-controlled union welfare fund, at 18 and 20 percent interest, repaid by the taxpayers. But No-Nose himself has been long missing, like many another soldier in the Brooklyn gang wars, so let him rest in peace.

He is mentioned here because his name was cited in a recent legislative report on New York City's day-care scandals. Official investigators like to bring out a Mafia connection because it's glamorous. Also, it deflects attention from the fact that, as will be seen, very solid citizens indeed—respected lawyers, promoters, and high city officials—have cooperated in a rip-off that figures ultimately to exceed one-third of a billion dollars of day-care funds. That is equivalent to one-third of all the money the federal government will spend on day care this year, and it's three times the reduced budget of New York City for day care.

One has misgivings about opening this can of worms. Scandals have always been used to justify the crippling of social programs. Indeed New York State, bled white by theft and waste in its welfare programs, has been slashing them across the board, so that children and working mothers and the elderly sick are being made to pay for the failures of politicians. The abuses that have been revealed in all of the great social programs of the 1960s—Medicare, Medicaid, Head Start, free lunches, job training—have been cited to prove that "you can't solve a problem by throwing money at it." The truth is that we have thrown money at politicians, not problems.

Organized child care in the United States has been at best a relief program since it began more than a century ago, with foundling homes. As recently as 1973, a report of the Day Care and Child Development Council of America said: "Too often, public institutions for children provide abysmally poor services, with nobody to care what goes on in the back wards." Things improved, paradoxically, during the Great Depression of the 1930's, when federal funds were made available for the first time through the Works Progress Administration to operate day-care services, primarily to provide jobs for unemployed teachers. This experience turned out to be a national resource during World War II, when child-care aid was granted to enable women to staff the arms factories.

After the war, the funds stopped. Congress assumed that women would now return to their homes, and most of the subsidized centers closed. Then, New York City women community leaders and working mothers played a pioneer role. Fighting City Hall and the State Capital, they attained grudging appropriations of local welfare funds that helped some of the nurseries to keep operating, in church basements, settlement houses, public housing, and brownstones. It was one of the few places in the country where public funds were used for such a purpose.

In the early 1960s, modest federal grants were made for child care, but most were used up by studies and drafting of standards. Then operating funds were appropriated in 1964 for the Head Start program, aimed at giving an educational and nutritional lift to the preschool children of the poor; despite many shortcomings, Head Start centers are rated among the better ones today.

A considerable expansion was opened up by the Social Security Act of 1967, which offered federal funds for child care, in essence to enable women who otherwise would be on welfare to take jobs. But no federal funds were available for the construction of new centers—and that was what led to the great New York rip-off.

A Bonanza for Landlords

Politicians and professionals alike quickly realized that the operating costs of new centers would include the rents; and the rents could be set high enough to cover the building costs, with Washington paying 75 percent. A state law was passed to underwrite mortgages for any non-profit group that proposed to build a center, provided it met all plans and regulations. That was the rub. Anthony Ward and Annice Probst of the Bank Street Day Care Consultation Service recall what happened.

"The red tape," Ward said, "was such that community groups couldn't get through. Inez Padilla had a fine program set for East New York which was turned down because the site was too close to the elevated subway tracks. Six months later, the city signed a lease for the same site with a private developer. A Bedford-Stuyvesant group had six projects turned down, and Catholic Charities had ten—they were even more innocent than we were. Only six nonprofit projects, out of 430, were ever approved."

This was 1969, an election year in New York City. Handsome John V. Lindsay was the liberal republican Mayor, and new programs of all kinds were mushrooming. Federal seed money was forthcoming and the banks were very generous with loans. On the ground that the community day-care groups were too slow about building new centers, City Hall authorized the Department of Real Estate to sign fifteen-year and twenty-year leases with private developers who would do the job. The rent, taxes, and utilities would be paid by the city's new Agency for Child Development, which would turn the premises over to community groups at no charge. These were the "direct leases" as opposed to the "indirect leases" of centers that found their own quarters at minimal cost to taxpayers.

Lindsay' Commissioner of Real Estate, Ira Duchan, wasted no time. He put a little ad in *The New York Times*, and the developers came running. But some were luckier than others. Ten of the first fifteen leases were awarded to Sam Getz, whose lawyer was Assemblyman Leonard Simon of Brooklyn. Curiously just at that time, Simon broke with the Democratic Party organization to support the re-election campaign of Mayor Lindsay who was a Republican at that time.

The figures cannot be precise because the identity of the buyers was concealed by private corporations, held in the name of lawyers. In the end, Getz built at least twenty-six centers. Another big beneficiary was Euclid Avenue Associates, which had strong ties with the Republicans through one of its principals, N. Hilton Rosen, and with the Democrats through its law firm, Shea, Gould, Climenko and Kramer. A partner in Shea, Gould was then Democratic city chairman, and the firm continues to be a party powerhouse. Still another multiple builder of the direct-lease centers was the aforementioned John Gurino, who was financed by a shady union welfare fund to which he paid up to 20 percent interest as its share of the take.

Sam Getz, the champion builder of day-care centers, turned out not to be interested in owning them. He sold all but three of his, often before they had even been occupied. The reason was that Duchan had been so generous with the rental terms that the properties became gold mines for well-heeled buyers. Here is how it worked:

In most cases the promoters were able to take Duchan's leases to the bank and borrow more money than the cost of the land and the construction combined. (The land was often picked up for a song at city auctions of tax-delinquent slum properties. In at least one case, the builder leased the site from the city, cheaply.) So the builders started off with a windfall profit—there was no investment of their own funds, and they were assured rentals over the terms of the leases, usually twenty years, with the city paying the taxes, utilities, and most of the maintenance.

Shoddy Construction

Duchan figured the rents at $3.75 a square foot, which some builders considered not too excessive, but he applied it also to the roofs and basements, so that the city would pay four-story rentals for two-story buildings. Neither his nor any other city agency supervised the planning or construction, so a characteristic of the new centers was their vast amounts of unusable space—wide corridors, windowless little offices, etc.—and leaking and unsafe roofs, flooded basements, poor kitchens, and general shoddiness.

In one typical project on Livonia Avenue in Brooklyn, an audit showed a nominal cost for site and construction of $956,021, which included the builder's profits. The mortgage came to $1,034,000, so the builder started out with a windfall of $78,000, and a lease guaranteeing him $147,000 a year in rent for twenty years, with the city paying the utilities, normal maintenance, and taxes. (For some curious reason, the city chose to pay the landlords 130 percent of their rent each month, so that they could pay the taxes when they fell due. An unrelated investigation revealed that many of the real-estate owners who rent to the city were delinquent in their tax payments.) And on opening day, the basement of this Brooklyn day-care center was flooded. It has remained unusable since.

The less the promoters spent on construction, the more they put into their own pockets. So, for example, they installed baseboard electric heating, which is the cheapest system to put in and by far the most expensive to use; New York City's electricity rates are the highest in the country; and this last hard winter, the virtually bankrupt city took a beating on this count alone.

In many of the centers, incidentally, the electrical work was done by Sheldon Biel, a politically well-connected contractor. Like some other subcontractors, he took part of his pay in the form of partnerships in the ownership of centers. This meant that the promoters could use for other ventures the cash that they normally would have had to pay for construction. It is notable, too, that an unusual number of the projects were insured by the City Title Insurance Company, in which the Brooklyn Democratic leaders Meade Esposito and Stanley Steingut were principals. Presumably as a sop to ghetto politicians, the liability insurance on the day-care centers themselves was placed by the city, without bidding, with Bowman Procope Associates, a well-connected black agency. (A church center, cut off from city funds because of the fiscal crisis last year, found that it could buy insurance at half the price that the city had been paying.)

People Pay

Now, city property records show an extraordinary "churning" of the titles of the direct lease centers. Ownerships changed hands with bewildering speed, as many as eighteen times in less than a year for a single center. Sometimes they passed to new owners, more often back and forth among the same principals. But, if these were such gold mines, why were the owners so eager to sell? Realty men smiled at the naiveté of my question. Property, especially while under construction, is a safer tax haven than a Swiss numbered account, they explained.

When a bill for construction or a mortgage payment falls due, for example, a taxpayer in the upper brackets may find it advisable to have the property in his name; the payment then becomes a deduction from his income. He may immediately transfer the property back to the corporation, so as to avoid personal future liability. Profits can be directed where they will do the most good, and outsiders who can use the write-offs may be brought in, for a price. Thus the ordinary taxpayer is taken by the day-care operation in two ways: by the direct outlays for rents and by the loss of tax revenues that otherwise would have been paid by the promoters and their syndicate partners.

By 1972, New York City was spending more for daycare than the maximum allowed by Social Security and had to dig into its own funds and those of the state for the difference. (The federal government paid 75 percent of the cost up to the maximum and the city and state shared the rest.) By 1975, the state put its own lid on, and the city's financial roof was caving in. It responded by ordering the closing of twenty-eight of the 435 subsidized centers and reducing the programs of others. (Six months later, it closed forty-nine more and cut back at seventeen, up to ninety more closings are threatened at this writing.)

Significantly, nearly all of the centers being closed were among those paying little or no rent, in churches, schools, housing projects, and such. Officials of the Agency for Child Development acknowledged that they had been told to leave the direct-lease centers alone. One exception was the Roc-Somers Day-Care Center, in a direct-lease building in Brooklyn. It was among the twenty-eight closed on December 31, 1975. But it reopened three moths later under a new management loyal to Councilman Sam Wright, a powerful Democrat. To provide it with children, the city closed two neighborhood centers, one of them in a school and the other in a housing project.

Investigations Prove Futile

As the crunch began in the fall of 1975, Inez Padilla, the day-care organizer who had been rebuffed in her effort to build a center in East New York, began an investigation. Along with colleagues in the Bank Street Service and with Wayne Barrett, an aide to State Senator Major Owens, a Brooklyn Democrat, she combed the city archives. Without experience or special training, they came up with a monumental study of interlocking ownerships and official negligence or worse.

Inez Padilla and her colleagues were upset when they presented their findings to city officials and were asked, "Why didn't you complain before?" They had. Way back in 1971, the day-care people in the Bank Street service had been outraged by the evidence of abuses in the building program. They weren't being consulted about the sites for centers, which were being built where the landlords wanted them, regardless of need. So there were four centers going up in one devastated neighborhood of the Bronx, while other areas, especially in Manhattan, were under-served. They weren't being consulted, either, about the design of the buildings, which was awful, or the quality, which was often worse.

"Our assumption was that the direct-lease program was a rip-off," says Tony Ward of Bank Street. So they went to the City Department of Investigation. In short order there were inquiries by that department, by the office of City Comptroller (now mayor) Abraham Beame and by the state comptroller. All found gross improprieties and abuses in the 138 direct-leases then granted: that the rents were excessive, that site-planning was inexistent, that construction was unsupervised and shoddy, that leases apparently had been granted to a few politically favored groups, that windfall profits had been made, that there was no provision for canceling leases if these centers had to be closed. All recommended that these short-comings be corrected forthwith. The Investigation report ended: "This department is continuing its investigation to determine if there is any evidence of improper or corrupt practices on the part of any City employees."

The Bank Street people assumed that the wrongs would be righted, and they went back to their work on improving the quality of day care. What did not occur to them was that Duchan and City Hall would not change their ways.

From 1972 through 1975, Duchan approved seventy-eight more direct-lease projects. Rents went up from $3.75 a square foot to $5 and then more than $6. In the end, the city was committed to pay a total of more than one-third of a billion dollars over the twenty years of the program, not counting utilities.

Far from negotiating rent reductions, as the official reports had recommended, Duchan actually amended at least twelve leases already signed, to grant increases on the order of 50 percent. When this came to light, he explained that the increases were necessary to meet rises in building costs, and so to enable the developers to qual-ify for bank mortgages. (The files on many of these transactions have turned up missing. The landlords who benefited, incidentally, later unanimously refused to negotiate the leases downward, to help the city in its crisis.) All those deals were approved by Mayor Beame, ignoring the earlier advice of Comptroller Beame.

Last fall, I called on Duchan, a stocky and placid man, and asked him why he had ignored the investigation reports. He replied that he had never seen them. He did explain, however, why he had so many bank accounts (at that time investigators had located more than thirty, and have reportedly found many more since). His wife, he said, just liked having lots of bank accounts, and they didn't amount to much.

I then asked Nicholas Scoppetta, who was now Commissioner of Investigation, what had become of the "continuing" inquiry into possible corruption that had been announced by his department in 1971. He said he had no record of any further investigation then, but one was on now, and the district attorney was involved too.

In fact, there was one indictment that arose almost accidentally from the 1971–72 probes. It was that of Salvatore Indiviglia, then chief architect of the Department of Social Services, who had approved all the direct-lease designs. He pleaded guilty to a reduced count of bribery, involving the receipt of $2300 from a partner in Euclid Avenue Associates, and served several months in jail. Typically, the partner, who had cooperated with the district attorney, was not charged, and was not publicly identified.

That is all that happened on the investigative front until Inez Padilla and her colleagues went to work in late 1975. When they reported their new findings there was a flurry of investigations by the same agencies that had looked into the problems in 1971–72, and they came up with the same shocking data. The city comptroller's office called the direct-lease program "an enormous give-away of public funds," but had no program for recapturing these funds except to withhold part of the rent until essential repairs were made in some particularly dilapidated new centers. (At that, landlords filed seventeen lawsuits to fight this move.) The state comptroller's office said, "We told you so." The office of Assembly Speaker Stanley Steingut pointed a finger at the Mafia, dragging in poor No-Nose DeLucia. But meanwhile, the office of the Governor and the Agency for Child Development were busy cutting off funds to day-care centers and lowering the income-eligibility standards for poor working mothers, in order to reduce the losses.

Nothing, they said, could be done to break the sanctity of the direct leases, which were now according for one dollar out of every five spent by the city for the whole program. Unless, that is, somebody could prove criminal conspiracy— which nobody seemed prepared to do. "Do you think," demanded a friend of Duchan's, "that he would have signed those leases on his own?"

As it happened, there was one indictment in the 1976 leasing scandal, as there had been in 1972, and again it was almost accidental. An inquiry into an unrelated case led to the arrest of Duchan's director of leasing, Michael R. Palumbo, for accepting $3,000 from a broker for William Achenbaum. The gratuity involved the leasing to the city of an office building that belongs to Achenbaum, who also owns a string of day-care centers. When I called him on the day of the Palumbo indictment, he was surprised.

"I really cannot understand Mr. Palumbo's having taken or not taken (graft)," he said, "since the negotiations were basically handled by the Commissioner of Real Estate. My meetings were with Commissioner Duchan."

Duchan, who had been consulted on the matter, left "on a motoring trip" and could not be reached for weeks. Soon after he returned, he was allowed to retire "for health reasons" on a full and irrevocable pension of $25,000 a year. The Department of Investigation had thirty days in which to file charges of impropriety or laxity that could have blocked the pension, but said it could find no evidence in so short a time. Soon afterward, Commissioner Scoppetta was promoted to deputy mayor . . .

Where Were the Feds?

Now, in principle, three-quarters of what New York City is spending for day care comes from Washington. And where were the Feds while all this was going on? An aide in the Department of Health, Education, and Welfare confided: "We look to the states to make sure that everything is being done that should be done. My personal view is that nobody is doing anything."

Actually, HEW did do a nationwide survey in 1975 and published it last August. Delving in it, one learns that twenty-seven states have no program for evaluating day-care centers, that only half visit centers at least once a year to see how they are doing, and that many states were unable to account for money spent. (New Jersey recently acknowledged that $1 million was missing.) In New York State, which spent $449 million on day care in fiscal 1976, the report said:

"State respondents cited the highly politicized nature of day-care services as a significant problem in program continuity. They felt that the state's commitment to day care depends too heavily on personal politics and preferences of public officeholders and not enough upon public need."

The objection appeared to be rather to the resistance of communities cutting back on day care than to the theft of public funds, for the report actually gave high marks to New York's fiscal management!

After the scandal broke, HEW went back to New York City for another look. Its specialists on child care found conditions good, but its safety inspectors found "disturbing" hazards in the fifteen centers visited. However, the HEW auditors, after reading the local investigative studies, came up with the amazing conclusion that costs in direct-lease centers were "not significantly different" from those in other centers.

This sheds more light on the caliber of HEW auditing, such as there is, than it does on the New York situation. The auditors found that the average cost in direct-lease centers was $66.88 per child per week, while that in the centers that provided their own housing was $60.38. That's already a difference of 10 percent, on the face of it. But what the auditors did not appear to realize was that the city set the budget for each center arbitrarily, without regard to its rental cost. So a center that was rent-free might get as much money per child as one where the landlord was collecting $23.51 per child per week, which is the average for direct-lease centers. And that does not include utilities, which are ten times higher in the shoddy direct-lease premises, or taxes, which the city pays only for direct-lease centers. The indirect-lease centers simply had that much more money to spend for child care.

The basic problem with HEW, in the view of many professionals in the field, is that for the eight years of the Nixon and Ford administrations, the department was headed by people who were philosophically hostile to the Great Society programs of the 1960s. Insofar as they were required by law to carry them out, they tossed billions of dollars to the states, with little or no effort to police its use. As a result, untold amounts were stolen or wasted, in Medicare, Medicaid, lunch programs, job training, and child care. When some of this was revealed by local investigations, the resulting scandals were exploited to discredit and cut back on these vitally needed services.

Official Neglect

Thus New York City last year laid off one thousand of the eight thousand staff workers in subsidized day-care centers and cut the number of children served by 7,300, to 36,000. It also changed the income and employment qualifications for mothers, so as to threaten the eligibility of half those remaining.

This was a source of self-congratulation to the state government. When a civic group appealed for a special state commission to investigate the direct-lease scandals and the day-care crisis, a spokesman for Governor Hugh Carey replied that such a good job of cost-cutting was being done that a special investigation "doesn't seem appropriate at this time."

Workers in the field agree that the philanthropic and educational establishments tend to look down on day care as a luxury for middle-class women or at best a necessary evil for the most disadvantaged poor. But no one has been listening to the voices of working women, of student mothers, of overworked housewives who cannot afford private care. When they are heard, it will be seen that quality care of preschool children is a normal function of any educational system, at least as important as colleges are to the health of our society.

This should be a high-priority issue for the Carter-Mondale administration. When he catches his breath, the vice president might well direct his efforts toward resurrecting his comprehensive child-development bill that was vetoed by Nixon. When that is done—

and eventually, I believe, it must be done—care must be taken to avoid theft and waste. Private promoters must be rigorously excluded, and auditing must be first-rate; yet community groups should be encouraged to run neighborhood programs free from unduly rigid guidelines.

In building such a national program, the record of New York should be studied as a rich source of information on what should and what should not be done.

5.
THE ROLE OF JOURNALISM

from MORE

Perhaps the most imminent threat to civil liberties today is the notion that the media pose a threat to civil liberties. Gag orders are issued in the name of justice; government files are sealed to protect people who might be indicted if their contents were known; bills are introduced to make it a crime to leak or publish damaging information.

The campaign is, in a way, flattering. It suggests that the media are so hungry for scandal that they let no consideration of justice stand in their way. Well, Lord knows we have our faults, but an excess of investigative zeal is not one of them. In the year of Watergate, as *Washington Post* publisher Katharine Graham has pointed out, "It got awfully lonesome." So why are Graham and such other lonely practitioners as *The Village Voice* suddenly switching sides? Why are they warning that, as a recent *Voice* headline put it, "Investigative Journalism Can Be Dangerous"?

One reason is that *The Washington Post* was vindicated, that some of the truth about Watergate, Vietnam, the C.I.A. and corporate bribery has been brought to light and that, here and there around the country, a scattering of investigators has been digging up bad news. This is upsetting to the Establishment and to many conventional citizens, including some of the journalists who had not reported the scandals now revealed on their own beats. It is natural that those who feel threatened should strike back. It is less natural that so dedicated a champion of the underdog as Nat Hentoff of the *Voice* should charge to the defense of endangered politicians. It is disturbing that under the headlines "Punish the Prosecutors!" he supports still another proposed law aimed at plugging leaks. To be sure, Hentoff shies away from a clause that would punish defense lawyers, as well as prosecutors, for "trying their cases in the press." But he goes along with the idea that the First Amendment threatens the rights of privacy and due process. I submit that Hentoff and his colleagues are confused about their priorities, confused about civil rights and confused about journalism.

Consider the situation in New York. At this moment, largely as a result of newspaper exposés, the speaker and the majority leader of the Assembly are under indictment and the Democratic state chairman and several judges are fighting grand jury subpoenas. On Christmas Eve, Governor Carey tried to sack Special Prosecutor Maurice Nadjari, only to run into a firestorm when Nadjari revealed that he had been investigating the Governor's circle. An opinion poll showed that an overwhelming majority of the public did not believe Carey's claim that he simply wanted a more effective cleanup of the judiciary. Yet a surprising number of political writers did buy that claim, at least in part. Without denying that the sale of judgeships was a traditional practice in New York, they made the central issues the ones that the pols had drawn: the alleged incompetence of the prosecutor, and the impropriety of Nadjari's leaks to the press.

Pious indignation is the mode. We must draw no inferences from the fact that the politicians are fighting to avoid testifying before a grand jury, and when indicted, to delay their trials. Above all, we must keep in mind the sacred presumption of innocence. Yet the indicted speaker and majority leader have not only kept their powerful posts in the Assembly, but also received warm testimonials from fellow pols. A rally for one of them was attended by two judges, a swarm of legislators and Congresswoman Bella Abzug, who is running hard for the Senatorial nomination. She explained: "Everyone is innocent until proven guilty."

The statement is at once an absurdity and the glory of our judicial system. In the real world, it simply isn't so; lots of guilty people are never convicted, and some innocent ones are found guilty. But our courts must act *as if it were true*, in order to bar punishment without due process of law. Apply this principle to the press, and we are dead; Hentoff could never get away with calling Nadjari a bum if he first had to persuade twelve jurors that it was true beyond a shadow of a doubt.

I forget which philosopher wrote that liberty is obedience to the law—a nice paradox meaning that only law can protect the individual against tyranny. That's what civil liberty is all about: the protection of the weak. To write about it in the abstract, as if it had nothing to do with the real world, is to fall into folly.

A remarkable example is the article in the *Voice* headed "The Dangers of Investigative Journalism." The writer, Phil Tracy, tells us that he came "precariously close" to publishing an anonymous tip that a bribe had been paid to get a suspended sentence for a friend of the governor. The man, it appears, had "involved himself in a series of financial transactions which were ultimately characterized by the district attorney's office as grand larceny and forgery." (Translation: the guy was a crook. Note that, where "financial transactions" are involved, the presumption of innocence persists even after conviction.) Luckily, the tip came in too close to deadline for Tracy to publish it that week, he says, and it didn't stand up on further inquiry. Conclusion; "I only hope that... the reformers—particularly newspapers—do not become so insensitive to the power that they have that they become almost as evil as the people they are seeking to uproot."

The problem posed here was an elementary one of journalistic responsibility and fair play, and Tracy flunked it. He managed to do precisely what he was saying that he had damned near done: he published an anonymous charge of a criminal conspiracy, naming names, and now wants a medal for calling it false, although he does not prove that, either. At the same time, he escaped a real story that was under his nose: "I further discovered [!] that in cases similar to this one, where the guilty party has made partial restitution eventually, judges often give suspended sentences."

It is, to be sure, an old story: "The law locks up both man and woman / Who steal the goose from off the common / But lets the greater felon loose / Who steals the common from the goose." It has become an acutely current issue now, however, in part because for the first time a very substantial number of the powerful have been exposed as lawbreakers. The Presidential pardon, the tennis-playing sentences, the acquittals and the lecture fees incurred by the mighty and the near-mighty cannot fail to impress the less privileged. A resulting cynicism about the law is surely a greater danger to our liberties than is an irresponsible press.

When prisoners rioted in an overcrowded city jail recently, *The New York Times* mentioned in passing that they had been waiting up to six months for trial. Presumption of innocence? Not for those too poor and friendless to post bail. As a matter of fact, bail is almost never required of persons of status who, in Tracy's words, may be involved in transactions that some district attorney may characterize as criminal. Out of twenty-four indicted to date in the New York nursing-home scandals, only one, to my knowledge, has been required to post bail. He was a kitchen helper, accused of lying to a grand jury about his boss's thefts of food. The boss drew a conditional discharge—even lighter than probation—on his confession to having stolen $60,000 from Medicaid. Another operator, who stole $187,000, drew probation from a judge who was tougher than the prosecutor. All four owners convicted so far—two of them notorious for abuse of patients—are still running nursing homes and will keep their licenses while their lawyers exhaust all the resources of due process, which will take years.

This is not to suggest that the rich and powerful should not have the same civil rights as the poor and weak, only that they don't have the same problems. Few prosecutors have the staffs, the time, and the will to go after what is misleadingly called "white collar crime." (The clerk who is caught tapping the till is in a different predicament altogether from the corporation president found to be conspiring to fix prices.) And those who do have the capacity point out that the courts are reluctant to send a solid citizen to prison. As a lawyer commented cynically, we reserve harsh punishment for slobs who cannot measure the risks of crime, while withholding it from those who can.

The problem is frankly acknowledged by Charles J. Hynes, New York's special prosecutor for nursing homes. A dedicated and scrupulous law man, he graciously credits his appointment to exposés in the media. Yet a recent speech of his was headlined "Hynes Details Steps to Curb Media Abuse" and described his need to "defuse the lynch mob attitude" and "pressure for indictments."

Et tu, Hynes? Considering that no publication had cried for the blood of a nursing-home promoter, nor had ever criticized Hynes since his appointment a year earlier, although he had yet to send a perpetrator to prison, his remarks might stir surprise. But most observers took Hynes to be trying to spare himself the obloquy that has been falling on the special prosecutor for abuses in the criminal justice system, Nadjari. In other words, Hynes was attacking the media because the media were attacking the media.

To oversimplify a bit, the criticisms of Nadjari boil down to two counts: that some of his indictments of judges have been thrown out by other judges, and that he leaks to reporters. As for the first count, it would be hard to determine what a good batting average is, since few prosecutors have ever indicted a judge, and there is no reason to believe that the judiciary is any more enthusiastic about cleaning house than is, say, the American Medical Association. (More broadly, it is easy for a prosecutor to bat close to 1.000 if he only goes after patsies. That goes for media crusaders as well.) Journalists should rejoice that, at last, somebody is going after crooks in black robes, while hoping that he does a good job of it.

As for the second count, there is no reason to suppose that Nadjari is any more prone to leak than virtually all the other district attorneys, sheriffs and police officials I have seen since I was a cub reporter in Arizona more than thirty years ago. Leak is a mild word for dragging a poor wretch in handcuffs before the cameras, an everyday practice that disgraces the law and should shame the media. All honor to Hentoff for denouncing it. But while it takes a willing press to make this misconduct worthwhile for lawmen, their offenses are different in kind. The task of the lawman is to enforce the rule of law, with all its restrictions. The task of the journalist is to report the news as fairly, accurately and meaningfully as he can. Both proceedings, unfortunately, inflict some punishment on the accused. That cannot be helped, but should be minimized.

Unfortunately, a great deal of journalistic energy is wasted on hunting the cheap scoop—the advance tip on who is going to be indicted. Good reporters try to dig up news that would not be printed, ever, if they didn't get it. In this effort, the leak plays a precious role. Most civil servants and corporation employees know things that the public ought to know, but never will unless they tip us off.

So do district attorneys, and members of grand juries. The obstacles to prosecuting crimes of politicians and corporations are so great that many improprieties and felonies known to them are never made public. It is proper that we require law enforcers, to whom we grant such enormous powers of prying, to keep their mouths shut. But I do not believe that this bars a reporter from publishing leaks from such sources. (Where an official cover-up is involved, as in the Pentagon Papers, Watergate or the crimes of the C.I.A., there is no problem. A reporter should seek out leaks, and publish them without hesitation.)

On the one hand, we should not ask prosecutors to do our work for us. On the other hand, we should not join the clamor against investigative reporting, as if it were a threat to our civil liberties.

There are, of course, leaks and leaks. Henry Kissinger, the champion leaker of state secrets who for years basked in the adoration of the press (remember Super K, and Henry the Sexpot?), now sobs about McCarthyism when he faces a bit of criticism. (Where was the professor when McCarthy was riding?) Agnew, Nixon, Mitchell, they were all victims of the media, all targets of treacherous leaks, all being found guilty without due process. Their defenders cried that in view of the lynch atmosphere stirred up by the press, it would be impossible for those heroes to get a fair trial. But none went to prison, or indeed suffered anything comparable to the fate of a poor slob in the toils of the law. That is a real danger to civil liberties, in that it encourages contempt for the law.

There is a French witticism that every state grants its subjects the right to cry "God save the King!"; the test of liberty is whether they may cry "Down with the King!" That is why the Founding Fathers placed freedom of speech in the First Amendment, well ahead even of due process. With freedom of speech, the rest of the Bill of Rights may be defended. Without it, there is no Bill of Rights. So let's worry a bit less about the dangers of investigative journalism and a bit more about the danger of *non*-investigative journalism.

6.
THE SHAME OF THE URBAN PRESS

The Nation, September 27, 1986

When a reporter asked the Mayor of New York whether he shouldn't have known about the massive corruption in his administration, he replied, characteristically, "Did *you* know?" Even in New York, that was not much of an answer, but it was a good question. In an era of overt corruption of government, it may fairly be said that the major media would rather not know about it.

In New York City, for example, everyone was aware that Mayor Koch had received millions of dollars in campaign contributions from donors who received billions of dollars in benefactions from his office, yet the media kept saying that his integrity could not be questioned. Indeed in January [1986], after one of Koch's cronies had attempted suicide and officials were being enveloped in a snow-fall of subpoenas, Joyce Purnick of *The New York Times* felt obliged to say of the Mayor in a column:

> He is recognized by everyone, even his die-hard political ene-mies, as impeccably honest. He also puts public service on a pedestal, prizes it more than any other profession and gets more plaudits than most public officials for the quality of his appointments.

It was prudent of Purnick not to be more specific, because there was no major department of the Koch administration untainted by scan-dal and flagrant incompetence, and scores of his top appointees would be gone before the leaves of autumn. To be sure, a less flat-tering portrait of the hero had been drawn by three City Hall reporters in a book, *I, Koch*, published last year. They described him as a bigot, a bully, an egomaniac and a twister from way back. But they acknowledged that this was not the picture they conveyed to the public when they were on the City Hall beat. They could not explain why.

Let's try.

To begin with, their bosses did not want the muck to be raked. In a democracy, it's not possible to bury all of the dirt all of the time, but heaven knows they do their best. It may be said that since Water-gate, to paraphrase Adam Smith, our media merchants seldom meet on the most innocent occasions without ending on a note of alarm at an imagined excess of investigative zeal. Take Wes Gallagher, former general manager of the Associated Press, who told an appreciative session of the American Newspaper Publishers Association that "the First Amendment is not a hunting license." Or consider the swan song of Michael J. O'Neill as editor of the New York *Daily News* and president of the American Society of Newspaper Editors. It was a tirade against reportorial nosiness. The press, he said, had undermined and demoralized authority, and must now "set matters straight." It should "make peace with the government," be "more positive, more tolerant of the frailties of human institutions," lest it "undermine public confidence and, without intending to, become a cause rather than just a reporter of national decline.

"On balance," he seesawed,

> investigative reporting probably has done more good than harm, though a wise member of the *New York Times* editorial board, Roger Starr, would dispute the point. He once suggested wistfully that journalism schools should ban Lincoln Steffens' famous book, *The Shame of the Cities*. He said that muckraking did so much damage to the cities that he hated to think what havoc modern investigative reporting might cause.

Starr made his meaning plainer in *The Rise and Fall of New York City*, which Mayor Koch, in a jacket blurb, called brilliant. The book says the city's downfall was due to rent control, welfare, and public hygiene, which, by keeping alive slum infants who otherwise would die, helped create a mammoth class of born criminals. But Starr was not against all crime. "Graft," he wrote, "is an important safety valve against the possibility of ineffective government. If a government is weak enough, the official who takes graft and accomplishes something in return can be a hero.... In a government as good as New York's has been, much graft is of a minor, rather benign sort." And so on.

Starr may have come by laissez-faire views naturally. Born and bred in the building-materials business, he became a leading propagandist for New York property owners and developers, defending Robert Moses' assault on the urban infrastructure, then became the city housing commissioner before finally becoming the *Times*'s chief editorialist on city affairs. But his neoconservative philosophy was neither original nor unique when he arrived at the *Times*.

Ken Auletta, a prominent New York journalist who deplored the post-Watergate vogue of investigative journalism, used to publish New Year's greetings to just about all the pols in town. In wishing them a happy 1977 in the *Village Voice*, he described pols in general as decent folks who had to worry about "zealous prosecutors who would indict them for 'crimes' they do not understand; about journalists who confuse custom with corruption; about constituents who come to lump them all together as common crooks."

He also had a kind word for each politician. Even then, it seems, Anthony Ameruso was notorious. Auletta greeted him thus: "The city's capable highway commissioner hails from the clubhouse. Shame! So did Al Smith." And Donald Manes rated this: "The Queens County leader (and borough president) doesn't bullshit his friends, or the press."

Most city reporters would have said the same about Ed Koch, the antimachine Democrat who would be elected mayor that year with the secret endorsement of the borough machines, who reappointed Ameruso against the advice of associates, and who became thick as thieves with Manes and the other county bosses of both parties.

The exposure by the Feds of corruption in Ameruso's department led to Manes's suicide early in 1986, which in turn set off a pinwheel of criminal investigations that for a season overwhelmed the media. Observing the fireworks, Andy Logan of the *New Yorker* recalled a scene from the 1981 Inner Circle revue staged by the City Hall press gang, in which reporters acting as party bosses sang: "Give us a little deal, will ya, Ed? / Grease up our little wheel, will ya, Ed? / Gosh, oh gee, /Why do you refuse? I can't see /What you've got to lose." There was the real Ed Koch, just down the hall from the press room, giving away the store to the politicians every day, but he kept saying he did not deal with bosses, so they believed him.

As with Auletta writing about Manes, it was a matter of being able to recognize bullshit when it was being laid on them.

7.
CITY TO ELDERLY: DROP DEAD

Newsday, August 2, 1991

Filthy streets and shabby parks tell all the world that New York, the richest and most dynamic city on earth, is too mean and stupid to keep up a civilized appearance. There is worse that does not meet the eye.

For example, New York *Newsday*'s story the other day about a couple in their 80s, waiting in vain for their daily hot meal. It said they were among 6,680 homebound persons who were cut off from this lifeline as of July 1. Mayor Dinkins has since announced that the hot meals will be restored, but he said nothing about home care for the disabled elderly or transportation to health clinics, both of which have been eliminated as a result of budget cuts.

In any case, we are talking about pin money. Igal Jellinek of the Council of Senior Centers figured they lost in the neighborhood of $8 million in budget cuts. Money like that could come from furniture allowances for the city's brass, not to mention their high-paid press agents, staffs, and consultants, not to mention travel allowances. Surely what they have already wasted on idle limos alone is more than what they will save by canceling the transportation of one thousand infirm people each day to doctors and senior centers.

A myth prevalent in the media holds that the elderly Americans are rich, selfish, and so powerful that they spark terror in politicians. All these characterizations are false.

The elderly are, on average, the poorest among adults, the least able to find work, and the most heavily burdened with medical costs despite the deceptive and tattered safety net of Medicare. As for selfishness, who has not noticed the gray hairs among the thousands of wonderful volunteers who gather petitions, toil in our parks, and bus to our halls of government to defend the quality of life for all generations?

Old people and children have much in common, like their relative poverty, their special need of services like clinics and libraries—and the fact that politicians speak so kindly about them. Did not Mayor Dinkins dedicate his administration to the children of New York?

Politicians butter up the elderly. They tour the centers, because that's where the voters are, and they receive senior delegations with warm assurances of sympathy. So why have programs for the elderly taken repeated hits over the past dozen years? Why has the Geezer Lobby, caricatured in the press as an 800-pound gorilla, been so ineffective?

A brutal explanation is that he who pays the piper calls the tune. Although a disproportionate number of them go to the polls, by then it's too late: The elderly as such don't contribute much to campaign funds.

Another reason is that the kind and gentle people march in dispersed order—here to save the libraries, there the after-school programs, the firehouse, meals on wheels. To each delegation, the budget makers say they agree, so what do you want us to cut instead? They wind up cutting everything except, for the moment, the cops and the jails.

On my annual visits to Europe, I marvel at how civic leaders there feel about the quality of life. In Paris, for example, a very conservative city government taxes employers to reduce fares on a splendid and ever-improving transit system. Even Budapest seems to employ more gardeners.

Here, the class that pulls the strings has but one theme for public policy: Keep taxes down. Let the city choke on its garbage, let its water mains burst and its bridges collapse, let its elderly go hungry and its untended children roam the sweltering streets, they don't see why *they* should pony up.

Some signs of decay do alarm them. A well-to-do East Sider asked me where the city might find the wherewithal to make our streets safe from crime. I remarked that the traffic under his window was choked with stretch limos, and his neighborhood was up to its ears in money.

"But that's *private* money!" he exclaimed.

And that's why some old people will go hungry, and children and mothers, too, and the streets will be filthy and the parks unkempt... until we change our mindset, and our leadership.

Index

ACKNOWLEDGMENTS

For painstaking and valuable advice on the manuscript, the author thanks Karen, Martha, and Peter Hess; Jim Naureckas of FAIR; Noam Chomsky; Jacob Levich; and the team at Seven Stories Press: Dan Simon and Tom McCarthy.

ABOUT THE AUTHOR

JOHN L. HESS is a veteran newspaperman and the author of *Vanishing France, The Case for de Gaulle, The Grand Acquisitors,* and, with his wife Karen, *The Taste of America.* After leaving *The New York Times* Hess worked in television and radio journalism, wrote a nationally syndicated column, and freelanced for *The Nation* and *Grand Street.* Today he continues his role as media watchdog with a daily spot on WBAI's Pacifica, New York public radio. Among other honors, he holds the French Ordre National du Mérite and the Meyer Berger Award of the Columbia School of Journalism. For samples of his recent journalism see www.sevenstories.com.